FROMMER'S

COMPREHENSIVE TRAVEL GUIDE

ATLANTA '93-'94

by Rena Bulkin

PRENTICE HALL TRAVEL

NEW YORK • LONDON • TORONTO • SYDNEY • TOKYO • SINGAPORE

FROMMER BOOKS

Published by Prentice Hall General Reference
A division of Simon & Schuster Inc.
15 Columbus Circle
New York, NY 10023

ISBN 0-671-84663-9
ISSN 1047-7888

Design by Robert Bull Design
Maps by Geografix Inc.

FROMMER'S ATLANTA '93-'94
Editor-in-Chief: Marilyn Wood
Senior Editors: Judith de Rubini, Alice Fellows
Editors: Thomas F. Hirsch, Paige Hughes, Sara Hinsey Raveret, Lisa
Renaud, Theodore Stavrou
Assistant Editors: Margaret Bowen, Peter Katucki, Ian Wilker
Managing Editor: Leanne Coupe

SPECIAL SALES Bulk purchases of Frommer's Travel Guides are available at
special discounts. The publishers are happy to custom-make publications for
corporate clients who wish to use them as premiums or sales promotions. We
can excerpt the contents, provide covers with corporate imprints, or create
books to meet specific needs. For more information write to Special Sales,
Prentice Hall Travel, Paramount Communications Building, 15 Columbus
Circle, New York, NY 10023

CONTENTS

LIST OF MAPS v

1 INTRODUCING ATLANTA 1

1. History 3
2. Famous Atlantans 11
3. Recommended Books & Films 12

SPECIAL FEATURES
● What's Special About
   Atlanta 2
● Dateline 3

2 PLANNING A TRIP TO ATLANTA 14

1. Information & Money 14
2. When to Go 15
3. What to Pack 26
4. Tips for the Disabled, Seniors, Singles,
   Gay Men & Lesbians, Students &
   Families 28
5. Getting There 30

SPECIAL FEATURES
● What Things Cost in
   Atlanta 14
● Atlanta Calendar of
   Events 16
● Frommer's Smart Traveler:
   Airfares 31

3 FOR THE FOREIGN VISITOR 32

1. Preparing for Your Trip 32
2. Getting to the U.S. 34

SPECIAL FEATURES
● Fast Facts: For the Foreign
   Traveler 34

4 GETTING TO KNOW ATLANTA 40

1. Orientation 40
2. Getting Around 45

SPECIAL FEATURES
● Fast Facts: Atlanta 46

5 ATLANTA ACCOMMODATIONS 50

1. Downtown 52
2. Midtown 63
3. Buckhead 75
4. Georgia Tech 85
5. Georgia's Stone Mountain 86
6. Druid Hills/Emory
   University/Brookhaven 88
7. Off I-20 90

SPECIAL FEATURES
● Frommer's Smart Traveler:
   Hotels 59
● Frommer's Cool for Kids:
   Hotels 63

6 ATLANTA DINING 91

1. Downtown 92
2. Midtown 99
3. Buckhead 111
4. Virginia-Highland 125
5. Sweet Auburn 131
6. Decatur 132
7. Chamblee 132
8. Specialty Dining 133

SPECIAL FEATURES
● *Frommer's Smart Traveler: Restaurants 96*
● *Frommer's Cool for Kids: Restaurants 100*

7 WHAT TO SEE & DO IN ATLANTA 137

1. The Top Attractions 138
2. More Attractions 165
3. Cool for Kids 176
4. Organized Tours 183
5. Sports & Recreation 185

SPECIAL FEATURES
● *Suggested Itineraries 137*
● *Did You Know . . . ? 138, 141*
● *Frommer's Favorite Atlanta Experiences 147*

8 STROLLING AROUND ATLANTA 190

1. Downtown 190
2. Sweet Auburn 194

9 ATLANTA SHOPPING 199

1. Shopping Areas 199
2. Department Stores & Malls 205
3. Shopping Around Town 207

10 ATLANTA NIGHTS 210

1. The Performing Arts 210
2. The Nightclub Scene 217
3. More Entertainment 222
4. Film & Video 224

INDEX 225

LIST OF MAPS

ATLANTA

Metropolitan Atlanta   26–27
City Layout   43
MARTA Rapid Rail   47
Downtown
    Accommodations   53
Midtown/Georgia Tech
    Accommodations   66–67
Buckhead
    Accommodations   79

Downtown Dining   95
Midtown/Virginia-Highland
    Dining   102–103
Buckhead Dining   115
Central Atlanta
    Sights   144–145
Georgia's Stone Mountain
    Park   153
Metropolitan Atlanta
    Sights   166–167

ATLANTA WALKING TOURS

Downtown   191
Sweet Auburn   196–197

INVITATION TO THE READERS

In researching this book, I have come across many wonderful establishments, the best of which I have included here. I'm sure that many of you will also come across wonderful hotels, inns, restaurants, guesthouses, shops, and attractions. Please don't keep them to yourself. Share your experiences, especially if you want to comment on places I have covered in this edition which have changed for the worse. You can address your letters to me:

Rena Bulkin
Frommer's Atlanta '93–'94
c/o Prentice Hall Travel
15 Columbus Circle
New York, NY 10023

A DISCLAIMER

Readers are advised that prices fluctuate in the course of time and travel information changes under the impact of the varied and volatile factors that affect the travel industry. The author and publisher cannot be held responsible for the experiences of readers while traveling. Readers are invited to write to the publisher with ideas, comments, and suggestions for future editions.

SAFETY ADVISORY

Whenever you're traveling in an unfamiliar city or country, stay alert. Be aware of your immediate surroundings. Wear a moneybelt and keep a close eye on your possessions. Be particularly careful with cameras, purses, and wallets, all favorite targets of thieves and pickpockets.

CHAPTER 1

INTRODUCING ATLANTA

- **WHAT'S SPECIAL ABOUT ATLANTA**
1. **HISTORY**
- **DATELINE**
2. **FAMOUS ATLANTANS**
3. **RECOMMENDED BOOKS & FILMS**

They call it the Big A, the capital of the New South, and the International Gateway City—all names evocative of Atlanta's dynamism, dash, and spirit. This ever-expanding city—the 13th largest metropolitan area in the United States—teems with energy. Its architecturally innovative downtown area is a sleek showplace of glittering glass skyscrapers, a setting worthy of the city's role as the South's major marketplace and its hub of finance, communications, and transportation.

This is the home of the world's largest airport. It's one of the nation's top meeting and convention cities and is headquarters for hundreds of businesses, including Delta Air Lines, Lockheed, Days Inns, Ritz-Carlton, Holiday Inn, Georgia-Pacific, Coca-Cola (never ask for a Pepsi here), Turner Broadcasting System, and Scientific Atlanta. Atlanta hosted the Democratic National Convention in 1988, and it is now gearing up to host Super Bowl XXVIII in 1994 and the Summer Olympics in 1996. It is the major shopping center of the Southeast region; home to 29 colleges and universities; and a southern crossroads where three interstate highways converge.

Atlanta is also called the Dogwood City, and this name evokes another of its alluring aspects. Coexisting with the bustling metropolis is a very southern city of magnolias and colonnaded white mansions. Every spring (and spring here can begin in February), the city blossoms with delicate pink dogwood buds, fragrant honeysuckle and yellow jasmine, and beautiful pink, white, and red azaleas. Drive a few miles out of the metropolitan area and you'll find yourself in verdant countryside.

Big-city Atlanta celebrates holidays with small-town exuberance. Annual events include chili and barbecue cookoffs, traditional Fourth of July picnics and parades, and Christmas chestnut roasts. The city's patron saint is *Gone With the Wind* author Margaret Mitchell (the book comes up almost on a daily basis), and history—especially Civil War history—is venerated. And while it's extremely dynamic, this is also a leisurely city where people are never in so much of a rush that they dispense with southern graciousness and hospitality. Atlanta is consistently ranked as one of the best places in the country to live—a sentiment that any resident will enthusiastically confirm.

To this appealing mix of urban sophistication and southern gentility add a vibrant cultural scene, with a growing theater

WHAT'S SPECIAL ABOUT ATLANTA

Architectural Highlights

- ☐ Peachtree Center, a downtown "urban village" comprising 14 city blocks.
- ☐ Swan House, designed in the manner of a 16th-century Palladian villa.
- ☐ The fabulous Fox Theatre, a lavish 1920s movie palace featuring replicas of art and furnishings from King Tut's tomb.

Parks and Gardens

- ☐ Piedmont Park, designed by noted landscape artist Frederick Law Olmsted and home of the beautiful Atlanta Botanical Garden.
- ☐ Grant Park, a Civil War battle site which now houses the zoo (see below) and Cyclorama, a 360-degree cylindrical painting of the Battle of Atlanta.
- ☐ Georgia's Stone Mountain Park, with 3,200 acres of lakes and wooded parkland, is the site of vast Mount Rushmore–like sculpture wide.

For Kids

- ☐ Zoo Atlanta, a 40-acre facility with animals housed in large open enclosures which simulate natural habitats.
- ☐ Birth Home of Martin Luther King, Jr.—along with the nearby Center for Non-Violent Social Change, an opportunity for kids to learn about America's foremost black leader and the history of the civil rights movement.

- ☐ Center for Puppetry Arts, a puppetry museum that offers first-rate productions.
- ☐ Yellow River Wildlife Game Ranch, an idyllic 24-acre animal preserve where kids can feed, pet, and mingle with friendly animals along a tree-shaded forest trail.
- ☐ Six Flags Over Georgia, a major theme park with over 100 rides, shows, and attractions.
- ☐ Fernbank Museum of Natural History, Atlanta's largest museum, with an IMAX Theater, children's discovery rooms, and many fascinating exhibits.

After Dark

- ☐ Coca-Cola Lakewood Amphitheatre, used for headliner entertainment, with most seating on a sloping lawn.
- ☐ Alliance Theatre, the largest resident professional theater in the Southeast.
- ☐ Atlanta Symphony Orchestra, one of America's most highly acclaimed orchestras.
- ☐ Kenny's Alley in Underground Atlanta, with about a dozen nightclubs—the perfect setting for an evening of clubhopping.
- ☐ New Georgia Railroad—a glamorous evening. A champagne dinner by candlelight, served aboard a vintage turn-of-the-century excursion train.

community; major art and science museums; prestigious symphony, ballet, and opera companies; big-league sports; a culinary spectrum that ranges from fried chicken 'n' biscuits to beluga caviar; hot nightlife; and a delightfully temperate climate.

Add further a clean and safe state-of-the-art urban mass-transportation system and visitor attractions that run the gamut from legacies of the Confederacy to black heritage sites (Martin Luther King, Jr., was born and is buried here), from historic homes to the futuristic SciTrek Museum, and from a newly refurbished zoo to tours of the high-tech CNN Center studios. And that's not to mention theme parks, a presidential library (Jimmy Carter's, of course), a magnificent botanical garden and conservatory, a winery that's a replica of a 16th-century French château, and Georgia's Stone Mountain Park, one of the nation's most gorgeous parks and Atlanta's third-largest tourist attraction.

1. HISTORY

It is most fitting that Atlanta in the 1990s is an international gateway/transportation hub. The city was conceived as a rail cross-roads for travel north, south, east, and west, and its role as a strategic junction has always figured largely in its destiny. It all began with a peach tree.

THE STANDING PEACHTREE

Today, just about everything in Atlanta is called "Peachtree" something, but the first Peachtree reference was in 1782 when explorers discovered a Cherokee village on the Chattahoochee River called Standing Peach-tree. Since peach trees are not native to the region, some historians maintain the village was actually named for a towering "pitch" tree (a resinous pine). Nevertheless, the Indian village became the location of Fort Peachtree, a tiny frontier outpost, during the War of 1812; a Peachtree Road connecting Fort Peachtree to Fort Daniel (in Gwinett County) was completed by 1813.

In 1826, surveyors Wilson Lumpkin and Hamilton Fulton first suggested this area of Georgia as a practical spot for a railroad connecting the state with northern markets.

DATELINE

- **1782** Explorers discover Cherokee village of Standing Peachtree.
- **1820s** Cherokee and Creek leaders cede millions of acres to white settlers in hopes of keeping peace.
- **1833** Atlanta's first permanent settler, Hardy Ivy, builds log cabin near present-day intersection of Courtland and Ellis streets.
- **1837** The town, newly named Terminus, is selected as site of railroad terminus connecting Georgia with the Tennessee River. The same year, 17,000 Native Americans are forced to march westward on a "Trail of Tears."

(continues)

DATELINE

• **1843** Terminus is renamed Marthasville.

• **1845** The first locomotive chugs into town; the city is renamed Atlanta.

• **1861** Georgia secedes from the Union. Civil War begins, and Atlanta becomes a major Confederate supply depot and medical center.

• **1864** Union forces under General William Tecumseh Sherman burn Atlanta.

• **1865** Civil War ends.

• **1877** Atlanta becomes the permanent capital of Georgia.

• **1886** Newspaper editor Henry Grady inspires readers with vision of a "New South." John S. Pemberton introduces Coca-Cola.

• **1888** Atlanta adopts the symbol of a phoenix rising from the ashes for its official seal.

• **1900** Atlanta University professor W. E. B. Du Bois founds the NAACP.

• **1904** Piedmont Park, designed by Frederick Law Olmsted as site of the Cotton States and

(continues)

This was not yet the heyday of railroads (canals were still the most popular mode of transport), and the report was more or less ignored for a decade. But in 1837, the state legislature approved an act establishing the Western & Atlantic Railroad here. Today a marker known as Zero Milepost in Underground Atlanta marks the W & A Railroad site around which a city grew. The new town was unimaginatively dubbed "Terminus." But future governor Alexander H. Stephens, visiting what was still dense forest in 1839, predicted that "a magnificent inland city will at no distant date be built here."

THE TRAIL OF TEARS

One aspect of the city's inception, however, was far from "magnificent." In the early 1800s, most of Georgia was still Native American territory. White settlers coveted the Cherokee and Creek lands they needed to expedite the railroad and further expand their settlements. To keep the peace, native leaders throughout the 1820s signed numerous treaties ceding millions of acres. They adopted a democratic form of government similar to the white man's, complete with a constitution and supreme court; erected schools and shops; built farms; and accepted Christianity. But the white frontierspeople cared little whether the Native Americans adapted—they wanted them to leave.

With Pres. Andrew Jackson's support, Congress passed a bill in 1830 forcing all southern tribes to move to lands hundreds of miles away on the other side of the Mississippi River. When the U.S. Supreme Court ruled against the order, Jackson ignored their ruling and backed the Georgia settlers. In 1832, the state gave away Cherokee farms in a land lottery; the white settlers assumed control over the land at gunpoint. The issue culminated in 1837, when 17,000 Native Americans were rounded up by federal soldiers, herded into camps, and forced on a cruel westward march called the "Trail of Tears." Some 4,000 died on the 800-mile journey to Oklahoma, and even those who survived suffered bitterly from cold, hunger, and disease.

Terminus and its surroundings were now firmly in the hands of the white settlers.

A CITY GROWS

Terminus soon began its evolution from a sleepy rural hamlet to a thriving city, a meeting point of major rail lines. In 1843, the town was renamed Marthasville, for ex-governor Wilson Lumpkin's daughter Martha. No one in Marthasville took note in 1844 when a 23-year-old army lieutenant, William Tecumseh Sherman, was stationed for two months in their area, but the knowledge he gained of local geography would vitally affect the city's history two decades later. The first locomotive, the Kentucky, chugged into town in 1845, and shortly thereafter the name Marthasville was deemed too provincial for a burgeoning metropolis. J. Edgar Thomson, the railroad's chief engineer, suggested Atlanta (a feminized form of Atlantic).

In 1848, the newly incorporated city held its first mayoral election, an event marked by dozens of street brawls. Moses W. Formwalt, a maker of stills and member of the Free and Rowdy party, was elected over temperance candidate John Norcross. But if Atlanta was a bit of a wild frontier town, it also had civic pride. An 1849 newspaper overstated things poetically:

Atlanta, the greatest spot in all the nation,
The greatest place for legislation,
Or any other occupation—
The very center of creation.

STORM CLOUDS GATHER: ANTEBELLUM ATLANTA

By the middle of the 19th century, the 31-state nation was in the throes of a westward expansion and the institution of slavery was a major issue of the day. In his 1858 debate with Stephen Douglas, Abraham Lin-

DATELINE

International Exposition, becomes Atlanta's central park.

- **1917** Fire destroys 73 square blocks of the city.
- **1929** Atlanta's first airport opens; Delta Air Lines takes to the skies and becomes Atlanta's home carrier.
- **1936** Margaret Mitchell's blockbuster novel, *Gone With the Wind*, is published.
- **1939** The movie version of *Gone With the Wind* premieres in Atlanta.
- **1952** The city of Atlanta incorporates surrounding areas, increasing its population by 100,000 and its size from 37 to 118 square miles.
- **1960** Sit-ins and boycotts protesting segregation begin. The million-square-foot Merchandise Mart is erected, the first of many downtown buildings designed and developed by John Portman.
- **1961** Ivan Allen, Jr., defeats segregationist Lester Maddox in mayoral election. Atlanta's public schools and the Georgia Institute *(continues)*

DATELINE

of Technology are peacefully desegregated.

• **1964** Atlanta native Martin Luther King, Jr., wins Nobel Peace Prize. The Beatles perform at Atlanta Stadium.

• **1965** 106 civic and cultural leaders die in plane crash at Orly Airport in Paris; the $18 million Atlanta-Fulton County Stadium is built.

• **1966** Baseball's Braves move from Milwaukee and the Falcons become a new NFL expansion team.

• **1968** Martin Luther King, Jr., is assassinated in Memphis.

• **1974** Atlanta's first black mayor, Maynard Jackson, is inaugurated. Atlanta Brave Hank Aaron hits his record-breaking 715th home run.

• **1976** Georgian Jimmy Carter elected president. Georgia World Congress Center, the nation's largest single-floor exhibit space, is completed.

• **1979** MARTA rapid-transit train system opens.

• **1980** New Hartsfield International-

(continues)

coln declared, "This government cannot endure permanently half slave and half free." A year later it was obvious that only a war would resolve the issue. In 1861 (a year that began dramatically in Atlanta—with an earthquake), Georgia legislators voted for secession and joined the Confederacy. In peacetime, the railroads had fashioned Atlanta into a center of commerce, known as the Gate City. In wartime, this transportation hub would emerge into perilous relief as a major Confederate military post and supply center—the vital link between Confederate forces in Tennessee and Virginia. Federal forces early on saw the city's destruction as essential to Northern victory.

On a lighter note, Atlanta made the following ridiculous bid to become the capital of the Confederacy: "The city has good railroad connections, is free from yellow fever, and can supply the most wholesome foods and, as for 'goobers,' an indispensable article for a Southern legislator, we have them all the time." The lure of plentiful peanuts notwithstanding, the Confederacy chose Richmond, Virginia, as its capital.

A CITY BURNS

Atlanta was not only a major Southern supply depot, it was also the medical center of the Confederacy. Throughout the city, buildings were hastily converted into makeshift hospitals and clinics, and trains pulled into town daily to disgorge sick and wounded soldiers. By 1862, close to 4,000 soldiers were convalescing here, and the medical crisis was further aggravated by a smallpox epidemic. That same year, Union spy James J. Andrews and a group of Northern soldiers disguised as civilians seized a locomotive called the General, with the aim of blocking supply lines by destroying tracks and bridges behind them. A wild train chase ensued, and the raiders were caught and punished (most, including Andrews, were executed). The episode came to be known as "the Great Locomotive Chase," one of the stirring stories of the Civil War and the subject of two subsequent movies. The General is today on view at the Big Shanty Museum in Kennesaw (details in Chapter 7).

The locomotive chase was an Atlanta victory, but the Northern desire to destroy the Confederacy's supply link remained intact. In 1864, Gen. Ulysses S. Grant ordered Maj. Gen. William T. Sherman to "move against Johnston's army to break it up, and get into the interior of the enemy's country as far as you can, inflicting all the damage you can against their resources." Georgians had great faith that the able and experienced Gen. Joseph E. Johnston, whom they called "Old Joe," would repel the Yankees. As Sherman's Georgia campaign got under way, an overly optimistic editorial in the *Intelligencer* scoffed at the notion of Federal conquest, claiming "we have no fear of the results, for General Johnston and his great and invincible satellites are working out the problem of battle and victory at the great chess board at the front." Johnston himself was not as sanguine. Sherman had 100,000 men to his 60,000, and the Union troops were better armed. By July, Sherman was forcing the Confederate troops back, and Atlanta's fall seemed a foregone conclusion. Johnston informed Confederate Pres. Jefferson Davis that he was outnumbered almost two to one and was in a defensive position. His candid assessment was not appreciated, and Davis removed him from command, replacing him with the pugnacious 32-year-old Gen. John Bell Hood. The change of leadership only further demoralized the ranks, and Sherman openly rejoiced when he heard the news.

Some disgruntled Confederate soldiers deserted. Hood abandoned the defensive tactics of Johnston, aggressively assaulting his opponent. His policy cost thousands of troops and gained nothing. In the Battle of Peachtree Creek on July 20, 1864, Union casualties totaled 1,710, Confederate, 4,796. Throughout the summer, the city suffered a full-scale artillery assault. Over 8,000 Confederates perished in the Battle of Atlanta on July 22, while Union deaths totaled just 3,722. And after hours of fierce fighting on July 28, the Confederates had lost another 5,000 men, the Federals, 600. The Yankees further paralyzed the city by ripping up train rails, heating them over huge bonfires, and twisting them around trees into useless spirals of mangled iron that came to be known as "Sherman's neckties." The most devastating bombardment came on August 9—"that red day . . . when all the fires of hell, and all the thunders of the universe seemed to be blazing and roaring over Atlanta."

By September 1, when Hood's troops pulled out of the area, first

IMPRESSIONS

The terminus of that railroad will never be anything more than an eating house.
—JAMES M. CALHOUN, 1836 (Calhoun later became mayor of Atlanta)

Atlanta lies . . . diamond like, in the very center of Georgia, yea, of the South, rough and unpolished . . . in the eyes of jealousy and prejudice, but destined . . . to becoming a bright and glittering jewel in the diadem of Southern cities.
—LUTHER J. GLENN, Atlanta Mayor, 1858 inaugural address

---

setting fire to vast stores of ammunition (and anything else that might benefit the Yankees), the town was in turmoil. Its roads were crowded with evacuees, its hospitals, hotels, and private residences flooded with wounded men. Crime and looting were rife, and food was almost unavailable; the price of a ham-and-eggs breakfast with coffee soared to $25! Rooftops were ripped off houses and buildings, there were huge craters in the streets, and many civilians were dead. The railroads were in Sherman's hands. On September 2, Mayor James M. Calhoun, carrying a white flag to the nearest Federal unit, officially surrendered the city. The U.S. Army entered and occupied Atlanta, raising the Stars and Stripes at city hall for the first time in four years. Claiming he needed the city for military purposes, Sherman ordered all residents to evacuate. Atlantans piled their household goods on wagons and, abandoning their homes and businesses, became refugees. Before departing Atlanta in November, Union troops leveled railroad facilities and burned the city, leaving it a wasteland—defunct as a military center and practically uninhabitable. The Yankees marched out of the city to the music of "The Battle Hymn of the Republic."

In January 1865, there was $1.64 in the treasury, the railroad system was destroyed, and most of the city was burned to the ground.

A CITY REBUILDS

Slowly, exiled citizens began to trickle back into Atlanta. Confederate money was worthless. At the inauguration of his second term in 1865, Lincoln pledged "malice toward none, charity for all"—but after his assassination later that year, this policy was replaced with one of harsh Republican vengeance. It wasn't until 1876 that Federal troops were withdrawn and Atlanta was freed from military occupation. Still, the city was making a remarkable recovery. Like the ever-resilient Scarlett O'Hara ("It takes more than Yankees or a burning to keep me down"), Atlanta rolled up its sleeves and began rebuilding. A Northern newspaper reported, "From all this ruin and devastation a new city is springing up . . . the streets are alive from morning till night with drays and carts and hand-barrows and wagons . . . with loads of lumber and loads of brick. . . ."

IMPRESSIONS

No one goes anywhere without passing through Atlanta.
—FRANCIS C. LAWLEY, *London Times* reporter, 1861

*I want to say to General Sherman, who is an able
man . . . though some people think he is kind of careless about
fire, that from the ashes he left us in 1864 we have raised a
brave and beautiful city; that we have caught the sunshine in our
homes and built therein not one ignoble prejudice or memory.*
—HENRY GRADY, *Atlanta Constitution* editor, 1886

In postwar years, Atlanta was filled with carpetbaggers and adventurers hoping to turn a quick buck, and with them came gambling houses, brothels, and saloons. But the city also boasted hundreds of new stores and businesses, churches, schools, banks, hotels, theaters, and a new newspaper, the *Atlanta Constitution.* Blacks chartered Atlanta University in 1867, today the world's largest predominantly black institution of higher learning. Moreover, the railroads were operative once again. Newspaper editor Henry Grady inspired readers with his vision of an industrialized and culturally advanced "New South." He was Atlanta's biggest civic booster. A new constitution in 1877 made Atlanta the permanent capital of the state of Georgia. Two years later, General Sherman visited the city he had destroyed and was welcomed with a ball and, lest he get any funny ideas, a grand military review.

In 1886 a new headache cure was introduced—a syrup made from the cocoa leaf and the kola nut which would eventually become the world's most renowned beverage, Coca-Cola. Atlanta adopted the symbol of a phoenix rising from the ashes for its official seal in 1888 and, the following year, dedicated the gold-domed state capitol and opened a zoo in Grant Park. Piedmont Park was built in 1904 as the site of the Cotton States and International Exposition—a $2.5 million world's fair–like extravaganza with entertainments ranging from Buffalo Bill and His Wild West Show to international villages. Former slave Booker T. Washington gave a landmark address, and John Philip Sousa composed the "King Cotton March" to mark the event.

THE TWENTIETH CENTURY

At the turn of the century, Atlanta's population was 90,000, a figure that more than doubled two decades later. Though a massive fire swept through the city and destroyed almost 2,000 buildings in 1917, the city was on a course of rapid growth. In 1929, Atlanta opened its first airport on the site of today's Hartsfield International, presaging the growth of a major air-travel industry. The same year, Delta Air Lines took to the skies and became Atlanta's home carrier. Margaret Mitchell's blockbuster Civil War epic *Gone With the Wind,* which went on to become the world's second-best-selling book (after the

Bible) and the basis for the biggest-grossing picture of all time, was published in 1936. Louis B. Mayer turned down a chance to make the film version for MGM, because "no Civil War picture ever made a nickel."

A more dire legacy of the Civil War and the institution of slavery was racial strife, and the early years of the 20th century were marked by violent race riots. Atlanta University professor W. E. B. Du Bois founded the NAACP in 1900. In 1939, black cast members were unable to attend the glamorous premiere of *Gone With the Wind* because the theater was segregated. And as late as 1960, segregation in Atlanta (as everywhere in the South) was still firmly entrenched and backed by state law. Unlike much of the South, though, the city has, for the most part, adopted a progressive attitude regarding race relations. Even before the civil rights movement there were black advancements—the hiring of black police officers, the election of a black to the Atlanta Board of Education, the desegregation of a public golf course in 1955, and, in 1959, the desegregation of public transit. Mayor Bill Hartsfield (who held office for almost three decades) called Atlanta "a city too busy to hate." And his successor, Mayor Ivan Allen, Jr., called on Atlantans to face race problems "and seek the answers in an atmosphere of decency and dignity."

Without screaming mobs, Atlanta peacefully desegregated its public schools and the Georgia Institute of Technology in 1961. Atlanta native Dr. Martin Luther King, Jr., headquartered his Southern Christian Leadership Conference here and made Ebenezer Baptist Church, which he co-pastored with his father, a hub of the movement. In 1974 Atlanta inaugurated its first black mayor, Maynard Jackson, and, following a term by another black mayor, Andrew Young, Jackson is once again in office.

In 1966 Atlanta went major league when the Braves and the Falcons came to town. Atlantans went wild in 1974 when Hank Aaron broke Babe Ruth's home-run record here.

The 1960s also saw the beginning of downtown development with the rise of the million-square-foot Merchandise Mart, designed by an innovative young Atlanta architect named John Portman. It became the nucleus for the nationally renowned Peachtree Center

---

IMPRESSIONS

It stinks, I don't know why I bother with it, but I've got to have something to do with my time.
—MARGARET MITCHELL, author of *Gone With the Wind*

Gone With the Wind *is very possibly the greatest American novel.*
—PUBLISHERS WEEKLY

We're going to ride these buses desegregated in Atlanta, Georgia, or we're going to ride a chariot in heaven or push a wheelbarrow in hell.
—REV. WILLIAM HOLMES BORDERS, civil rights leader, 1957.

complex. Portman's futuristic design for the downtown Hyatt Regency (1967) introduced a towering atrium-lobby concept that revolutionized hotel architecture in America. Today Peachtree Center—a 13-city-block "pedestrian village"—comprises three Portman-designed megahotels, the 5.9-million-square-foot Atlanta Market Center (including the Apparel Mart and the high-tech-oriented INFORUM), 200,000 square feet of retail space, a restaurant row, and six massive office towers, its various elements connected by covered walkways and bridges. This is an open-ended project, still very much in a process of expansion.

MARTA rapid-transit trains began running in 1979. Today just about every part of Atlanta is accessible by bus or subway.

In 1980, a revitalized black neighborhood called Sweet Auburn became a National Historic District, its 10 blocks of notable sites including Martin Luther King, Jr.'s boyhood home, his crypt, the church where he preached, a museum, and the center for Non-Violent Social Change. It is probably *the* major black history attraction in the country.

Media mogul Ted Turner inaugurated CNN here in 1980, following with Superstation TBS, Headline News, and TNT. The High Museum of Art opened its doors in 1983. And in 1989, Underground Atlanta, a retail/restaurant/entertainment complex with a historical theme, garnered national attention.

In the 1990s, when other big cities are struggling to survive, Atlanta continues to soar. The 1994 Super Bowl (see box on p. 185 for ticket information) is expected to bring in $150 million in revenue and lure 85,000 visitors. And the city is very busy gearing up for the 1996 Olympics (expected to generate $3.5 billion) with new hotels, tour packages, and megastadiums. Of the last, most notable are the $214 million, 70,500-seat Georgia Dome and the 10,000-seat open-air Olympic Velodrome at Stone Mountain Park. An Olympic Village is also being erected on the campus of the Georgia Institute of Technology. In addition, the city is getting a major new sightseeing attraction—the Fernbank Museum of Natural History—and several other museums are expanding their premises.

Atlanta in the nineties remains a forward-looking city that is constantly renewing itself—a dynamic metropolis where the past is honored and the present enthusiastically embraced. The city's motto is "Resurgens." The phoenix has risen from the ashes and taken wing.

2. FAMOUS ATLANTANS

Henry Louis "Hank" Aaron   (b. 1934) An outfielder with the Milwaukee (later Atlanta) Braves, Aaron broke Babe Ruth's record in 1974 with his 715th home run. He retired in 1976 with 755 homers.

Henry Woodlin Grady   (1850–1889) Managing editor of

the *Atlanta Constitution*, Grady preached post–Civil War reconciliation, and worked passionately to draw Northern capital and diversified industry to the agrarian South. His name is synonymous with the phrase "The New South."

Joel Chandler Harris (1848–1908) Called "Georgia's Aesop," he created Uncle Remus, the wise black raconteur of children's fables. His tales of Br'er Rabbit and Br'er Fox were the basis for Disney's delightful animated feature *Song of the South*.

Robert Tyre "Bobby" Jones (1902–1971) Golf's only Grand Slam winner, he was the founder of the Masters Tournament. Jones has been called the world's greatest golfer; he retired from the game in 1930 but his record remains unsurpassed. He also held academic degrees in engineering, law, and English literature.

Martin Luther King, Jr. (1929–1968) Civil rights leader, minister, orator, and Nobel Peace Prize winner, King preached Mohandas Gandhi's doctrine of passive resistance.

Margaret Mitchell (1900–1949) Author of the definitive southern blockbuster novel, *Gone With the Wind*. Originally a journalist, Mitchell began writing "the book" in 1926 when a severe ankle injury forced her to give up reporting. *GWTW* is, next to the Bible, the world's best-selling book.

John C. Portman (b. 1924) Architect/developer who revolutionized hotel design in America with his lofty atrium-lobby concept and almost singlehandedly designed Atlanta's skyline. He has been called "Atlanta's one-man urban-renewal program."

Robert Edward "Ted" Turner III (b. 1938) Dubbed "the mouth from the South," America's most dynamic media mogul, Ted Turner, owns 24-hour cable news networks CNN and Headline News, along with entertainment networks Superstation TBS and TNT, not to mention a portion of MGM and the Atlanta Braves and Atlanta Hawks.

Robert W. Woodruff (1889–1985) Coca-Cola Company president, philanthropist, and leading Atlanta citizen for over half a century. He put Coca-Cola on the map worldwide; promoted civil rights; and gave over $400 million to Atlanta educational, artistic, civil, and medical projects such as Emory University, the Woodruff Arts Center, and the High Museum.

3. RECOMMENDED BOOKS & FILMS

BOOKS

Bridges, Herb, *Frankly My Dear . . . Gone With the Wind Memorabilia* (Mercer University Press, 1986).
Bryan, T. Conn, *Confederate Georgia* (UGA Press, 1953).

Coleman, Kenneth, *Georgia History in Outline* (UGA Press, 1960).

Gardner, Gerald and Harriette, *Pictorial History of Gone With the Wind* (Bonanza Books, 1980).

Garrison, Webb, *The Legacy of Atlanta: A Short History* (Peachtree Publishers, Ltd., 1987).

Jackson, Maynard, Jane Sobel, and Art Klonsky, *Atlanta* (Bolton Pub. Services, Inc., 1985).

Kahn, Clifford, Harlan Joye, and Bernard West, *Living Atlanta: An Oral History of the City 1914–1918* (UGA Press, 1990).

Key, William, *The Battle of Atlanta and the Georgia Campaign* (Peachtree Publishers, Ltd., 1981).

Martin, Harold H., *Atlanta & Environs: A Chronicle of Its People and Events* (UGA Press, 1987).

McCarley, J. Britt, *The Atlanta Campaign/CW Driving Tour of Atlanta Battlefields* (Cherokee Pub. Co., 1989).

McKenzie, Barbara, *Flannery O'Connor's Georgia* (UGA Press, 1980).

Miles, Jim, *Fields of Glory: A History and Tour of the Atlanta Campaign* (Rutledge Hill Press, 1989).

Shavin, Norman, and Bruce Galphin, *Atlanta: Triumph of a People* (Capricorn Corporation, 1985).

Sibley, Celestine, *Atlanta: A Brave and Beautiful City* (Peachtree Publishers, Ltd., 1986).

————. *Peachtree Street USA* (Peachtree Publishers, Ltd., 1986).

FILMS

Many films focus on Atlanta. The two most famous are *Gone With the Wind* (1939) and *Driving Miss Daisy* (1989).

CHAPTER 2

PLANNING A TRIP TO ATLANTA

1. INFORMATION & MONEY
- **WHAT THINGS COST IN ATLANTA**

2. WHEN TO GO
- **ATLANTA CALENDAR OF EVENTS**

3. WHAT TO PACK

4. TIPS FOR THE DISABLED, SENIORS, SINGLES, GAY MEN & LESBIANS, STUDENTS & FAMILIES

5. GETTING THERE
- **FROMMER'S SMART TRAVELER: AIRFARES**

I f you're going to a beach resort, there's little need to plan your vacation—you can wing it. But when visiting a city where dozens of sightseeing attractions and activities vie for your time, planning is the key to optimum enjoyment.

1. INFORMATION & MONEY

As soon as you know you're going to Atlanta, write to or call the **Atlanta Convention & Visitors Bureau (ACVB),** 233 Peachtree St. NE, Suite 2000, Atlanta 30303 (tel. 404/222-6688 or toll free 800/ ATLANTA). They'll send you a copy of *Atlanta Now* (a visitor's guide), a *Metro Atlanta Attractions Guide,* a map, and a 2-month calendar of events; they can also advise you on anything from Atlanta's hotel and restaurant scene to the best tour packages available. You can call weekdays between 8am and 6pm.

WHAT THINGS COST IN ATLANTA	U.S. $
Taxi from airport to downtown, for one person	15
Bus from airport to downtown	8
Double at the Ritz-Carlton Atlanta (very expensive)	155–200
Double at the Wyndham Hotel Midtown (expensive)	135
Double at the Comfort Inn (moderate)	79–129

	U.S. $
Double at Travelodge Atlanta Downtown (inexpensive)	74–84
Double at Cheshire Motor Inn (budget)	35–46
Three-course dinner at the Hedgerose Heights Inn, including tip, no wine (very expensive)	45
Three-course dinner at Pricci, including tip, no wine (expensive)	35
Three-course dinner at Peasant Restaurant & Bar, including tip, no wine (moderate)	25
Three-course Dinner at Rocky's Brick Oven Pizza, including tip, no wine (inexpensive)	17
Three-course dinner at The Varsity (budget)	4
Theater ticket at the Alliance	17–34

2. WHEN TO GO

THE CLIMATE

Atlanta's temperate climate is a delight year round. The city enjoys four distinct seasons, but the variations are less extreme than elsewhere. It seldom snows much in winter, and sweltering summer hot spells are short-lived, with few days reaching, let alone surpassing, the 90°F mark. Spring and autumn are long seasons, and, in terms of natural beauty and heavenly climate, they're optimum times to visit. Annual rainfall is about 48 inches, and the wettest months are December through April and July.

Atlanta's Average Daytime Temperature and Rainfall

	Jan	Feb	Mar	Apr	May	June	July	Aug	Sept	Oct	Nov	Dec
Temp. °F	45	46	52	60	69	77	79	79	73	63	52	43
Rainfall "	4.4	4.5	5.3	4.4	3.1	3.8	4.7	3.6	3.2	2.4	2.9	4.3

ATLANTA
CALENDAR OF EVENTS

Note: Some events, such as the Georgia Renaissance Festival, begin in one month and continue for several months thereafter. These are listed in the month of inception. So do look back a few months prior to your visit for ongoing events.

JANUARY

☐ **Martin Luther King Week,** the second week of the month, is a major happening. It begins with an interfaith service and includes plays, musical tributes, seminars, films, a parade down Peachtree Street to Auburn Avenue, and speeches by notables (including Mrs. Coretta Scott King). For details, contact the King Center (tel. 404/524-1956).

☐ **Ringling Brothers Barnum & Bailey Circus** comes to the Omni Coliseum for 22 performances each year in late January or early February. Dial 404/681-2100 for information, 404/249-6400 for tickets.

FEBRUARY

☐ **Cathedral Antiques Show.** For four days in the first week of February (some years the last week in January), 30 to 35 dealers of high-quality antiques display their wares at the Cathedral of St. Philip. The merchandise ranges from 18th- and 19th-century furnishings to Oriental rugs. A sit-down lunch, served in a genteel setting, is available each day. Admission is $6 per day, or you can attend the preview party for $20 and come back all four days for free. For details, call 404/365-1000.

☐ **Atlanta Flower Show.** One of the South's premier gardening events, it takes place at the Atlanta Apparel Mart and Inforum for four days, usually including Valentine's Day but sometimes as late as early March. It offers 200,000 square feet of stunning land-scapes and gardens displaying both flowers and vegetables. Other displays might include anything from a bamboo forest to a wildlife refuge. Garden-related products and patio furniture are sold, and there are demonstrations of gardening techniques, photography exhibitions, and events for children. Admission is $8 for adults, $6 for seniors, $3 for children under 12. For information call 404/220-2115.

MARCH

☐ **Atlanta Boat Show.** Sponsored by the Southern Exposition Management Company (SEMCO), this event takes place for nine days early in the month. It's the largest inland marine show in the

United States, featuring houseboats, yachts, cabin cruisers, salt-water craft, pleasure craft, rowboats, and canoes, not to mention displays of fishing gear, waterskiing equipment, and other water-related items. There are fashion shows of swimsuits and boating attire, plus fishing and skiing clinics. Admission is $6 for adults, $3 for children 12 and under, $5 for seniors. For details, call 404/998-9800.

✪ **St. Patrick's Day Parade** *A major production here, with some 7,000 marchers each year and 150,000 viewers. The mayor and other local politicians attend, and there are sports celebrities, high school bands, majorettes, clowns, cloggers, drill teams, and bagpipers. The parade culminates at Underground Atlanta with concerts of Irish music, dance, and other festivities. If you want to do a St. Patrick's Day pub crawl, two good choices offering the requisite green beer, bagpipe players, and Irish fare are* **Limerick Junction,** *822 N. Highland Ave. (tel. 874-7147) and* **County Cork Pub,** *56 E. Andrews Dr. (tel. 262-ABAR).*

Where: The parade begins at Peachtree Street and Ralph McGill Boulevard. When: March 17. How: Just show up. Check the local paper for details.

APRIL

✪ *THE ATLANTA DOGWOOD FESTIVAL Culminating in Piedmont Park on a weekend in mid-April, this is a biggie, with many events taking place the week prior. Activities include concerts, house and garden tours, juried art and crafts shows, an International Village (showcasing worldwide crafts, cuisine, and talent), and bicycle tours of Buckhead to view azaleas and dogwoods in bloom. On the final weekend, three stages are set up for musical performances in the park, and there are food booths, hot-air balloon races, kite-flying contests, and children's activities.*

Where: Several locations around town and in Piedmont Park. When: Nine days in early April. How: Admission is free. For details, call 404/952-9151 or check the local papers for a full listing of events.

☐ **Antebellum Jubilee.** Demonstrations of early American/Southern arts and crafts, a re-created Civil War encampment, and concerts on the dulcimer, harp, zither, and musical saw are all part of this annual celebration at Georgia's Stone Mountain Park the first two weekends in April. All festival activities are included in the price of regular admission to the plantation. For details, call 404/498-5702.

☐ **The Easter Egg Hunt** is another early April happening, held on the south lawn of the Old Courthouse in Decatur. There are prizes for those who collect the most eggs. Admission is free. For details, call 404/371-8386.

☐ **Easter Sunrise Services** are held at the top and the base of Georgia's Stone Mountain at 6:30am. Park gates open at 4am and the skylift begins operation at 4:30am (though it seems more appropriate to walk up if you're in good shape). For details, call 404/498-5702.

☐ **Lasershow,** also at Stone Mountain Park, is a sight-and-sound spectacular of laser lights and fireworks choreographed to popular, patriotic, country, and classical music. It begins on April weekends (Friday, Saturday, and Sunday nights at 9pm). Don't miss it. Admission is free. Beginning in early May through Labor Day, Lasershow can be seen nightly. For details, call 404/498-5702.

☐ **The Sweet Auburn Festival,** a 4-day event in mid-April, features a parade, historical and cultural activities, children's activities, and music. For details, call 404/577-0625.

☐ **The Inman Park Festival** takes place the last weekend in April in an Atlanta suburb noted for its gorgeous turn-of-the-century Victorian mansions. Activities include a tour of homes, music (jazz bands, cloggers), an arts-and-crafts festival/flea market, a parade, a Saturday-night street dance, and food vendors. Tickets are about $10, good for all events both days. For more information, call 404/242-4895.

✪ *THE GEORGIA RENAISSANCE FESTIVAL* This re-creation of a 1700s English county fair in a 30-acre "village" called Willy Nilly features a juried crafts show with over 100 craftspeople demonstrating 16th-century skills; continuous entertainment on five stages; period foods; and a cast of costumed characters including kings and queens, jousters, jugglers, storytellers, giant stilt walkers, and knights in shining armor.

Where: In Fairburn—10 miles south of the airport on I-85, exit 12. *When:* On seven weekends, from the last Saturday in April through the first Sunday in June (plus Memorial Day). *How:* You can purchase tickets at the door. Admission is $10 for adults, $5 for ages 5 to 12, under 5 free. For details, call 404/964-8575.

MAY

☐ **Blue Sky Concerts** are free performances of jazz, classical, bluegrass, and rock music, held at noon every Wednesday in May on the south lawn of the Old Decatur Courthouse. Bring a blanket and a picnic lunch. For more information, call 404/371-8386.

☐ **Concerts on the Square,** a similar series at the courthouse, takes place every Saturday night in May at 7:30pm. It traditionally opens with a performance by the Dekalb Symphony Orchestra. For details, call 404/371-8386.

☐ **The Gardens for Connoisseurs Tour,** proceeds of which go to the Atlanta Botanical Garden, visits outstanding private gardens the weekend of Mother's Day. Tickets are $15. For details, call 404/876-5859.

☐ **Springfest.** There's good food to eat at this event, which includes the annual BBQ Pork Cookoff. It takes place on a weekend early in May at Georgia's Stone Mountain Park. Continuous live entertainment on three stages (emphasizing folk and country music and featuring some biggish names, like Stella Parton), a vast arts and crafts show, children's activities, and southern food booths round out the events. All activities are free. For information, call 404/498-5702.

☐ **The Dekalb Sheriff's Posse Rodeo,** A 4-day event mid-month, is also set in the confines of Stone Mountain Park. Buckin' broncos, barrel riding, calf roping, and more. For details, call 404/498-5702.

☐ **The Atlanta Film & Video Festival,** which takes place for five days in mid-May at Image Film/Video Center, 75 Bennett St. NW, Suite M1, features about three dozen films and videotapes by some of the country's most important independent media artists. Admission is $6.50 per film, with discounts available for students and seniors. For details, call 404/352-4225.

☐ **Decatur Arts Festival,** a 3-day event on the south lawn of the Old Decatur Courthouse, takes place Memorial Day weekend. It features an art show on the lawn, various juried shows nearby, a garden tour, storytellers, mimes, jugglers, puppet shows, clowns, children's art activities, great food, and performances by music, dance, and theater groups. A great family outing. For details, call 404/371-8386.

☐ **A Taste of the Southeast.** Part of Stone Mountain Park's Memorial Day weekend celebrations, this happening has music, dance, regional foods, art, crafts demonstrations, and more. For details, call 404/498-5702.

☐ **The Atlanta Jazz Festival** takes place the last weekend in May and the first weekend in June, with free ongoing concerts in Grant Park (at the main stage next to Cyclorama) on Saturday and Sunday from 3 to 10pm. The afternoon begins with local performers and goes on to major stars by evening—for example, Wynton Marsalis, Sun Ra, Nancy Wilson, Dizzy Gillespie, Max Roach, and Sonny Rollins. Arrive early to get a good space, and bring a blanket and a picnic. Big names also perform on the Friday nights preceding these weekends at an Atlanta theater determined annually. Tickets for Friday night shows are $8 to $12. Events additionally include an annual concert (admission is charged) featuring major jazz artists at the Chastain Park Amphitheatre at Powers Ferry Road and Stella Drive. And during the festival week there are free noontime jazz concerts at Woodruff Park. For details on any of the above, call 404/653-7160.

JUNE

☐ **The Gay Pride Parade,** always on a Sunday in early June, goes from the Civic Center to Piedmont Park. The whole month is event-filled (June is National Gay Pride Month), including a gay prom, a gay business expo, performances by the Gay Men's Chorus, and musical entertainment/art market in Piedmont Park. For details, call 404/662-4533.

☐ **The Annual Shakespeare Festival** offers two or three productions between mid-June and mid-August, performed in a 400-seat theater tent at Oglethorpe University, 4484 Peachtree Rd. Preceding the performances, there's entertainment on the lawn (music and farcical vignettes). Everyone brings a pre-performance picnic or arranges in advance to purchase it on the premises. The company, made up of Actors Equity pros for the most part, offers both traditional and innovative Shakespearean productions. Picnic grounds open at 6:30pm, the pre-show begins at 7pm, the actual show at 8pm. Admission is $16 to $20 for adults, $3 less for seniors, and half price for students and children under 12. Call for tickets as far in advance as possible, especially for weekend performances (tel. 404/264-0020 or 404/233-1717). To order a picnic, call 404/396-6627.

✪ *A TASTE OF ATLANTA* *The Southeast's largest outdoor food festival lets you sample fare from over 60 noted Atlanta restaurants. While strolling about tasting ribs, fajitas, Indian curries, and more, guests enjoy continuous live entertainment, an arts and crafts fair, cooking demonstrations, and a "Great Atlanta Waiters Race." There's a children's area featuring kid's favorite foods, magicians, clowns, crafts, and games. And an area called "A Taste of Chocolate" specializes in desserts. Proceeds from the event benefit the National Kidney Foundation of Georgia.*

  Where: CNN Center of Marietta Street and Techwood Drive. When: Three days in mid-June. How: Admission is $5 (free for children under 12), and food tastings are 50¢ to $2. For details, call 404/248-1315.

☐ **The Stone Mountain Village Annual Arts & Crafts Festival** (see Chapter 9, "Atlanta Shopping") is held on Father's Day weekend. Over 200 Southeast craftspeople and antique dealers display their wares, local community groups set up fabulous food booths, and entertainment is offered continually in the Village Gazebo. For details, call 404/296-8058. A small admission (about $2) is charged; under 12 free.

☐ **Beach Party.** Decatur's not on the ocean, but that doesn't stop its residents from throwing this bash every year on the Friday closest to June 21 on the south lawn of the Old Decatur Courthouse. The lawn is covered with sand, plastic palms and volleyball courts are erected, a disc jockey provides music, food and drink is sold, and there are sandcastle-building, hula hoop, and dance contests. There are wading pools and other activities. For details, call 404/371-8386.

☐ **Fox Summer Electrolux Film Festival.** Don't miss this event at the fabulous Fox Theatre (see Chapter 7). About a dozen films are shown from June through August, mostly on Monday and Thursday nights, and the shows include vintage cartoons, a sing-along organ concert (follow the bouncing ball), and a feature film at just $5.50 per ticket. Coupon books are available at a discount, a good bet for families. For details, call 404/881-2100.

JULY

☐ **Independence Day** is celebrated from July 1 to July 4 at Georgia's Stone Mountain Park's **Fantastic Fourth Celebration**—a star-spangled festival of free concerts (some featuring well-known artists like Sha Na Na, the Platters, and the Coasters), beach parties (with beauty, hula hoop, and dance contests; there is a real beach here), a traditional July 4th picnic, and, of course, fireworks and the nightly Lasershow. Mimes, jugglers, cloggers, and clowns perform throughout the park. For details, call 404/498-5702.

You can also celebrate **the Fourth in Decatur.** Festivities begin with a Pied Piper Parade (led by the mayor in a fire truck) departing at 6pm from the Decatur Baptist Church on Courthouse Square. Decorate yourself, your bicycle, or your car and join in. The parade is followed by a concert at 7:30pm (bring a picnic and blanket) and a great fireworks display. Everything is free. For details, call 404/371-8386.

An old-fashioned **Fourth of July Parade** takes place in Stone Mountain Village, from Mountain Street at the foot of the west gate of Stone Mountain Park along Main Street through the Village shop area. There are bands, floats, cloggers, baton twirlers, and more. The parade begins at 10am. For details, call 404/296-8058.

☐ **The National Black Arts Festival** is a 7- to 10-day affair (even-numbered years only) in late July and early August, with events (most of them free) taking place, throughout the city. Billed as "a celebration of the works of artists of African descent," it features dozens of events—concerts, theater, film, dance (both African and African American companies), art and folk-art exhibitions, children's activities, African puppet shows, and that's not the half of it. For details, call 404/730-7315.

AUGUST

☐ **The Atlanta International Food & Wine Festival,** a 3-day weekend event in early August, takes place at various posh

Buckhead hotels determined annually. It features over 150 booths exhibiting international wines and foods, with upscale tastings, seminars and speeches by wine writers, and winemaker dinners at host hotels. Profits go to charities. Admission is $30 to $35, including all tastings. Seminars and dinners are additional. For details, call 404/873-4482.

SEPTEMBER

☐ **The Montreux Atlanta International Music Festival** (patterned after the Montreux jazz festival in Switzerland), is a 6-day affair (including Labor Day) featuring jazz, blues, gospel, reggae, and zydeco (Cajun) music in Piedmont Park and local theaters. Both regional and internationally known artists perform, and the fun usually includes late-night jam sessions at local hotels. Piedmont Park events are free. Like the **Atlanta** Jazz Festival in May and June (see above), this also includes a paid concert with big-name artists at Chastain Park Amphitheatre. For details, call 653-7160.

☐ **Blue Sky Concerts** and **Concerts on the Square.** The fall schedules of these concert series (see May) begin in Decatur. Concert times are the same as above. The final Saturday night concert is all "golden oldies." For details, call 404/371-8386.

☐ **The Yellow Daisy Festival** at Georgia's Stone Mountain Park is a vast outdoor arts-and-crafts show (over 400 exhibitors) with musical entertainment, a flower show, great food, storytellers, and puppetry. It takes place in early September. About 300,000 people attend each year. For details, call 404/498-5702.

☐ **Sesame Street Live.** Early to midmonth this show comes to the Omni Coliseum. Call 404/249-6400 for tickets.

☐ **Georgia Music Festival.** This statewide celebration of music takes place for 10 days midmonth. Events include jazz, gospel, bluegrass, country, and rock concerts, as well as dancing, seminars, and contests at varied locations. It culminates with the Georgia Music Hall of Fame Awards banquet/concert at Atlanta's World Congress Center. For details, call 404/656-9044.

○ **ARTS FESTIVAL OF ATLANTA** One of the nation's largest outdoor art events, this avant-garde visual and performing arts festival features regional, national, and international artists. There's a vast Artist Market, in addition to indoor gallery shows and outdoor sculpture exhibits. Three stages are set up for music, dance, and theater performances. Children's activities are numerous. And food concessions throughout the park offer everything from funnel cakes to fajitas.
   Where: Piedmont Park (plus special exhibits on billboards and in MARTA stations). **When:** Nine days, beginning the second or third week of September. **How:** All events are free. For details, call 404/885-1125.

☐ **Arts Alive** takes place on one selected evening in late September or early October. On that night there are over 20 performances—theater, dance, symphony, chamber music—at various Atlanta locations. A $30 ticket provides entry to the performance of your choice and to a postshow gala (at a site determined annually) featuring great food from local caterers and restaurants, an art show, performers, and bands for dancing. Quite a night out. For information and tickets, call 404/586-8536.

OCTOBER

☐ **The Heritage Festival** takes place in early October on the south lawn of Courthouse Square in Decatur. It celebrates the old days with candlemaking, blacksmithing, and other crafts demonstrations; bluegrass music and other entertainment; and food booths. Admission is free. For details, call 404/371-8386.

☐ **The American Association of University Women's Annual Book Fair** is a 4-day event in Lenox Square Mall around the first week in October. AAUW collects and categorizes over 50,000 used books each year for the fair. All are in good condition, some are valuable, and prices are low. Proceeds go to charity. Admission is free. Hours are 9:30am to 9:30pm. Call 404/355-1861 to find out the fair's location in the mall.

☐ **The Atlanta Miller Lite Chili Cookoff** is held at Georgia's Stone Mountain Park on a weekend day early in the month. You can sample thousands of varieties of chili, Brunswick stew, and chili dogs. Entertainment varies each year but will likely include cloggers, country music, jalapeño-eating contests, and other folksy fun. For details, call 404/498-5702.

☐ **The Annual Scottish Festival and Highland Games,** held midmonth at Stone Mountain, is a gathering of the clans comprising three days of military tattoos, Highland dancers, pipe and drum concerts, Scottish harping and fiddling, sword dancing, reels, lilts, and athletic events such as the hammer throw and caber toss. For details and admission charges, call 404/634-7402 or 396-5728.

NOVEMBER

☐ **Walt Disney's World on Ice** comes to the Omni Coliseum early in November. To charge tickets, call 404/249-6400.

☐ **Veteran's Day Parade.** Atlanta mounts an impressive version of this parade each year, on the 11th. It's led by a grand marshal, such as Sen. Sam Nunn. And of course there are floats, drill teams, marching bands, clowns, color guards, and more. The parade begins at 10:30am at Peachtree and West Peachtree streets and proceeds south to Woodruff Park. For details, call 404/321-6111, ext. 6257.

☐ **The High Museum Antique Show & Sale,** at the Apparel Mart on a weekend in mid-November, features over 35 exhibitors—outstanding international antique dealers all. In addition, it offers lectures (some of them at luncheons), a tour of homes rich in decorative arts, daily high teas, and a Sunday brunch. Admission to the show and high tea is $6 per day at the door. For details, call 404/898-1152.

☐ **Holiday Celebrations** in Atlanta kick off with a dazzling array of events at Stone Mountain Park from late November through December 30. A "tree of lights" atop the mountain is visible from miles away; the park's roads offer a stunning display of lights, animated scenes, music, and traditional decorations; and activities include visits with Santa, candlelight plantation tours, carriage rides, holiday sing-along train rides, a special Lasershow, and lots of entertainment. For details, call 404/498-5702.

Christmas is heralded in Atlanta by the **Lighting of the Great Tree** (a traditionally decorated 80-foot pine topped by an 8-foot star) on Thanksgiving night. There are choirs singing Christmas carols. It all takes place at Underground Atlanta at Peachtree Fountains, across from Five Points MARTA station. Arrive early via MARTA; traffic comes to a standstill as hundreds of thousands converge to view the spectacle. For details, call 404/523-2311.

The last Friday in November, the **Fidelity Tree Lighting** takes place in front of the Fidelity Bank at Commerce Drive and Clairmont Avenue in Decatur. In addition to lighting a 60-foot tree, festivities include caroling, choruses, and food vendors. The fun begins at 7:30pm. Decatur's seasonal events also feature a **Candlelight Tour of Homes, a Bonfire and Christmas Carol Sing-Along** (with a marshmallow roast around a blazing fire), a **Breakfast with Santa** at a local Holiday Inn, and strolling carolers. For details, call 404/371-8386.

DECEMBER

☐ **Christmas at Callanwolde,** at Callanwolde Fine Arts Center, 980 Briarcliff Road NE, is held during the first two weeks in December (details in Chapter 7). Noted interior and floral designers decorate the Tudor mansion, and shops (sweets, toys, pottery, garden, etc.) are set up in different rooms. Activities also include concerts on the 3,752-pipe Aeolian organ, children's breakfasts with Santa, caroling and hymn singing, and other entertainment. Admission: $8 adults, $6 seniors, $5 children 12 and under. For details, call 404/872-5338.

☐ **Country Christmas.** The Atlanta Botanical Garden throws this fete on the first Sunday in December. The garden house is beautifully decorated, and highlights of the afternoon include carolers, bell ringers, children's theater, entertainers, chestnuts roasting on an open fire, horse-drawn carriage rides, cranberry and popcorn stringing, and strolling mimes, musicians, and magicians. Christmas crafts like wreath making are demonstrated, and you can shop for handcrafted gifts and homemade baked goods. Refreshments include mulled wine and cider. Of course there's a giant tree. And throughout December, there's a vast poinsettia display here. Admission is free. For details, call 404/876-5858.

○ *EGLESTON CHILDREN'S CHRISTMAS PARADE AND FESTIVAL OF TREES* Both of these events raise money for Egleston Children's Hospital. The parade is a major to-do with award-winning bands, lavish holiday-themed floats, helium-balloon comic characters, Santa Claus, carolers, costumed storybook characters, clowns, and celebrity guest appearances (for example, Marie Osmond). The parade kicks off the 9-day Festival of Trees for which Atlanta artists, interior designers, florists, and corporations innovatively decorate and donate trees, wreaths, and Christmas vignettes which are exhibited and auctioned off. The festival also features national entertainers (like Shari Lewis and Lambchop, Sesame Street actors, and Mary Lou Retton), musical performances, children's activities, an antique carousel, the "pink pig" monorail ride, ice-skating demonstrations, and an international area of heritage displays from 28 countries.

Where: The parade proceeds from Marietta and Spring streets to West Peachtree Street and Ralph McGill Boulevard. The Festival of Trees takes place at the Georgia World Congress Center, 285 International Blvd. *When:* The parade begins at 10:30am the first Saturday in December; the 9-day festival follows. *How:* For details on the parade, call 404/264-9348 or check the local papers. Admission to the Festival of Trees is $6 for adults, $4 for children under 12. For details, call 404/325-NOEL.

□ **The Sugar Plum Festival** in Stone Mountain Village takes place on a weekend early in the month. There are strolling carolers, a 15th-century St. Nick with his elves, cloggers, bell choirs, dance performances, and much more. Many shops offer gratis holiday refreshments, and, throughout the season, shops are candlelit Thursday nights. You can't beat this "village" for Christmas shopping, either. For details, call 404/296-8058.

□ **The Peach Bowl Game.** The final event of the year, some time between Christmas and New Year's (occasionally in early January) at the new Georgia Dome. It's one of 18 postseason college football games played around the country. For information, call 404/586-8500; for tickets, 404/249-6400.

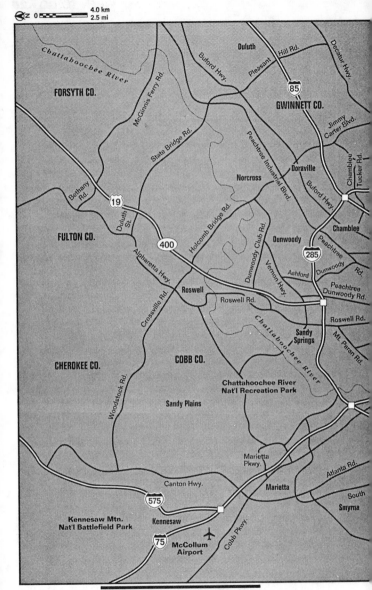

3. WHAT TO PACK

The most important aspect of a traveler's wardrobe is comfort. It can get very unpleasant trekking around even the most fascinating attractions when your shoes hurt or your clothing is too warm. In

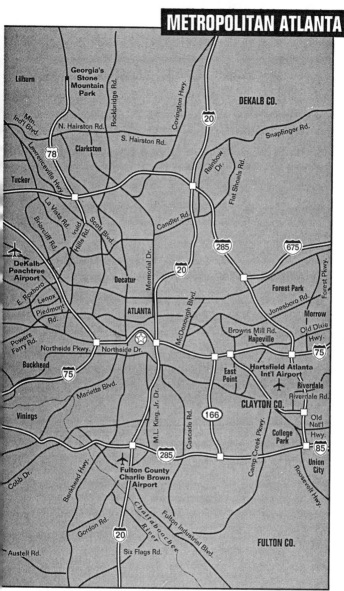

summer especially, the ideal ensemble is sneakers, shorts, and a T-shirt—in other words, the least amount of clothing you can wear in public without causing a commotion. You might, however, wish to carry a light jacket or shawl in hot weather, since interior spaces are always frigidly air-conditioned.

In winter, pack a coat, hat, and boots, but don't get carried away—this isn't Wisconsin. A fold-up umbrella is always a good idea, and if you don't use it, so much the better. People definitely dress up for dinner and evening entertainments (theater, concerts), so be sure to bring along one or two elegant outfits for nighttime wear. Jackets and ties for men are essential. This is no hick town—Atlanta is the fashion capital of the South.

One thing I like to pack is a 75- or 100-watt light bulb, especially if I'm staying at a moderately priced or budget hotel where bedside lamps seldom provide adequate wattage for reading. You don't need to pack a travel iron. Almost all hotels these days provide irons at the front desk. Find out if your hotel offers hairdryers before you pack one.

One final note: If you are taking along any vital medication—or anything else that would be devastating to lose—carry it in your hand luggage. Better safe than sorry.

---

4. TIPS FOR THE DISABLED, SENIORS, SINGLES, GAY MEN & LESBIANS, STUDENTS & FAMILIES

A free newspaper called **Creative Loafing,** available in some restaurants and in front of some MARTA stations, lists numerous events around town each issue and has special sections for "Gay and Lesbian Activities," "Seniors," and "Singles."

FOR THE DISABLED Some nationwide resources include the following: For accessibility information contact the **Travel Information Service,** Moss Rehabilitation Hospital, 1200 W. Tabor Road, Philadelphia, PA 19141 (tel. 215/456-9602), which charges nominally for mailing materials. **The Itinerary,** P.O. Box 2012, Bayonne, NJ (tel. 201/858-3400), is a bimonthly magazine for disabled travelers costing $10 per year.

Recommended tour packages include **Evergreen Travel Service/Wings on Wheels Tours,** 19505 44th Avenue, West Lynnwood, WA 98036 (tel. 206/776-1184) and **Whole Person Tours,** P.O. Box 2012, Bayonne, NJ 07002 (tel. 201/858-3400).

Two general books with helpful information are *Access to the World: A Travel Guide for the Handicapped* by Louise Weiss (H. Holt & Co.) and *Travel for the Disabled: A Handbook of Travel Resources & 400 Worldwide Access Guides* by Helen Hecker (Twin Peaks Press).

FOR SENIORS Bring some form of photo ID as many city attractions, theaters, transportation facilities, hotels, and restaurants grant special senior discounts.

If you haven't already done so, think about joining the **American Association of Retired Persons (AARP),** 1909 K Street NW,

Washington, DC 20049 (tel. 202/872-4700). Among other things, they publish a helpful publication called *Travel Easy: The Practical Guide for People Over 50.*

Another good source of discount information is *The Discount Guide for Travelers Over 55* by Caroline and Walter Weinz (E. P. Dutton).

Elderhostel, a national organization that offers low-priced educational programs for people over 60 (your spouse or significant other must be at least 50). Most of these focus on government and American history. Contact Elderhostel headquarters at 75 Federal St., Third Floor, Boston, MA 02110 (tel. 617/426-7788).

FOR SINGLE TRAVELERS The main problem for single travelers is meeting up with other people. There is, of course, the bar scene (see Chapter 10). Another good way to meet people is to go on a hike, river-rafting trip, or other such excursion, many of which are listed in the *Atlanta Journal-Constitution* "Weekend" section. You'll find other people-meeting activities listed there as well.

Another tip: choose a bed-and-breakfast facility; it's easy to meet people over coffee and muffins in the communal dining room.

FOR GAY MEN & LESBIANS Atlanta has a large gay community and you can access it via a free magazine called **Etcetera,** like *Creative Loafing* (see above) available in front of MARTA stops and in some restaurants. If you'd like a copy in advance of your trip, send $2 for a current issue to P.O. Box 8916, Atlanta, GA 30306. Or, when you arrive call 525-3821 to find out where you can pick up an issue near your hotel. You can also call that number for information on gay resources in town ("we call ourselves the gay 411," an *Etcetera* representative assured me).

FOR STUDENTS The key to securing discounts is valid student ID. Be sure to carry such and keep your eyes open for special student prices at attractions, theaters, transportation facilities, etc.

FOR FAMILIES Careful planning makes all the difference between a successful, enjoyable vacation and one that ends with exhausted, irritable parents and cranky kids. Here are just a few hints to help:

Get the kids involved Let them, if they're old enough, write to the tourist offices for information and color brochures. Give them a map on which they can outline the route; let them help decide the itinerary.

Packing Although your home may be toddler-proof, accommodations are not. Bring portable gates for stairways and other off-limits areas, and also some blank plugs to cover outlets.

En route Carry a few simple games to relieve boredom while traveling. A few snacks will also help and will save money. Check Amtrak for special family discounts; the airlines, too, have reduced airfares for those under 17; both let under-2s travel free.

Accommodations Children under a certain age usually

stay free in their parents' room. Look for establishments that have pools and other recreational facilities. Reserve equipment such as cribs and playpens in advance.

Resources What to do with the kids this year: *Traveling with Children in the U.S.A.* by Leila Hadley (Morrow), *Travel with Children* by Maureen Wheeler (Lonely Planet), and *How to Take Trips with Your Kids* by Joan and Sanford Portnoy (Harvard Common Press).

5. GETTING THERE

BY AIR

Atlanta-Hartsfield International Airport, 10 miles south of downtown, is the world's largest and second-busiest airport and transfer hub. It connects with every major metropolitan area of the United States, as well as with Europe, Mexico, Canada, the Caribbean, and Asia. The airport is bordered by I-75 and I-85, which converge going toward downtown. I-285, known as the Perimeter because it rings the city, is also accessible from the airport.

Delta, which is based at Hartsfield, is the major carrier to Atlanta ("We call home over 500 times a day" is their motto), connecting it to pretty much the entire country. As we go to press, there's a major airline price restructuring going on throughout the country, and fares are going up and down. With everything up in the air (so to speak), quoting typical fares here would be meaningless. It is always a good idea to book your flight as far in advance as possible, since advance-purchase fares are often substantially lower. When you call, also inquire about money-saving packages that include hotel accommodations, car rentals, tours, and other like expenses, with your airfare. Delta, especially, will be offering some very attractive packages for the Super Bowl and the Olympics. For Delta reservations and flight information, call toll free 800/221-1212.

BY TRAIN

Amtrak operates the *Crescent* daily between Atlanta and New York, with stops in Washington, D.C., Philadelphia, and other intermediate points. The *Crescent* also goes beyond Atlanta to many points south. And other Amtrak trains connect with most of the country. To find out if your city connects via rail with Atlanta, call toll free 800/USA-RAIL. The Amtrak station is at 1688 Peachtree Street, just off I-85.

Like the airlines, Amtrak also offers discounted fares. A limited number of seats are set aside for these special fares, so the sooner you reserve them, the greater your likelihood of success. Many people reserve these fares months in advance, so the minute you know the

**FROMMER'S SMART TRAVELER:
AIRFARES**

VALUE-CONSCIOUS TRAVELERS SHOULD TAKE
ADVANTAGE OF THE FOLLOWING:

1. Book as far ahead as possible to take advantage of lower advance-purchase fares.
2. Always ask for the lowest-priced fare, not just a discount fare.
3. Keep calling the airline to check fares. Availability of inexpensive seats changes daily, and as the departure date draws nearer, more seats are sold at lower prices.
4. Ask about senior citizen discounts (usually 10%) and discounts for children and youths (up to age 24 at some airlines).

dates of your trip, make your reservations. The fares are refundable, so you don't lose anything by reserving far in advance. There are some restrictions as to the dates you may travel.

Do inquire about money-saving packages, which might include hotel accommodations, car rentals, tours, even an air-rail combination with your train fare.

BY BUS

Greyhound buses connect the entire country with Atlanta. The bus terminal is in the heart of downtown Atlanta at 81 International Blvd., at Williams Street. For information/reservations call 404/522-6300 in Atlanta. There's no toll-free number; check your local directory for the Greyhound office in your city.

The fare structure on buses is complex and not always based on distance traveled. The good news is that when you call Greyhound, they'll always give you the lowest-fare options. Most of these are advance-purchase fares, so, once again, call as soon as you know your travel dates. Discount fares may involve restrictions on the date of travel or the departure time, and some are not refundable.

BY CAR

Three major interstate highways (I-20, I-75, and I-85) converge close to the center of downtown Atlanta. For car-rental information, see "Getting Around" in Chapter 4.

CHAPTER 3

FOR THE FOREIGN VISITOR

1. **PREPARING FOR YOUR TRIP**
2. **GETTING TO THE U.S.**
* **FAST FACTS: FOR THE FOREIGN TRAVELER**

Coming into the United States, like coming into any foreign country, can be confusing, especially if you aren't totally at ease with the language or familiar with the customs. The following information is intended to help the foreign visitor have as easy an entry and as comfortable a stay as possible.

1. PREPARING FOR YOUR TRIP

ENTRY REQUIREMENTS

DOCUMENTS Canadian nationals need only proof of Canadian residence to visit the United States. Citizens of Great Britain and Japan need only a current passport. Citizens of other countries, including Australia and New Zealand, usually need two documents: a valid **passport** with an expiration date at least six months later than the scheduled end of their visit to the United States and a **tourist visa** available at no charge from a U.S. embassy or consulate.

To get a tourist or business visa to enter the United States, contact the nearest American embassy or consulate in your country; if there is none, you will have to apply in person in a country where there *is* a U.S. embassy or consulate. Present your passport, a passport-size photo of yourself, and a completed application, which is available through the embassy or consulate. You may be asked to provide information about how you plan to finance your trip or show a letter of invitation from a friend with whom you plan to stay. Those applying for a business visa may be asked to show evidence that they will not receive a salary in the United States. Be sure to check the length of stay on your visa; usually it is six months. If you want to stay longer, you may file for an extension with the Immigration and Naturalization Service once you are in the country. If permission to stay is granted, a new visa is not required unless you leave the United States and want to reenter.

MEDICAL REQUIREMENTS No inoculations are needed to

enter the United States unless you are coming from, or have stopped over in, areas known to be suffering from epidemics, particularly cholera or yellow fever.

If you require treatment with medications containing narcotics or drugs requiring a syringe, carry a valid signed prescription from your physician to allay any suspicions that you are smuggling drugs. Ditto for syringes.

CUSTOMS REQUIREMENTS An adult visitor who stays a minimum of 72 hours may bring in the following items duty free: 1 liter of wine or hard liquor; 200 cigarettes or 100 cigars (but no cigars from Cuba) or 3 pounds of smoking tobacco; $100 worth of gifts. These exemptions are offered to travelers who spend at least 72 hours in the United States and who have not claimed them within the preceding 6 months. It is altogether forbidden to bring into the country foodstuffs (particularly cheese, fruit, cooked meats, and canned goods) and plants (vegetables, seeds, tropical plants, and so on). Foreign tourists may bring in or take out up to $10,000 in U.S. or foreign currency with no formalities; larger sums must be declared to Customs on entering or leaving.

TRAVEL INSURANCE (BAGGAGE, HEALTH & ACCIDENT)

All travel insurance is voluntary in the United States. Given the very high cost of medical care, however, I cannot too strongly advise every traveler to arrange for appropriate coverage before setting out. There are specialized insurance companies that will, for a relatively low premium, cover:

- loss or theft of your baggage;
- trip-cancellation costs;
- guarantee of bail in case you are arrested;
- sickness or injury costs (medical, surgical, and hospital);
- costs of an accident, repatriation, or death.

Such packages (for example, "Europe Assistance" in Europe) are sold by automobile clubs at attractive rates, as well as by banks and travel agencies.

A SPECIAL SERVICE

The Georgia Council for International Visitors, 999 Peachtree Street NE, between 9th and 10th streets (tel. 873-6170), is a volunteer-staffed multilingual service designed to aid foreign visitors. Their language bank allows them to offer services in 42 languages. Services include providing a translator or interpreter; help with questions about hotels, restaurants, sights, and transportation; and an escort to a doctor's office. In fact, they will try to assist foreign visitors in any way they are needed. Hours are Monday to Friday from 9am to 5pm.

2. GETTING TO THE U.S.

Travelers from overseas can take advantage of the **APEX (Advance Purchase Excursion) fares** offered by all the major U.S. and European carriers.

Some large American airlines (for example, TWA, American Airlines, Northwest, United, and Delta) offer travelers—on their transatlantic or transpacific flights—special discount tickets under the name **Visit USA**, allowing travel between any U.S. destinations at minimum rates. They are not on sale in the United States, and must, therefore, be purchased before you leave your foreign point of departure. This system is the best, easiest, and fastest way to see the United States at low cost. You should obtain information well in advance from your travel agent or the office of the airline concerned, as the conditions attached to these discount tickets can be changed without advance notice.

The visitor arriving by air, no matter what the port of entry, should cultivate patience and resignation before setting foot on U.S. soil. Getting through immigration control may take as long as two hours on some days, especially summer weekends. Add the time it takes to clear Customs and you will see that you should make very generous allowance for delay in planning connections between international and domestic flights—an average of two to three hours at least.

In contrast, for the traveler arriving by car or by rail from Canada, the border-crossing formalities have been streamlined to the vanishing point. And for the traveler by air from Canada, Bermuda, and some places in the Caribbean, you can sometimes go through Customs and Immigration at the point of departure, which is much quicker and less painful.

For further information about travel to and arriving in Atlanta see "Getting There" in Chapter 2, and "Arriving" in Chapter 4, Section 1.

FAST *FOR THE FOREIGN TRAVELER*

Accommodations See Chapter 5. *Note:* For foreign students, the **Atlanta Convention and Visitors Bureau,** 233 Peachtree St. NE, Suite 2000 (tel. 404/521-6600), offers (subject to availability) discounted rooms at 11 Atlanta hotels. Rates are $25 to $35 single, $30 to $45 double. You must stop by during office hours (Monday to Friday, 8:30am to 5:30pm) to participate.

Automobile Organizations Auto clubs will supply maps, suggested routes, guidebooks, accident and bail-bond insurance, and emergency road service. The major auto club in the United

States, with 850 offices nationwide, is the **American Automobile Association** (AAA). To join in Atlanta, call 404/843-4500 or toll free 800/336-4357. Membership costs $50 for the first year, $40 for each consecutive year after that. AAA can provide you with a "Touring Permit" that validates your driver's license. Members of some foreign auto clubs that have reciprocal arrangements with AAA enjoy AAA's services at no charge.

Automobile Rentals   To rent a car you need a major credit card, or you'll have to leave a sizable cash deposit ($100 or more for each day). A valid driver's license is required, and you usually need to be at least 21 (sometimes older) to rent a car; some companies do rent to younger people but add a daily surcharge. Be sure to return your car with the same amount of gas you started out with; rental companies charge excessive prices for gasoline. All of the major car rental companies are represented in Atlanta. **Atlanta Rent-A-Car** (tel. 404/763-1160) offers particularly low prices (see Chapter 4, Section 2 for details).

Business Hours   Offices are usually open Monday through Friday from 9am to 5pm. **Banks** are open Monday through Friday from 9am to 3pm and sometimes on Saturday mornings. The **post office** is open Monday through Friday from 8:30am to 5pm and on Saturday from 8:30am to noon. **Shops** are generally open from 10am to 5 or 6pm. Those in malls tend to stay open late, to about 9pm Monday through Saturday and until 5 or 6pm on Sunday. Museum days and hours of operation vary (see individual listings in Chapter 7, "What to See and Do in Atlanta").

Climate   See Chapter 2, Section 2.

Consulates   At press time, 45 countries have official representation in Atlanta, including: **Canadian Consulate General,** Suite 400, South Tower, One CNN Center, Atlanta, GA 30303 (tel. 404/577-6810); **Consulate of France,** 285 Peachtree Center Avenue, Suite 2800, Atlanta, GA 30303 (tel. 404/522-4226); **Consulate General of the Federal Republic of Germany,** 229 Peachtree Street NE, Suite 1000, Atlanta, GA 30303-1618 (tel. 404/659-4760); **British Consulate General,** 245 Peachtree Center Avenue, Marquis One Tower, Suite 2700, Atlanta, GA 30303 (tel. 404/524-5856); **Honorary Consulate of Italy,** 1106 W. Peachtree Street NW, Atlanta, GA 30309 (tel. 404/875-6177); and the **Consulate of Mexico,** One CNN Center, 410 South Tower, Atlanta, GA 30303 (tel. 404/688-3258). For complete information, contact the **Atlanta Chamber of Commerce,** P.O. Box 1740, Atlanta, GA 30301 (tel. 404/586-8470).

Currency & Exchange   The U.S. monetary system has a decimal base: one American **dollar** ($1) = 100 **cents** (100¢).

Dollar **bills** commonly come in $1 ("a buck"), $5, $10, $20, $50, and $100 denominations (the last two are not welcome when paying for small purchases and are not accepted in taxis or at subway ticket booths).

There are six coin denominations: 1¢ (one cent or "penny"); 5¢ (five cents or "nickel"); 10¢ (ten cents or "dime"); 25¢ (twenty-five cents or "quarter"); 50¢ (fifty cents or "half dollar"—rare); and the rare—and prized by collectors—$1 pieces (both the older, large silver dollar and the newer, small Susan B. Anthony coin).

Traveler's checks denominated in dollars are accepted without demur at most hotels, motels, restaurants, and large stores. But as any experienced traveler knows, the best place to change traveler's checks is at a bank.

Credit cards are the method of payment most widely used: VISA (BarclayCard in Britain), MasterCard (EuroCard in Europe, Access in Britain, Diamond in Japan), American Express, Diners Club, Carte Blanche, Discover, and Transmedia, in descending order of acceptance. You can save yourself trouble by using "plastic" rather than cash or traveler's checks in 95% of all hotels, motels, restaurants, and retail stores. A credit card can also serve as a deposit for renting a car, as proof of identity (often carrying more weight than a passport), or as a "cash card," enabling you to draw money from banks that accept them.

Currency Exchange Thomas Cook Currency Services (formerly Deak International) offers a wide variety of services: more than 100 currencies, commission-free traveler's checks, drafts and wire transfers, check collections, and precious metal bars and coins. Rates are competitive and service excellent. They have an office at 245 Peachtree Center Ave. in Atlanta; for other locations or information call toll free 800/582-4496. Many hotels will exchange currency if you are a registered guest.

Note: The "foreign-exchange bureaus" so common in Europe are rare even at airports in the United States and nonexistent outside major cities. Try to avoid having to change foreign money, or traveler's checks denominated other than in U.S. dollars, at small-town banks, or even at branches in a big city; in fact leave any currency other than U.S. dollars at home—it may prove more nuisance to you than it's worth.

Drinking Laws Every state, and sometimes every county and community, has its own laws governing the sale of liquor. The only federal regulation (based on a judgment of the U.S. Supreme Court on June 23, 1987) restricts the consumption of liquor in public places anywhere in the country to people ages 21 or over.

In Georgia, no alcohol is served at bars, restaurants, or nightclubs between 2:55am Saturday and 12:30pm Sunday.

Electric Current U.S. wall outlets give power at 110 to 115 volts, 60 cycles, compared to 220 volts, 50 cycles, in most of Europe. Besides a 110-volt converter, small appliances of non-American manufacture, such as hairdryers or shavers, will require a plug adapter with two flat, parallel pins.

Emergencies In all major cities (including Atlanta), you can call the police, an ambulance, or the fire department through the single emergency telephone number 911. Another useful way of reporting an emergency is to call the telephone-company operator by dialing 0.

If you encounter such travelers' problems as sickness, accident, or lost or stolen baggage, it will pay you to call **Travelers Aid,** an organization that specializes in helping distressed travelers, whether American or foreign. In Atlanta, you can reach this organization by calling 404/527-7400 (it's a 24-hour number). For further details on Travelers Aid, see Chapter 4, "Getting to Know Atlanta."

See also the **Georgia Council for International Visitors,** above.

Gasoline (Petrol)   One U.S. gallon equals 3.75 liters, while 1.2 U.S. gallons equal one imperial gallon. You'll notice several grades (and price levels) of gasoline at most stations. Most rental cars take the least expensive type of unleaded.

Holidays   Banks, government offices, post offices, and many stores, restaurants, and museums are closed on the following legal national holidays: January 1 (New Year's Day), Third Monday in January (Martin Luther King Day), Third Monday in February (Presidents' Day, Washington's Birthday), Last Monday in May (Memorial Day), July 4 (Independence Day), First Monday in September (Labor Day), Second Monday in October (Columbus Day), November 11 (Veterans Day/Armistice Day), Fourth Thursday in November (Thanksgiving Day), and December 25 (Christmas Day).

Legal Aid   If you are stopped for a minor infraction (for example, of the highway code, such as speeding), never attempt to pay the fine directly to a police officer; you may be arrested on the much more serious charge of attempted bribery. Pay fines by mail, or directly into the hands of the clerk of the court. If accused of a more serious offense, it is wise to say and do nothing before consulting a lawyer. Under U.S. law, an arrested person is allowed one telephone call to a party of his choice. Call your embassy or consulate.

Mailboxes   are blue with a red-and-white logo, and carry the inscription "U.S. MAIL." A first-class **stamp** costs 29¢.

Medical Emergencies   See "Emergencies," above, and "Fast Facts" in Chapter 4, Section 2.

Newspapers and Magazines   With a few exceptions, such as the *New York Times, USA Today,* the *Wall Street Journal,* and the *Christian Science Monitor,* daily newspapers in the United States are local, not national.

There are also innumerable newsweeklies like *Newsweek, Time,* and *U.S. News & World Report,* as well as specialized periodicals, such as the monthly magazines devoted to a single city. In Atlanta, the major daily is the *Atlanta Journal-Constitution.* The city magazine is called *Atlanta.*

The airmail editions of foreign newspapers and magazines are on sale only belatedly, and only at airports and international bookstores in the largest cities.

Radio and Television   Audiovisual media, with three coast-to-coast networks—ABC, CBS, and NBC—joined in recent years by the Public Broadcasting System (PBS) and the cable network CNN, play a major part in American life. In the big cities, televiewers have a choice of about a dozen channels (including the UHF channels), most of them transmitting 24 hours a day, without counting the pay-TV channels showing recent movies or sports events. In smaller communities, the choice may be limited to four TV channels (there are 1,200 in the entire country), and a half dozen local radio stations (there are 6,500 in all), each broadcasting a particular kind of music—classical, country, jazz, pop, or gospel—punctuated by news broadcasts and frequent commercials.

Safety   In general, the United States is about as safe as most other countries, particularly in rural areas, but there are "danger zones" in the big cities that should be approached only with extreme caution.

As a general rule, isolated areas such as gardens and parking lots should be avoided after dark. Elevators, rest rooms at bus and train stations, and public-transport systems in off-hours, particularly between 10pm and 6am, are also potential crime scenes. You should drive through decaying neighborhoods with your car doors locked and the windows closed. Never carry on your person valuables like jewelry or large sums of cash; traveler's checks are much safer.

Taxes   In the United States there is no VAT (value-added tax) at the national level. Every state, and each city in it, has the right to levy its own local tax on purchases, including hotel and restaurant checks. In Atlanta hotel tax is 13%. That includes room tax (7%) and sales tax (6%).

Telephone, Telegraph, Telex   You will find public telephones at street corners, in bars, restaurants, public buildings, stores, service stations, and along highways. Outside the metropolitan areas public telephones are more difficult to find. Stores and gas stations are your best bet. Local calls from public telephones in Atlanta cost 25¢.

Before calling from a hotel room, always ask the hotel phone operator if there are any telephone surcharges. These are best avoided by using a public phone, calling collect, or using a telephone charge card.

For local **directory assistance** ("information"), dial 411; for long-distance information, dial 1, then the appropriate area code and 555-1212. To make a long-distance call, dial 1, then the area code, followed by the number.

For **long-distance** or **international calls,** stock up with a supply of quarters; the pay phone will instruct you when you should put them into the slot. For long-distance calls in the United States, dial 1, followed by the area code and number you want. For direct overseas calls, first dial 011, followed by the country code and the number of the person you wish to call.

For **reversed-charge** or **collect calls,** and for **person-to-person calls,** dial 0 (zero, not the letter "O"), followed by the area code and number you want; an operator will then come on the line and you should specify that you are calling collect, or person-to-person, or both. If your operator-assisted call is international, ask for the overseas operator.

Like the telephone system, **telegraph** and **telex** services are provided by private corporations like ITT, MCI, and, above all, Western Union. You can bring your telegram to the nearest Western

Union office (there are hundreds across the country), or dictate it over the phone (a toll-free call, 800/325-6000). You can also telegraph money, or have it telegraphed to you very quickly, over the Western Union system.

Most hotels have **fax** machines available to their customers (ask if there is a charge to use it). You will also see signs for public faxes in the windows of small shops.

Telephone Directories There are two kinds of telephone directories, White Pages and Yellow Pages. In the **White Pages,** residences and businesses are listed in alphabetical order. The inside front cover lists emergency numbers for police, fire, and ambulances, as well as other vital numbers (poison-control center, crime-victim's hotline, etc.). The first few pages include community service numbers and a guide to long-distance and international calling, complete with country area codes.

The **Yellow Pages** lists local services and businesses by type of activity (for example, "restaurants," "plumbers," and so on). It's extremely comprehensive. It also includes city plans and area maps showing ZIP codes and public transportation routes.

Time The United States is divided into four **time zones** (six, if Alaska and Hawaii are included). From east to west, these are: Eastern Standard Time (EST), Central Standard Time (CST), Mountain Standard Time (MST), Pacific Standard Time (PST), Alaska Standard Time (AST), and Hawaii Standard Time (HST). Always keep changing time zones in mind if you are traveling (or even telephoning) long distances in the United States. For example, noon in New York City (EST) is 11am in Chicago (CST), 10am in Denver (MST), 9am in Los Angeles (PST), 8am in Anchorage (AST), and 7am in Honolulu (HST). Atlanta is on Eastern Standard Time.

Daylight Saving Time is in effect from 2am on the first Sunday in April to 2am on the last Sunday in October, except in Arizona, Hawaii, part of Indiana, and Puerto Rico.

Tipping This part of the American way of life is based on the principle that you must expect to pay for any service you get. Here are some rules of thumb: cab drivers, 15% of fare, bellhops and redcaps, at least 50¢ per bag and $2 to $3 for a lot of luggage; restaurants, bars, and nightclubs, 15% to 20% of the check; valet parking, $1.

CHAPTER 4

GETTING TO KNOW ATLANTA

1. ORIENTATION
2. GETTING AROUND
● **FAST FACTS:**
   ATLANTA

Atlanta is a fairly compact city rather than a sprawling metropolis. After a few days in town, you'll know your way around.

1. ORIENTATION

ARRIVING

In the International Gateway City, transportation is state-of-the-art and getting to your hotel from plane, train, or bus is a cinch.

BY AIR Hartsfield International Airport is just 10 miles south of downtown. It's a beautiful and well-planned airport, with ample parking space (and low parking charges), retail shops, facilities for the handicapped, and banking and currency-exchange facilities.

There are several options for getting from the airport to your hotel. The cheapest, if your luggage is manageable, is to take Atlanta's subway (**MARTA**), which has a stop right in the airport. The fare is just $1. Almost all hotels are very close to MARTA rail stations.

A taxi from the airport to a downtown or midtown hotel costs $15 for one passenger, $8 each for two or more. To Buckhead hotels, the fare is $25 for one passenger, $26 for two, $9 each for three or more.

Atlanta Airport Shuttle Vans (tel. 524-3400 or toll free 800/842-2770) operate between the airport and most downtown and midtown hotels. They depart from the Delta baggage claim/ground transportation area in the North Terminal. You can catch one about every 30 minutes in either direction from 8am to midnight seven days a week. Cost is $8 one way, $14 round trip; children under 3 ride free. It's a very well organized system, with destinations clearly marked and helpful attendants on hand. Vans also ply the route between the airport and Buckhead hotels. Cost is $12 one way, $20 round trip, free for children under 3. Some properties further afield are also served. Call 768-7600 for information about transport to suburban locations. When you leave Atlanta, check with your hotel desk about departure times; for some hotels, reservations are required a day in advance.

BY TRAIN Amtrak trains arrive in Atlanta at 1688 Peachtree Street, just off I-85. From this very central location, you can take a taxi to your hotel or to the nearest MARTA station (Arts Center). For information, call 404/881-3060 or toll free 800/USA-RAIL.

BY BUS The Greyhound bus terminal, 81 International Blvd. at Williams Street, is in the heart of downtown. The Peachtree Center MARTA station is about two blocks away, and taxis are available. For information, call 404/522-6300. There's no toll-free number; check your local directory for the Greyhound office in your city.

TOURIST INFORMATION

For information about hotels, restaurants, and attractions, contact the **Atlanta Convention & Visitors Bureau (ACVB),** 233 Peachtree St. NE, Suite 2000, Atlanta 30303 (tel. 404/222-6688 or toll free 800/ATLANTA). Call or write in advance to obtain a copy of *Atlanta Now* (the official visitor's guide), a *Metro Atlanta Attractions Guide,* a map, and a 2-month calendar of events. You can call weekdays between 8am and 6pm.

In town, you can visit ACVB information centers at:

Peachtree Center Mall, 231 Peachtree St. Open Monday to Friday 10am to 5pm.

Lenox Square, 3393 Peachtree Rd. Open Monday to Friday 10am to 5pm.

Underground Atlanta, 65 Upper Alabama St. Open Monday to Saturday 10am to 9:30pm, Sunday noon to 6pm.

FOR TROUBLED TRAVELERS The **Travelers Aid Society** is a nationwide, nonprofit social-service organization geared to helping travelers in difficult straits. Their services might include reuniting families separated while traveling, providing food and/or shelter to people stranded without cash, even emotional counseling. If you're in trouble, seek them out. They have three locations in Atlanta: near Underground Atlanta at 40 Pryor St. SW, between Decatur and Wall streets (tel. 404/527-7400, a 24-hour number), open Monday to Friday 8am to 8pm, Saturdays and holidays, 10am to 6pm; at the Greyhound Bus Terminal, 81 International Blvd. at Williams Street (tel. 404/527-7411), open the same hours; and at the airport (tel. 404/766-4511), open Monday to Friday from 9:30am to 6pm.

CITY LAYOUT

Atlanta is girded by a beltway called I-285, always referred to as the Perimeter. As a tourist, you'll be spending most of your time within the confines of the Perimeter. Two interstate highways (I-75 and I-85) converge just above the airport and proceed north, forking off just northwest of Piedmont Park: I-75 goes west, I-85 east. A fourth interstate highway just below the downtown area, I-20, is an east-west artery that cuts all the way through Georgia (and Atlanta), connecting South Carolina with Alabama.

As for the major streets, there's a joke that all directions here begin with "Go to Peachtree. . . ." That's because there are a few dozen Peachtrees—Peachtree Street, Lane, Road, Avenue, Circle, Drive, Plaza, and Way, not to mention West Peachtree Street, Peachtree Industrial Boulevard, Peachtree Memorial Drive, Peachtree Battle Avenue, Peachtree Valley Road, etc., etc., etc. So be sure to emphasize which Peachtree you're looking for when you ask for directions. That being said, Peachtree Street (which becomes Peachtree Road above midtown) and Piedmont Avenue are Atlanta's two major north-south arteries. Peachtree is a two-way thoroughfare, while Piedmont has two-way traffic above 14th Street, but south-to-north only below 14th Street. Major east-west streets include Memorial Drive, North Avenue, Ponce de Leon Avenue, 14th Street, and, in Buckhead, East and West Paces Ferry drives. With map in hand, you'll find getting around Atlanta very easy.

ATLANTA NEIGHBORHOODS IN BRIEF   You can't really get the feel of a city until you understand the characteristics of its neighborhoods. Herewith, a brief rundown of Atlanta's diverse districts.

Downtown   Atlanta's financial and business hub, this beautifully planned area of sleek skyscrapers includes the futuristic Peachtree Center hotel / convention center / trade mart / office-tower complex. Here, too: Underground Atlanta, an exciting mix of shops, restaurants, and nightclubs fronted by a 138-foot light tower; Omni Coliseum, featuring sports action and big-name entertainment; the mammoth Georgia World Congress Center, one of the largest meeting and exhibition halls in the nation; the 70,500-seat Georgia Dome, built for Olympic events and Super Bowl XXVIII; CNN Center, Ted Turner's media HQ; Georgia-Pacific Center, housing the downtown branch of the High Museum of Art; the golden-domed, century-old State Capitol, a major landmark; the downtown branch of the Atlanta Historical Society; and the SciTrek Museum. In the general area are Oakland Cemetery (it's mentioned in *Gone With the Wind*, and Margaret Mitchell is one of the many notables buried here) and Grant Park (the zoo and Cyclorama). This is a downtown that pulsates with big-city excitement, but its scale is human—and you can still find a place to park.

Sweet Auburn   This famous black neighborhood, also called the Martin Luther King, Jr., Historic District, is just below downtown's central area. Under the auspices of the National Parks Service, it was designated a park in 1980 to honor King, whose boyhood home, crypt, and church are located here. In spite of the yoke of segregation, affluent black businesspeople and professionals

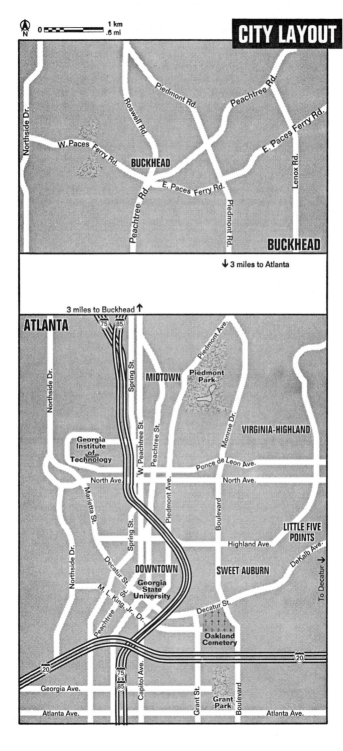

flourished here from the early part of the 20th century through the 1950s. Today it's one of Atlanta's major sightseeing draws.

Midtown   Though its boundaries have never been definitively decided, midtown basically encompasses the area north of downtown from about Ponce de Leon Avenue to 26th Street. It includes Piedmont Park, Atlanta's major recreation area; the Woodruff Arts Center, home of the Atlanta Symphony Orchestra, the Alliance Theatre, and the High Museum of Art; the famed Fox Theatre, a 1920s Moorish-motif movie palace; Ansley Park, a 230-acre residential greenbelt area, designed at the turn of the century by Frederick Law Olmsted; and Colony Square, an office/hotel/retail complex. AT&T, IBM, and Southern Bell maintain corporate offices in midtown.

Buckhead   Named for an 1838 tavern called the Buck's Head, this is Atlanta's silk-stocking district—one of America's most beautiful and affluent communities. It begins about 6 miles north of downtown. Here you'll find tree-shaded residential areas of magnificent mansions surrounded by verdant acreage, elite shops and boutiques (including Lenox Square and Phipps Plaza malls, two exclusive shopping enclaves), superb restaurants, and first-class hotels. Buckhead is also a nightlife center for the yuppie set (clubs abound) and a burgeoning business area. Its major sightseeing attraction is the Atlanta Historical Society, centered on a Palladian villa designed by noted architect Phillip Schutze and surrounded by 32 woodland acres. The Greek Revival Governor's Mansion is also in Buckhead.

Virginia-Highland   Every major American city has a district that claims kinship with New York's Greenwich Village. In Atlanta it's the Virginia-Highland section, so named for its central avenues, northeast of downtown. Here you'll find ethnic eateries, dozens of antique shops, bookstores, sidewalk cafés, art galleries, lively bars and bistros, and browsable shops selling everything from healing crystals to recycled clothing. Virginia-Highland is colorful, casual, and completely unpretentious.

Little Five Points   Just below Virginia-Highland, Little Five Points offers similar offbeat ambience and emporia. It is also the location of the Jimmy Carter Library/Carter Presidential Center, which opened in 1986 to house the correspondence and memorabilia of this Georgia-born president. Many Victorian homes make for an architecturally interesting stroll. The neighborhood is centered at the junction of Euclid and Moreland avenues.

Decatur   Founded in 1823 by Commodore Stephen Decatur, a dashing naval hero of the War of 1812 who died in a duel, this quaintly charming village centers on an old courthouse square. About a 15-minute drive east from downtown, Decatur is the scene of numerous annual events, festivals, and concerts, and it houses the sprawling Dekalb Farmer's Market, an international food market that must be seen to be believed. Like Virginia-Highland and Little Five Points, Decatur weaves color and texture into Atlanta's tapestry of neighborhoods.

2. GETTING AROUND

If you're here for a few days, you'll get a pretty good feel for the layout of the city. It's not complicated. And getting around the city is easy and affordable.

BY PUBLIC TRANSPORTATION

The Metropolitan Atlanta Rapid Transit Authority (MARTA) operates an extensive and efficient subway and bus network, making it possible to reach just about any part of town by public transportation.

MARTA RAPID RAIL MARTA's subway or rapid-rail service began in 1979. The stations are clean and safe, and it's a pleasure to use. Eventually, this will be a 61-mile, 45-station system. At press time, the rail system extends 38.6 miles and includes 33 stations. There are two lines: South-north Orange Line trains travel between the airport and Doraville; east-west Blue Line trains travel between Indian Creek (east of Decatur) and Hightower. The lines intersect at Five Points Station in downtown Atlanta. Fare is just $1 for any ride, payable in exact change, tokens, or TransCards. Tokens, available at the stations, cost $9.50 for ten. A weekly TransCard, available at the RideStore in the Five Points Station, good for unlimited bus and rail travel for one week, is $9.

MARTA trains generally arrive and depart every 8 to 10 minutes during operating hours: Monday to Saturday from 5am to 1am, Sunday and holidays from 6am to 12:30am. Free transfers are available between bus and rail when you board a bus or enter a rail station. Parking is available at many rail stations; it costs $1 per day and is free in the evening and on the weekend.

For MARTA schedule and route information, call 848-4711 Monday to Friday from 6am to 10pm, Saturday and Sunday from 8am to 4pm. For information regarding the elderly and the disabled, call 848-3340.

BUSES Basically, you can get anywhere in Atlanta by bus. MARTA buses operate on a 1,550-mile network of 150 routes. The fare system is the same as described above for rail service. To find out what bus to take, call 848-4711 for route information (same hours as above). Drivers do not carry change; you must have exact change, a token, a transfer, or a TransCard. Special shuttle buses operate from downtown in conjunction with major-stadium sports events; call the above number for details.

BY TAXI

Taxi fares are a bit complicated in Atlanta. In the so-called Downtown Zone (roughly east to west between Piedmont Avenue and

Northside Drive, north to south from 14th Street to Ralph Abernathy Boulevard), you pay a flat rate of $4 for one or two passengers, $2 for each additional rider. That's fine if you're going from one end of this extensive zone to the other; unfortunately, though, you pay the same if you only go one block.

There's also a flat rate for rides between downtown or midtown and the airport: $15 for one passenger, $8 each for two or more. Between the airport and Buckhead, the rate is $25 for one passenger, $26 for two, $9 each for three or more.

Outside these specified zones, Atlanta cabs charge a $1.50 drop when you get in and 20¢ for each additional ⅙ mile for the first passenger and a flat rate of $1 for each additional passenger, adult or child.

There are many taxi companies in town. If you need to call for a taxi, try Yellow Cabs (tel. 521-0200) or Checker Cabs (tel. 351-1111).

If you have a complaint about taxi service, call 658-7600.

BY CAR

You don't desperately need a car in Atlanta. The transit system (MARTA) is very good. However, a car is certainly a convenience, and, in most places you'll visit, parking isn't a problem. Given my druthers, I prefer to have one. All of the major car-rental companies are, of course, represented here and reachable via toll-free numbers. One local company, however, offers good service, very competitive rates, and a full range of compact and midsize cars and vans.

Atlanta Rent-A-Car (tel. 404/763-1160) has been in Atlanta for over 10 years. They have 11 locations in town, including one close to the airport, and they'll pick you up anywhere in the city if you want to rent. At press time, their compact cars begin at just $19.95 a day with 100 free miles, or $9 a day and 19¢ a mile with no free miles. The same car costs $99.95 a week with 500 free miles. It's always best to reserve in advance.

 ATLANTA

Area Code 404.

Airport Atlanta is served by the **Hartsfield-Atlanta International Airport,** 10 miles south of downtown. It is the world's third-busiest airport and transfer hub. (Flights to just about everywhere are routed through the city; in fact, there's a saying, "Even if you fly to hell, you still have to go through Atlanta.")

Babysitters Most hotels will arrange babysitters for you. If yours doesn't, a highly recommended service is **A Friend of the Family** (tel. 255-2848). All of their sitters are carefully screened, bonded, and at least 21 years of age. On request, they can send someone who is also trained in CPR and first aid and/or who speaks

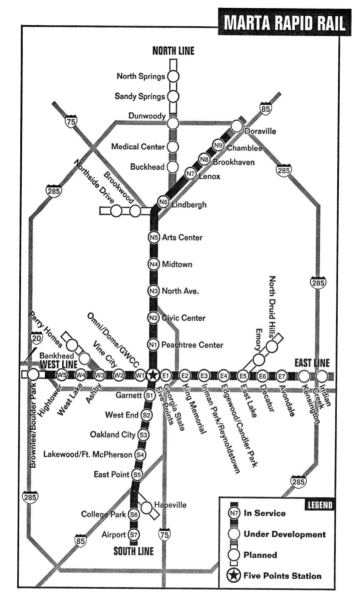

MARTA RAPID RAIL

NORTH LINE

North Springs
Sandy Springs
Dunwoody
Doraville
Medical Center
N9 Chamblee
Buckhead
N8 Brookhaven
N7 Lenox
Northside Drive
Brookwood
N6 Lindbergh
N5 Arts Center
N4 Midtown
N3 North Ave.
Omni/Dome/GWCC
N2 Civic Center
Perry Homes
N1 Peachtree Center
Bankhead
Vine City
North Druid Hills
WEST LINE
Emory
EAST LINE
W5 W4 W3 W2 W1 E1 E2 E3 E4 E5 E6 E7
Indian Creek
Brownlee/Boulder Park
Hightower
West Lake
Ashby
Garnett S1
Georgia State
Five Points
King Memorial
Inman Park/Reynoldstown
Edgewood/Candler Park
East Lake
Decatur
Avondale
Kensington
West End S2
Oakland City S3
Lakewood/Ft. McPherson S4
East Point S5
Hapeville
College Park S6
Airport S7
SOUTH LINE

LEGEND
N7 In Service
Under Development
Planned
★ Five Points Station

a foreign language. You can interview the sitter in advance on the phone or in person. Rate is $6 to $8 per hour, with a 4-hour minimum, plus a $15 agency fee. Advance notice of 24 hours is appreciated but not required. A Friend of the Family also provides pet care, companions for adults, and shopping companions or services.

Banking   There is a 24-hour NCR bank machine at **World Congress Center,** 285 International Blvd. (tel. 841-7420).

Buses See "Getting Around," above.

Car Rentals See "Getting Around," above.

Climate See "When to Go," in Chapter 2.

Dentists The **Georgia Dental Association of Atlanta** (tel. 458-6166) offers a free referral service. They'll refer you to a dentist close to your hotel, or if need be, one who can accommodate special needs (for example, a dentist who does cosmetic work, offers home visits or senior-citizen discounts, keeps emergency hours, or otherwise specializes). The service operates weekdays from 8:30am to 5pm. At other times, inquire at your hotel desk.

Doctors The **Medical Association of Atlanta** (tel. 881-1714), with over 2,000 member physicians in town, runs a free referral service for every kind of medical specialty and subspecialty. Hours are Monday to Friday from 9am to 4pm. At other times, inquire at your hotel desk. (See also "Hospitals," below.)

Drinking Age You must be at least 21 to consume liquor in Georgia. (See also, "Liquor Laws," below.)

Drugstores **Treasury Drugs,** 1026 Ponce de Leon Ave. at Highland Avenue (tel. 876-0381), is open 24 hours and offers full pharmaceutical services.

Emergencies To report a fire, summon the police, or procure an ambulance, simply dial 911.

Eyeglasses Head over to **Opti-World,** in the Around Lenox Shopping Center (enter the Lenox Square Mall on Peachtree Road, just below Lenox Road, look for Neiman-Marcus, and veer to the right; tel. 262-2020). This eyeglass department store offers 1-hour service on contacts and eyeglasses (including bifocals and trifocals), stocks the largest selection of frames in Atlanta (from designer to economy), provides on-premises eye examinations by independent doctors of optometry, maintains a complete contact-lens center, and gives 15% discounts to senior citizens and college students.

Hairdressers To some of us, a gifted hairdresser can be the most essential of services. **Stan Milton,** 721 Miami Circle NE, off Piedmont Road (tel. 233-6241), is one of Atlanta's most talented and celebrated stylists. He's done dozens of makeovers for local TV personalities, and his devoted clientele comes from all over the South. He's wonderful at finding your optimum look. The salon also does a beautiful job on perms and hair coloring, and an excellent staff proffers every salon service—facials, manicures/pedicures, waxing, massage, video imaging (letting you see yourself in different styles before you take the plunge), and full days of beauty services. The salon is elegant but very relaxed and friendly. I appreciate Milton's commitment to the environment; he uses only products that are natural, chemical free, and biodegradable. While you're here, ask for a complimentary makeup application. Haircuts are $20 to $55 for women, $15 to $25 for men, and $10 to $15 for children. Perms are $45 to $65. Reserve as far in advance as possible.

Hospitals **Piedmont Hospital,** 1968 Peachtree Road, just above Collier Road (tel. 605-3297), offers 24-hour full emergency-room service. It also offers a free physician-referral service for all medical problems (tel. 605-3556) weekdays between 9am and 5pm.

In addition, Piedmont maintains a minor-illness emergency room downtown: the **Medical Care Center,** 115 Peachtree St., in the Candler Building (tel. 577-1990). This is for minor problems only—cuts, slight burns, illness, splinters, and the like. It's open weekdays from 8:30am to 6pm. If need be, they'll send a cab for you.

Libraries The **Atlanta Fulton Public Library,** 1 Margaret Mitchell Sq., at Forsyth Street and Carnegie Way (tel. 730-1700), is the city's central branch. In addition to the usual well-stocked library inventory, it has a large collection of African-American records, books, and photographs; many books in Spanish; and city newspapers from all over the world. The High Collection of first-edition children's books can be seen by appointment. Two only-in-Atlanta library features are an extensive collection of first and rare editions of *Gone With the Wind* and a permanent exhibit on Margaret Mitchell. In addition, the library features frequent art exhibits, classes, films, lectures, and storytelling; inquire when you visit. Open Monday from 9am to 6pm, Tuesday to Thursday from 9am to 8pm, Friday and Saturday from 10am to 5pm, and Sunday from 2 to 6pm.

Liquor Laws No alcohol is served at bars, restaurants, or nightclubs between 2:55am Saturday and 12:30pm Sunday. The drinking age is 21.

Multilingual Visitor Assistance Call 873-6170.

Newspapers/Magazines The major newspaper in town is *The Atlanta Journal-Constitution.* You'll also find it helpful to pick up a current issue of *Atlanta* magazine when you're in town; it has all the current theater, movie, club, gallery, and museum listings, among other informative data. And keep an eye out for *Creative Loafing,* an offbeat free publication available in shops, restaurants, and on the street; it offers much interesting info.

Police See "Emergencies," above.

Population 2.8 million.

Road Conditions Call 656-5267, a 24-hour number.

Taxis Call **Yellow Cabs** (tel. 521-0200) or **Checker Cabs** (tel. 351-1111).

Tickets For tickets to almost all sports and performing arts events, call **Ticketmaster** (tel. 249-6400).

Time Call 976-1221. Atlanta is on Eastern Standard Time.

Transit Information To find out how to get from point A to point B via MARTA (bus and rail), dial 848-4711; via Amtrak, dial 872-9815 or 800/872-7245; via Greyhound/Trailways, dial 522-6300.

Weather Call 976-1221.

CHAPTER 5

ATLANTA ACCOMMODATIONS

1. **DOWNTOWN**
- **FROMMER'S SMART TRAVELER: HOTELS**
2. **MIDTOWN**
- **FROMMER'S COOL FOR KIDS: HOTELS**
3. **BUCKHEAD**
4. **GEORGIA TECH**
5. **GEORGIA'S STONE MOUNTAIN**
6. **DRUID HILLS/EMORY UNIVERSITY/ BROOKHAVEN**
7. **OFF I-20**

As a major convention city, Atlanta is capable of accommodating vast numbers of visitors. It has 55,337 rooms at 340 properties (up from 29,000 rooms only 10 years ago), and several new hotels are being built as I write. These accommodations exist at all levels; there are budget digs (though not as many as I'd like to see), bed-and-breakfast lodgings, and bastions of luxury. Presented below are my choices in all price brackets, each one offering excellent value in its category.

Note: Although 100% occupancy is a rarity in Atlanta, booking well in advance assures you a room in the hotel of your choice.

Savvy travelers can save considerably on hotel rates. Be sure to take advantage of weekend rates. Even top-of-the-line hotels often slash prices 30% to 50% on weekends—and at some properties "weekends" include Friday, Saturday, and Sunday nights. Always inquire about the availability of these rates when you reserve. That doesn't mean you can only travel on weekends; rather, you can usually get the lower rate for that segment of your stay. Be sure to verify that your reservation has been made at the weekend rate before hanging up the phone (if possible, request written confirmation), and check on it again when you register at the hotel. At many properties, you can't just show up at the desk for checkout Monday morning and expect to pay weekend rates; you have to be so registered in advance. In addition, weekend rates are often subject to availability, so reserving considerably in advance is advisable.

Also inquire about reduced-price packages (they may include extras such as meals, parking, theater tickets, and golf fees) and reduced rates for senior citizens, families, and active-duty military personnel.

Many preferential rates are available only when you reserve via toll-free reservation numbers. These numbers are supplied in all applicable listings below. Days Inns offer drastically reduced Super Saver rates if you reserve 30 days or more in advance (subject to availability).

Weekend and special rates aren't the whole picture. Keep in mind the perspective of the hotelier. A hotel makes zero dollars per night on an empty room. Hence, though they don't bruit it about (for obvious reasons), most hotels are willing to bargain on rates rather than leave a room unoccupied. Haggling won't work when hotels are running close to 100% occupancy, but whenever a rate is quoted it's a good idea to ask, "Can I get a better deal?" If the reservations clerk can't help you, ask to speak to the desk captain. I'm not saying you won't risk a snub or two, but those who persevere can nurse wounded feelings all the way to the bank. An especially advantageous time to secure lower rates is late afternoon or early evening on the day of your arrival, when a hotel's likelihood of filling up with full-price bookings is remote.

HOW TO READ THE LISTINGS

The hotels listed below are divided first by location, then alphabetically by price category within a given district. Since most Atlanta attractions are within the downtown/midtown/Buckhead areas, almost all of the hotels here are in, or close to, those sections of town. (See Stone Mountain listings for camping.) When within walking distance, the nearest MARTA subway stop is listed.

Hotels listed in the **budget** category are those charging $60 or less for a double room. Those with rates ranging from $60 to $85 are rated **inexpensive** (don't blame me, I didn't create inflation), $85 to $115 rooms make up the **moderate** grouping, $115 to $150 I've listed as **expensive,** and anything above that ranks as **very expensive.** Any extras included in the rates (for example, breakfast or other meals) are listed for each property. Add 13% hotel tax to the rates listed, and keep in mind that the prices quoted are subject to change. If you have a car, be sure to consider the price of parking in your hotel selection.

RESERVATION SERVICES

FOR FOREIGN STUDENTS ONLY The **Atlanta Convention and Visitors Bureau,** 233 Peachtree St. NE, Suite 2000 (tel. 404/521-6600), has an International Youth Travel Program for students of any age or country with valid student identification. It offers, subject to availability, rooms in 11 Atlanta hotels at discounted rates of $25 to $35 single, $30 to $45 double. You must stop by in person during office hours (Monday to Friday between 8:30am and 5:30pm) to participate.

BED & BREAKFAST **Bed & Breakfast Atlanta,** 1801 Piedmont Ave. NE, Suite 208 (tel. 404/875-0525 or toll free 800/967-3224), is a professional reservation service that carefully screens facilities in the Atlanta area. Their list comprises close to 100 homes and inns, all accommodations offering private bath. They include a turreted Queen Anne–style Victorian home with nine fireplaces near the Carter Library; a three-bedroom, two-bath pool house in "Miss Daisy's" Druid Hills; a 1930s bungalow near Piedmont Park; an elegant 1920s Tudor-style home in Buckhead, a fully furnished garden cottage in Ansley Park; and a sunny contemporary home with pool and sauna in the Emory University area. They even have kosher homes on their roster. Owners Madalyne Eplan and Paula Gris have been running B&B Atlanta since 1979. All rates include continental breakfast, in many cases extended considerably beyond the usual roll and coffee. Reserve as far in advance as possible for the greatest possible selection. Call during office hours, which are Monday to Friday from 9am to noon and 2 to 5pm.

The rates run the gamut from $40 to $125, single or double. Weekly and monthly rates are available (in guesthouses and apartments) for long-term visitors. There's no fee. American Express, MasterCard, and VISA are accepted.

1. DOWNTOWN

Downtown hotels primarily cater to the business/convention traveler, but a tourist will also enjoy the services and facilities of these properties.

VERY EXPENSIVE

ATLANTA HILTON & TOWERS, 255 Courtland St., between Baker and Harris Sts., Atlanta, GA 30303. Tel. 404/659-2000 or toll free 800/HILTONS. Fax 404/222-2868. 1,224 rms, 41 suites. A/C TV TEL **MARTA:** Peachtree Center.

$ Rates: $165–$185 single, $185–$205 double; Tower rooms $205 single, $225 double; business-class rooms $125 single, $145 double. Each additional person $20. Children stay free in a room with parent. Weekend rate (available Fri–Sat) $99 per room per night (for up to four people), sometimes extended to include additional nights in low season. AE, CB, DC, MC, DISC, ER, V. **Parking:** $9 valet, $8 self.

One of Atlanta's top convention hotels, with 104,000 square feet of meeting and exhibit space, the Hilton is also a glamorous downtown enclave where famed guests have included everyone from Michael Jackson to Rob Lowe (this is the site of his famous videotape). It's a hotel very much in the Hilton tradition, with a plushly furnished lobby, paneled in rich mahogany. A bank of glass elevators provides a futuristic note. Cheerfully decorated rooms, in a variety of color schemes, offer clocks, radios, and remote-control TVs with Spectravision movies, plus video checkout and account-review functions; you can even order up breakfast via video.

A special floor of the Hilton is geared to business travelers, offering speedy private registration, concierge services, nightly bed turn down, in-room bars/refreshment centers, and complimentary continental breakfast in a private lounge.

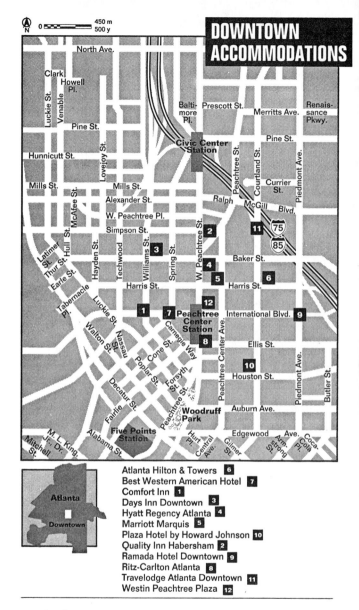

DOWNTOWN ACCOMMODATIONS

Atlanta Hilton & Towers **6**
Best Western American Hotel **7**
Comfort Inn **1**
Days Inn Downtown **3**
Hyatt Regency Atlanta **4**
Marriott Marquis **5**
Plaza Hotel by Howard Johnson **10**
Quality Inn Habersham **2**
Ramada Hotel Downtown **9**
Ritz-Carlton Atlanta **8**
Travelodge Atlanta Downtown **11**
Westin Peachtree Plaza **12**

The above services are also featured in the Tower section of the hotel. Here the lounge is even more luxurious and provides panoramic downtown views. In addition to continental breakfast, Tower guests enjoy complimentary cocktail-hour hors d'oeuvres in the lounge and superior in-room amenities.

Dining/Entertainment: The Hilton's premier restaurant is the very highly acclaimed Nikolai's Roof, a 30th-floor dining room offering spectacular skyline vistas. It evokes the opulent reign of Tsar Nicholas II, who employed the most brilliant chefs of France. Only multicourse prix-fixe dinners are offered. Trader Vic's, a South Seas–Polynesian restaurant found at numerous Hiltons, here offers its exotic signature setting of tapa-bark walls, thatched roofing, and primitive carvings. Potent rum drinks are a specialty. Dinner only. The Café de la Paix, a very pretty lobby-level eatery centered around a vast planter, serves buffet meals at breakfast and lunch and Sunday champagne brunch. Adjoining the Café are the Acapulco Bar and the Coffee House, the Hilton's casual dining facility, open daily from 6am to 2am. A pianist entertains nightly at the Bogart-and-Bergman-themed Casablanca Bar. It offers billiards, happy-hour hors d'oeuvres, and a large-screen TV on which sports events are aired. Finally, there's Another World, a plush disco adjoining Nikolai's.

Services: Room service from 6am to 2am, nightly bed turndown on request, babysitting, lobby information desk, valet parking.

Facilities: Four outdoor tennis courts, a $\frac{1}{10}$-mile outdoor jogging track, outdoor pool/sundeck, exercise room (stationary bikes and weights), sauna, whirlpool, business center, shops, shoeshine stand, airport shuttle.

HYATT REGENCY ATLANTA, 265 Peachtree St. NE, between Baker and Harris Sts., Atlanta, GA 30303. Tel. 404/577-1234 or toll free 800/233-1234. Fax 404/589-1754. 1,278 rms, 56 suites. A/C MINIBAR TV TEL **MARTA:** Peachtree Center.

$ Rates: $150–$190 single, $160–$200 double; Regency Club $190–$210 single or double. Each additional person $20. Children under 18 free. Weekend rate (Fri–Sun) $79 per room per night. Packages and promotional rates often available via the toll-free number. AE, CB, DC, DISC, ER, MC, V. **Parking:** $10.

Designed in 1967 by famed Atlanta architect John Portman, this hotel was the prototype not only for future downtown hotels in the city, but for architectural design in America. It features a 23-story open-air atrium lobby filled with lush greenery which thrives in the sunlight streaming through a lofty skylight. The indoor-garden motif is further enhanced by balconies draped with vine-covered trellises. Another Portman innovation is the central bank of bubble-glass elevators lit by marquee lights which glide silently up and down the atrium.

The Hyatt accommodates guests not only in this original building, but in two later additions—the 24-story International Tower and the 22-story Ivy Tower. Rooms in all three Hyatt buildings feature plush modern furnishings and are equipped with remote-control color cable TVs offering HBO and Spectravision movies (video checkout, account review, and message retrieval are further options), clock radios, and safes.

Floors 20 to 22 of the main building are Regency Club floors, a hotel within the hotel providing a comfortable private lounge wherein guests enjoy complimentary Continental breakfasts and afternoon hors d'oeuvres with wine and beer. Concierges are on duty throughout the day, and Club floor guests enjoy upgraded amenities. Yet another special Hyatt feature are rooms geared to businesswomen; on the lower floors, the rooms offer hairdryers, clotheslines, and makeup mirrors.

Dining/Entertainment: The blue dome capping Polaris, the Hyatt's revolving rooftop restaurant, is a landmark on the city's skyline. It's a lovely setting, with each mauve-velvet upholstered chair and banquette providing full window views. Open for dinner only, Polaris offers a classic menu featuring steak, seafood, and prime rib. You can enjoy the same spectacular views over cocktails in the adjoining lounge. Overlooking the hustle and bustle of the lobby is the Kafe Köbenhavn, designed for informal dining. Open from 6am to 2am, it features international specialties in addition to basic coffee-shop fare. Another lobby-level facility is the Ampersand Lounge, open daily from 11am to 2am for cocktails. Monday-night football games are aired on a large-screen TV here. A handsome curved stairway descending from the Ivy Tower lobby leads to Clock of 5's, an elegant dining room with seating in plush forest-green semicircular banquettes. Featuring an essentially steak-and-seafood menu, with an emphasis on market-fresh and regional specialties, the Clock is also notable for bountiful lunch buffets and a raw bar at night. And finally, one level below the lobby is Avanzare, a charming Italian restaurant with an 1,800-gallon living-reef saltwater aquarium along one wall. Fresh pasta, fresh-baked breads and pastries, and premium wines by the glass are featured. Open for lunch weekdays, dinner nightly.

Services: Room service from 6am to 12:30am, lobby concierge, valet parking, airport shuttle, babysitting, weekend children's activities.

Facilities: Full health club, tennis/golf nearby by arrangement, barber shop and beauty salon, gift shop, Delta Air Lines desk, large outdoor pool with sun deck and whirlpool, business center, convention facilities. The Hyatt connects to the vast Peachtree Center shopping mall via a covered walkway.

MARRIOTT MARQUIS, 265 Peachtree Center Ave., between Baker and Harris Sts., Atlanta, GA 30303. Tel. 404/521-0000 or toll free 800/228-9290. Fax 404/521-6870. 1,674 rms. 80 suites. A/C TV TEL **MARTA:** Peachtree Center.
$ Rates: $165 single; $180 double; Concierge Level rooms $190 single or double. Extra person $20. Children under 12 free. Weekend rate (Fri–Sat) $89 per room per night, including free parking and continental breakfast. AE, CB, DC, DISC, MC, V. **Parking:** $9.

A dramatic downtown landmark, the Marriott Marquis, with its towering tapered-glass exterior, is my personal favorite of Atlanta's Portman-designed megahotels. Fronted by a vast fountain that looks like a flying saucer, it focuses within on a soaring

48-story atrium in which a massive plum-colored fiber sculpture cascades through space from the skylight ceiling to a point just above the lobby. Another vertical design element is a central bank of illuminated bullet-shaped glass elevators, intended as a form of functional kinetic sculpture. Vines draped over interior balcony railings create a hanging-garden effect. And light classical piano music played in all public areas combines with these natural elements to further humanize a modern environment that might otherwise overwhelm.

The very attractive rooms have just undergone a total renovation, so everything is spanking new. Contemporary artwork hangs on the pale-peach walls; custom-designed bedspreads and drapes, of imported Belgian fabrics, are amber and peach, with lavender and plum accents; carpets are a muted aubergine hue. Furnishings are handsome walnut pieces. Amenities include digital bedside clocks and radios and remote-control color cable TVs with HBO and Spectravision movies. You can also pick up messages, review your account, or pay your bill via video. Closets have folding-mirror doors, and, inside, you'll find an iron, ironing board, and safe.

Floors 42 and 43 comprise the Concierge Level, with its own plushly furnished private lounge (a wall of windows afford stunning views). Your rate here includes an extensive continental breakfast, snacks and juices throughout the day, a lavish hors d'oeuvres spread at cocktail hour, and late-night desserts and coffee. Rooms offer special amenities, as well as services such as nightly bed turn down.

The hotel connects to the Peachtree Center mall via a covered walkway.

Dining/Entertainment: The Garden Level, above the lobby, is a vast, marble-floored expanse. Here you'll find all the hotel's restaurants and lounges as well as the entrance to the Peachtree Center. The Atrium Café, open for all meals, is an indoor sidewalk café, bordered by a large marble planter; it features light fare. Pompano's, an elegant seafood restaurant entered via a glass-walled arcade with gorgeous aquariums of variegated tropical fish at either end, seats diners amid a forest of ficus trees. The Arbors, a plant-filled restaurant with a lovely garden ambience and windows overlooking fountains, is the hotel's casual restaurant, offering steak, seafood, and sandwiches. La Fuente features traditional Mexican fare in an adobe-walled, south-of-the-border setting. In nice weather, you can enjoy fajitas al fresco at umbrella tables on the adjoining patio. The Garden Lounge on this floor is an elegant piano bar. And up a brass-railed stairway, seemingly suspended in space, is the Grandstand Bar. Champions, the Marquis's major nightclub and an exciting sports-themed bar, is covered more extensively in Chapter 10, "Atlanta Nights."

Services: 24-hour room service, limousine, valet parking, *USA Today* delivered daily to your room, airport shuttle, babysitting, lobby concierge.

Facilities: Full health club, large swimming pool under a retractable skylight roof with an adjoining whirlpool, business center, game room, florist, drugstore, Delta Air Lines desk, travel agent, clothing boutiques, magic shop, gift shop, unisex hair stylist, shoe-shine stand.

RITZ-CARLTON ATLANTA, 181 Peachtree St. NE, at Ellis St. (main entrance on Ellis), Atlanta, GA 30303. Tel. 404/659-0400 or toll free 800/241-3333. Fax 404/688-0400. 447 rms, 24 suites. A/C MINIBAR TV TEL **MARTA:** Peachtree Center.

$ Rates: $155 single, $155–$200 double; Club Level $200 single or double. Children under 18 free. Weekend rate (Fri–Sat) $99 per room per night. AE, CB, DC, DISC, ER, MC, V. **Parking:** $12.

It's hard to believe that this very traditional-looking hostelry—with Persian rugs strewn on marble floors, silk-tapestried and African mahogany-paneled walls hung with a collection of museum-quality 18th- and 19th-century paintings, and valuable antiques throughout the public areas—was built as late as 1984. The impeccable service also harks back to another, more gracious, era; you'll be cosseted as never before. Elegantly residential rooms, many with bay windows, are furnished in beautiful mahogany pieces (some have four-poster beds) and equipped with every amenity. Your remote-control TV (with movie and other cable channels) is concealed in a handsome armoire, and you'll find a clock radio, terry robe, scale, fresh flowers, and an extra phone in the bath; additional phone lines are available if needed. The telephone service offers call waiting, conference calling, and a do-not-disturb feature wherein calls are routed to the hotel operator.

The two top floors of the Ritz-Carlton (24 and 25) constitute the Club Level, a hotel within a hotel featuring upgraded room amenities, a private elevator, and a plush concierge-staffed lounge where guests enjoy a lavish complimentary continental breakfast, afternoon tea, cocktails with hors d'oeuvres, and late-night cordials. Of course, the rooms and lounge on these high floors offer great city views.

Dining/Entertainment: The hotel's premier dining room is the Restaurant, an equestrian-themed setting with 19th-century, gilt-framed hunt paintings on pine-green walls. Highly acclaimed, it offers traditional haute-cuisine items such as roasted quail, braised pheasant, and grilled salmon medallions. It's open for lunch and dinner (a pianist entertains at the latter). After dinner, you might retreat to the adjoining Bar where a jazz trio plays Tuesday to Saturday night till 1am. A very reasonably priced lunch buffet is served in the Bar weekdays. The warmly intimate peach and earth-toned Café on the lobby level, open daily from 6:30am to midnight, is the hotel's informal dining room. It's a gem, with glittering crystal chandeliers overhead, lavish floral arrangements, and shaded table lamps and wall sconces enhancing the cozy ambience. A harpist and flautist entertain here during Sunday brunch. An afternoon tea, complete with fresh-baked scones and watercress sandwiches, is served in the lobby lounge daily; a pianist entertains here from 11:30am to 4:30pm.

Services: 24-hour room service, twice-daily maid service, nightly turn down with a Godiva chocolate and a rose, complimentary shoeshine, your regional paper delivered to your door on request, evening pressing service, babysitting, car rental, limousine, valet parking, multilingual concierge staff.

Facilities: Florist/gift shop, airport shuttle, on-premises fitness center (Stairmasters, treadmills, exercise bikes, sauna, steam, free weights), use of the nearby state-of-the-art Peachtree Center Athletic Club ($12 per visit), business center.

THE WESTIN PEACHTREE PLAZA, 210 Peachtree St., at International Blvd., Atlanta, GA 30303. Tel. 404/659-1400 or toll free 800/228-3000. FAX 404/589-7586. 1,020 rms, 48 suites. A/C TV TEL **MARTA:** Peachtree Center.

$ Rates: $155–$195 single, $180–$220 double; club level $220 single, $245 double. Weekend (Fri–Sun) 50% off regular rates. Extra person $25. Children under 18 free. Inquire about packages. AE, CB, DC, DISC, ER, JCB, MC, V. **Parking:** $11.50.

Though the John Portman–designed Westin is a 73-story megahotel with over 1,000 rooms, it is invitingly residential within. The atrium lobby, under a 5-story skylight and utilizing acres of pink-hued Portuguese marble, divides into softly lit alcoves wherein plush sofas, fine artworks, rich mahogany paneling, and Persian rugs combine to create warmly intimate seating areas. Numerous trees and plants add an indoor garden look, and glittering marquee-lit facades evoke Copenhagen's Tivoli Gardens.

Rooms are decorated in muted earth tones with peach and burgundy accents. Handsome armoires house remote-control color cable TVs offering Spectravision movies and a gratis step-training exercise video (the step is provided). And in-room amenities include TV speakers in the bath, two phones (desk and bedside), voice-mail messaging, wall vaults, and AM/FM alarm clock radios. Medium and deluxe rooms are on higher floors, and the latter have minibars. Executive Level (floors 43–47) guests enjoy a stunning concierge-staffed lounge offering FAX and copy machines plus complimentary continental breakfast, cocktail-hour hors d'oeuvres, and evening desserts. In-room amenities and services are also upgraded.

Dining/Entertainment: The revolving Sun Dial Restaurant, on the 71st and 72nd floors, offers a breathtaking 360-degree city-skyline panorama. Plushly furnished with burgundy velvet horseshoe booths, and designed so that every table provides optimum views, it features sophisticated American cuisine; a strolling balalaika group entertains at dinner. The revolving Sun Dial Lounge, on the 73rd floor, is a romantic setting for exotic cocktails and light appetizer fare. Several other facilities are on the lobby level. The highly acclaimed Savannah Fish Company, with seating overlooking a splashing 100-foot horizontal waterfall, specializes in fresh seafood. Noted pianist Steve Jacobs entertains nightly in the lobby, near the Café—a delightful restaurant serving both buffet and à la carte American meals plus an award-winning Japanese breakfast. The Oak Bar, a plush venue of warm woods and rich leathers, specializes in liqueurs and coffee drinks. And the International Bar features an array of beers, wines by the glass, and nightly raw bar offerings.

Services: Concierge, 24-hour room service, airport shuttle.

Facilities: Fully equipped health club; beautiful large pool (under a retractable skylight for year-round indoor/outdoor use) and tropically planted sun deck; comprehensive business center; car rental; 17,000-square-foot shopping gallery which connects with Macy's; Peachtree Center Mall (see Chapter 9) is a block away.

MODERATE

BEST WESTERN AMERICAN HOTEL, 160 Spring St., at International Blvd., Atlanta, GA 30303. Tel. 404/688-8600 or toll free 800/621-7885. Fax 404/658-9458. 301 rms, 26 suites. A/C TV TEL **MARTA:** Peachtree Center.

$ Rates: $79 single, $89 double; Executive Club level $15 additional per night. Extra person $10. Children under 18 free. Weekend rate (Fri–Sun) $59 per room (up to four people). AE, CB, DC, DISC, MC, V. **Parking:** $7.

When it was first built in 1962 as an Americana Hotel, this was downtown's most glamorous property, attracting guests like Mary Martin, Carol Channing, Doris Day, and Pearl Bailey. Today, in the shadow of downtown's modern megahotels, the American seems decidedly retro, its public areas reflecting late-fifties/early-sixties interior-decorating ideas such as mirrored columns and blond wood paneling. However, everything's in tip-top shape after a $2 million renovation in 1991.

Rooms are decorated in a variety of styles and color schemes. They're all neat, clean, and homey-looking, with full-length mirrors, desks and tables, and color cable TVs offering Spectravision movies. Some rooms have sofas and loveseats. Windows that open are a nice feature. Floors 8 and 9 comprise an Executive Club Level with a

---

 FROMMER'S SMART TRAVELER: HOTELS

VALUE-CONSCIOUS TRAVELERS SHOULD TAKE ADVANTAGE OF THE FOLLOWING:

1. Weekend rates. Even top-of-the-line hotels slash prices 30% to 50% on weekends—and at some properties weekends include Friday, Saturday, and Sunday nights.
2. Reduced-price packages and reduced rates for senior citizens, families, and active-duty military personnel.
3. Preferential rates, available only when you reserve via toll-free reservation numbers.
4. Bargaining for lower rates.

private concierge-staffed lounge; guests on these floors enjoy a complimentary continental breakfast and cocktail-hour hors d'oeuvres here daily, free newspapers, express checkout, and nightly bed turn down with chocolate mints.

Dining/Entertainment: The pubby, wood-paneled Gatsby's Restaurant and Lounge, vaguely evoking the 1920s (walls are covered with news headlines heralding Lindbergh's flight, ads for Pierce Arrow cars, and *Saturday Evening Post* covers) is open daily from 6:30am to 10:30pm; typical American fare is served. There's also a poolside coffee shop, brightly decorated in yellow, called the Outside Inn. It's open 6:30am to 2pm.

Services: Airport shuttle, concierge, valet parking, room service during restaurant hours.

Facilities: Medium-size outdoor pool/sun deck, guest privileges (for a $10 fee) at the very comprehensive Peachtree Athletic Center, small on-premises workout room (with some Universal and Nautilus equipment, exercise bikes, and a Stairmaster), barber; full range of audiovisual equipment available.

COMFORT INN, 101 International Blvd., at Williams St., Atlanta, GA 30303. Tel. 404/524-5555 or toll free 800/535-0707 or 800/228-5150. 260 rms. A/C TV TEL **MARTA:** Peachtree Center or Omni.

$ Rates: $69–$119 single, $79–$129 double. Extra person $10. Children 18 and under stay free. Weekend rate (Fri–Sun) $59 per room. AE, DC, DISC, MC, V. **Parking:** $6.

A chain of moderately priced hotels created by the Quality Inn group in 1981, Comfort Inns are based on the theory that a low-cost hotel needn't be a no-frills hotel. This 11-story property, opened in 1985, is a good example. It's garnered three-star ratings from both Mobil and AAA. Entered via a lobby with a fountain, it offers appealing mauve-carpeted rooms with oak furnishings, very pretty teal-and-mauve shell-motif bedspreads, and watercolors depicting scenes of France on grasspaper-covered walls. Each room has both a desk and a table with two chairs (or sleeper sofa), a full-length mirror on the closet door, remote-control color TV offering Spectravision movies, a radio, and an alarm clock. The Greyhound bus station is just across the street, the Omni Coliseum two blocks away.

Dining/Entertainment: Bistro 101, the on-premises eatery, is rather charming, with tables amid potted ferns and copper cookware on the walls. Many seats overlook the pool. It offers typical American fare. In the adjoining Blind Zebra Bar, sporting events are aired on the TV (proximity to the Omni Coliseum attracts many sports-minded guests).

Services: Room service during restaurant hours.

Facilities: Electric shoeshine machines on each floor, a nice-size outdoor pool/sun deck with adjoining whirlpool, a "Discover Atlanta" video machine in the lobby, a gift shop, and airport shuttle.

DAYS INN DOWNTOWN, 300 Spring St., at Baker St., Atlanta, GA 30308. Tel. 404/523-1144 or toll free 800/

325-2525. Fax 404/577-8495. 262 rms. A/C TV TEL **MARTA:**
Peachtree Center.

$ Rates: $79–$119 single, $89–$129 double. Extra person $10.
Children under 18 in parent's room pay $1. Reduced rates may be
available if you reserve at least 30 days in advance. AE, DC, DISC,
MC, V. **Parking:** $5.

This very central Days Inn allows visitors to stay in the heart of the
business district at a very moderate cost. The rooms, decorated in a
burgundy/mauve/forest-green color scheme, have handsome oak
furnishings and grasspaper-style wall coverings. Remote-control col-
or TVs offer HBO and Spectravision movies, as well as other cable
channels. Most rooms have refrigerators, and those on floors 3 to 10
have balconies. All have either two double beds or one queen-size
bed; rooms with the latter offer love seats with ottomans and clock
radios. Although you don't get all the luxury-hotel frills here,
accommodations are clean and spiffy-looking, facilities very ample.

Dining/Entertainment: A Wendy's restaurant adjoins the
property and provides room service. There's also a comfortable
lounge in the hotel, open 5pm to midnight, where sporting events are
aired on a large-screen TV.

Facilities: Large outdoor pool with sundeck.

**PLAZA HOTEL BY HOWARD JOHNSON, 70 Houston St.,
at Courtland St., Atlanta, GA 30303. Tel. 404/659-
2660** or toll free 800/241-3828. Fax 404/524-5390. 213 rms, 6
suites. A/C TV TEL **MARTA:** Peachtree Center.

$ Rates: $81–$119 single, $91–$129 double. Extra person $10.
Children under 12 stay free. Weekend rate (Fri–Sun) $49–$69
single, $59–$79 double. AE, CB, DC, DISC, MC, V. **Parking:**
Free.

An 8-story cream stucco building that forms a courtyard around its
swimming pool, the Plaza is looking spiffy after a recent $5 million
renovation. Public areas, hung with architectural and historic prints
of Atlanta, include a wide resortlike mezzanine with comfortable
furnishings. Rooms, 90% of them with balconies, are charmingly
decorated in hues of burgundy, raspberry, teal, and mauve, with
handsome walnut and cherrywood pieces in traditional styles and
framed botanical prints gracing the walls. Your remote-control color
TV offers Spectravision movie options. Especially nice are six
poolside king rooms with lanais (ask for one when you reserve).

Dining/Entertainment: The Courtyard Café, a very pretty
garden-motif restaurant with balcony seating overlooking the pool,
serves all meals. A similarly decorated lounge adjoins.

Services: Airport shuttle, room service during restaurant hours.

Facilities: Small business center, outdoor pool/sun deck, baby
pool; for a fee, guests can use the state-of-the-art Phoenix Health
Club up the street in the Georgia-Pacific Building.

**QUALITY INN HABERSHAM, 330 Peachtree St. NE, be-
tween Baker St. and Ralph McGill Blvd., Atlanta, GA
30308 Tel. 404/577-1980** or toll free 800/241-4288. Fax

404/688-3706. 91 rms. A/C TV TEL **MARTA:** Peachtree Center or Civic Center.

$ Rates (including continental breakfast): $80 single, $90 double. Extra person $10. Children 18 and under free. Weekend rate (Fri–Sat) $59 per room per night. AE, CB, DC, DISC, ER, JCB, MC, V. **Parking:** Free.

Just a few blocks from the center of downtown, this pleasant hotel offers a lot for its price range. From a cozy lobby lounge with velvet-upholstered sofas to cheerful hallways adorned with ficus trees, its public areas are well cared for and aesthetically pleasing. The mauve-carpeted rooms, with floral-print teal-and-mauve bedspreads, are large and nicely furnished, each equipped with a desk, two armchairs or a sofa, a remote-control color cable TV with HBO movies, wet bar/refrigerator, and an in-room coffee maker. Marble baths are amply supplied with shampoo, soaps, toothpaste, mouthwash, and deodorant.

Dining/Entertainment: In a comfortably furnished room off the lobby, complimentary continental breakfast—danish, rolls, bagels, juice, fresh fruit, cold cereals, tea or coffee—is served each morning. There's a TV here, should you care to watch the "Today" show over the morning meal. Or, weather permitting, you might breakfast outdoors at patio tables.

Services: Room service 5 to 10pm, free newspaper delivered daily to your room.

Facilities: A workout room with exercise bikes, weights, exercise machines, and sauna.

RAMADA HOTEL DOWNTOWN, 175 Piedmont Ave. NE, at International Blvd., Atlanta, GA 30303. Tel. 404/659-2727 or toll free 800/228-2828. Fax 404/659-2727. 467 rms, 6 suites. A/C TV TEL **MARTA:** Peachtree Center.

$ Rates: $79–$99 single, $99–$119 double. Extra person $10. Children 12 and under free. Weekend rate (Fri–Sun) $65 per room per night. Packages available via the toll-free number. AE, CB, DC, DISC, MC, V. **Parking:** Free, in a 330-car indoor lot.

This 6-story hotel opened in the early 1960s, its 7-story addition ten years later. It's a particularly nice property, entered via a large lobby with intimate, lamplit seating areas. Much of the staff has been here since the hotel's inception, always a sign of a well-run operation. Recently renovated rooms offer AM/FM alarm clock radios and remote-control cable TVs with free movie channels.

Dining/Entertainment: The Pantheon, a pretty plant-filled restaurant-in-the-round, serves typical American fare at all meals. A lounge called Raphael's adjoins. And complimentary coffee is available in the lobby weekdays from 7 to 9am.

Services: Room service 6:30am to 2pm and 5 to 10pm, complimentary copy of *USA Today* at the front desk each morning, airport shuttle, complimentary toiletries on request at the front desk.

Facilities: Lobby gift shop, large outdoor swimming pool with nicely landscaped sun deck.

INEXPENSIVE

TRAVELODGE ATLANTA DOWNTOWN, 311 Courtland St. NE, between Baker St. and Ralph McGill Blvd., Atlanta, GA 30303. Tel. 404/659-4545 or toll free 800/255-3050. Fax 404/659-5934. 71 rms. A/C TV TEL **MARTA:** Peachtree Center.

$ Rates (including continental breakfast): $66–$72 single, $74–$84 double. Extra person $8. Children under 18 free. Weekend rate (Fri–Sun) $39 per room per night. AE, CB, DC, DISC, ER, MC, V. **Parking:** Free.

Operated by the Clark family since 1964, this small TraveLodge offers a moderately priced hotel alternative in the heart of downtown. Its teal-carpeted rooms were recently renovated, and they look clean and fresh. Each is equipped with an AM/FM radio, a personal safe, and a remote-control color TV with HBO movie channel. Complimentary continental breakfast—juice, coffee, and doughnuts—is served in the lobby each morning; there's a 24-hour eatery just down the street, and numerous other restaurants are within walking distance. Free daily newspapers are another plus. And facilities include an outdoor pool and sun deck.

2. MIDTOWN

Midtown hotels tend to be low-key, catering to tourists and their families rather than conventioneers. Joggers and other outdoor

 FROMMER'S COOL FOR KIDS:
HOTELS

Residence Inn Buckhead *(see p. 82)*. This place has not only a swimming pool but also accommodations with fully equipped kitchens—a potential money-saver when you're traveling with family. Rates here include breakfast, and there are barbecue grills and picnic tables on the premises. It's like having your own Atlanta apartment, with parking at your door. The property also contains basketball, volleyball, and paddle-tennis courts, and VCRs and movies can be rented at the front desk.

Hyatt Regency Atlanta *(see p. 54)* and **Marriott Marquis** *(see p. 55)*. Kids might also enjoy these massive downtown hotels, with their glass elevators, swimming pools, and HBO and Spectravision movies on TV.

enthusiasts will appreciate proximity to Piedmont Park. The Woodruff Arts Center is also in this section of town.

VERY EXPENSIVE

MARRIOTT SUITES, 35 14th St. NE, between Peachtree and W. Peachtree Sts., Atlanta, GA 30309. Tel. 404/876-8888 or toll free 800/228-9290. Fax 404/876-7727. 259 suites. A/C MINIBAR TV TEL **MARTA:** Midtown.

$ Rates (including continental breakfast): $159 single, $174 double. Extra person $15. Children under 18 free. Weekend rates (Fri–Sat) begin at $75 per room per night. Discounted rates and packages may be available through the toll-free number. AE, CB, DC, DISC, ER, MC, V. **Parking:** $8.

⭐ It would be hard to come by a more simpatico place to stay than this very hospitable, all-suite hotel. Each spacious suite has a full living room, with an extra phone on the desk (equipped with call waiting), a comfortable convertible sofa, a wet bar/refrigerator (stocked with complimentary sparkling water, juice, and milk), and a big console TV. Both this TV and the one in your bedroom are remote-control cable sets offering Spectravision and HBO movies, plus video account review, checkout, and message retrieval. Bedrooms, set off from the living areas by lace-curtained French doors, are furnished in traditional dark mahogany pieces. Most have king-size beds. Suites are decorated in a mauve/dusty aqua color scheme, with very pretty pale-gray, iris-motif bedspreads picking up accents of these hues. Other in-room amenities: coffee makers (delicious shortbread cookies are provided daily), full-length folding-mirror closet doors, large marble baths with adjacent dressing rooms and hairdryers, and clock radios. Jimmy Carter was a guest here during the Ethiopian peace negotiations, which took place at the Carter Center.

Dining/Entertainment: Off the lobby is the plant-filled, lavender-and-teal Windows, serving lavish buffet breakfasts and à la carte lunches and dinners daily. Steak and seafood are featured, along with sandwiches, burgers, and salads. In the adjoining lounge area, complimentary continental breakfast and cocktail-hour hors d'oeuvres are offered daily.

Services: Room service from 6 to 9:30am and 5:30 to 11pm, nightly bed turndown on request with Godiva chocolates and a book of bedtime stories, airport shuttle, valet parking, *USA Today* delivered to your door each morning.

Facilities: Lobby gift shop, sizable health club, connecting indoor/outdoor swimming pools and sun deck, whirlpool, coin-op washer and dryer.

SHERATON COLONY SQUARE HOTEL, 188 14th St. NE, at Peachtree St., Atlanta, GA 30361. Tel. 404/892-6000 or toll free 800/422-7895. Fax 404/892-6000, ext. 7651. 430 rms, 31 suites. A/C TV TEL **MARTA:** Arts Center.

$ Rates: $119–$139 single, $139–$159 double; Colony Club

$149–$169 single, $169–$189 double. Extra person $20. Children of any age free in room with parent. Weekend packages at reduced rates. AE, CB, DC, DISC, MC, V. **Parking:** $10.

Built in 1974 as an opulent anchor of the Colony Square complex (which includes a mall of 20 shops and restaurants), this theatrically themed property is very popular with entertainers playing at the adjacent Woodruff Arts Center. Sheraton Colony Square has hosted Willie Nelson, Frank Sinatra, Dionne Warwick, and Linda Ronstadt, not to mention Presidents Reagan, Ford, and Carter.

Rooms are simply gorgeous, decorated in earth tones with gray velvet armchairs and hassocks, beautiful marble desks, and silk throw pillows on the beds. In a handsome armoire, you'll find your remote-control color cable TV with Spectravision movies. Other in-room amenities include alarm clocks, AM/FM radios, walk-in closets, brass butlers, full-length mirrors, electric shoe buffers, and, in the baths, upscale toiletries and cosmetic mirrors. A live ficus tree in each room is a nice residential touch.

Floors 18 and 19 comprise the Colony Club, a hotel-within-a-hotel with its own luxurious concierge-staffed lounge offering buffets at breakfast and cocktail hour. Guests on these floors enjoy upgraded amenities, nightly bed turn down, and copies of the *Wall Street Journal* delivered to their doors each morning.

Dining/Entertainment: Trellises is the hotel's lovely plant-filled restaurant, with upholstered bamboo seating at marble tables and philodendrons growing up trellises. Open for breakfast, lunch, and dinner daily, it features an American/continental menu; the food is notably good. Light fare and piano music are offered in the cozy adjoining Bistro Lounge. In the cozy lamplit Lobby Bar, complimentary hors d'oeuvres are served with cocktails from 4 to 8pm nightly.

Services: Room service 6:30am to 1am, *USA Today* delivered to your door each morning, concierge desk, valet parking, airport shuttle.

Facilities: Business services, nice-size outdoor pool and sun deck, fully equipped on-premises health club with treadmills, exercise bikes, Stairmasters, and a full complement of Nautilus equipment.

EXPENSIVE

WYNDHAM HOTEL MIDTOWN, 125 10th St. NE, just east of Peachtree St., Atlanta, GA 30309. Tel. 404/873-4800 or toll free 800/822-4200. Fax 404/870-1530. 191 rms. A/C TV TEL **MARTA:** Midtown.

$ Rates: $125 single, $135 double; Executive King rooms $150. Extra person $10. Children 12 and under free. Weekend rates (Fri–Sun) $59 per room per night. AE, CB, DC, MC, V. **Parking:** $9.

An 11-story Georgia red-brick building, faced with bronze glass, the luxuriously appointed Wyndham opened in 1987. Its rooms, many with bay windows, are furnished in mahogany pieces and decorated

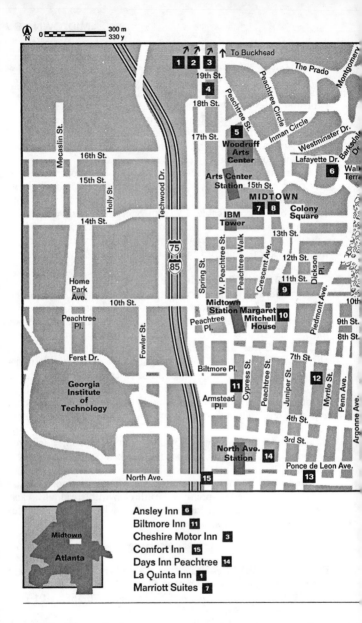

Ansley Inn	**6**
Biltmore Inn	**11**
Cheshire Motor Inn	**3**
Comfort Inn	**15**
Days Inn Peachtree	**14**
La Quinta Inn	**1**
Marriott Suites	**7**

in mauve color schemes with celadon carpeting. Each has an armchair and hassock, a handsome armoire concealing a remote-control color TV with cable and movie channels, a bedside clock radio, and a coffee maker. Executive King rooms feature separate parlors with sofas, extra TVs and phones, refrigerators, and stocked wet bars.

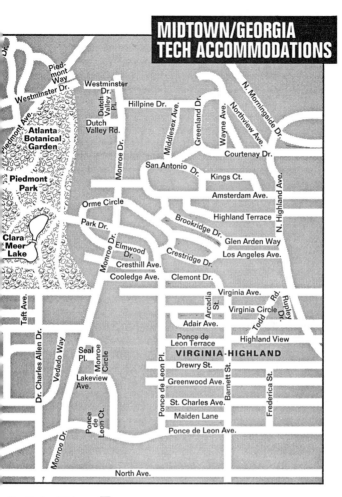

MIDTOWN/GEORGIA TECH ACCOMMODATIONS

Quality Inn Midtown **4**
Residence Inn Midtown **9**
Shellmont Bed and Breakfast Lodge **12**
Sheraton Colony Square Hotel **8**
Travelodge Peachtree **5**
Woodroff Bed & Breakfast **13**
Wyndham Hotel Midtown **10**

Dining/Entertainment: An art nouveau entranceway heralds the spacious, marble-floored Juniper Street Café, featuring buffet breakfasts and lunches as well as an à la carte menu at lunch and dinner. A lunchtime pasta bar offering three pastas, three sauces, and about a dozen toppings is a unique feature. There's outdoor seating at umbrella tables. Inside, tables set with white linens are lit by shaded lamps at night. The adjoining Butler's bar and lounge, furnished with comfortable gray leather chairs, specializes in premium wines by the glass.

Services: Comprehensive business services, including complete audiovisual setups; airport shuttle; valet parking; room service during restaurant hours.

Facilities: 7,000-square-foot fitness center with Nautilus equipment, steam and sauna, whirlpool, large indoor pool.

MODERATE

RESIDENCE INN MIDTOWN, 1041 W. Peachtree St., at 11th St., Atlanta, GA 30309. Tel. 404/872-8885 or toll free 800/331-3131. Fax 404/872-8885, ext. 1805. 66 suites. A/C TV MINIBAR TEL **MARTA:** Midtown.

$ Rates (including continental breakfast): Suites $119 one bedroom, $149 two bedrooms. Rates are reduced for stays of more than six nights. AE, DC, DISC, MC, V. **Parking:** Free.

Marriott's excellent Residence Inns are designed to offer travelers the ultimate in homeyness and hospitality. Staying here is like having your own apartment in Atlanta. This particular inn occupies a 7-story brick building with green-awninged windows fronted by a landscaped courtyard. A very inviting lobby, softly lit, with plush sofas and Persian rugs on oak floors, sets a warm tone. Superb housekeeping is in evidence everywhere; the place is gleaming.

Accommodations, off peach hallways with white doors, are spacious suites decorated in soft pastel hues with accents of burgundy and forest green. Handsome oak and mahogany furnishings are mostly antique reproductions, such as Chippendale-style beds, and both bedrooms and living rooms (the latter with Casablanca-style fans overhead) have their own TVs (remote-control color cable sets with HBO) and telephones. Kitchens are fully equipped. All rooms have full-length mirrors and French doors leading to balconies, and many have large walk-in closets.

Dining/Entertainment: An extended continental breakfast—muffins, croissants, fresh fruit, juice, yogurt, cereal, pancakes, and tea or coffee—is included in the rates; it's served in a pleasant breakfast room off the lobby, where hot tea and coffee are provided all day. Monday to Thursday night from 5:30 to 7:30pm, there are gratis beer-and-wine parties in the lobby with a wide array of hot and cold hors d'oeuvres. And every Wednesday night there's a complimentary rooftop barbecue dinner. All of these events provide a pleasant opportunity to meet and mingle with fellow guests. In addition, there's a cozy on-premises restaurant/bar, Stang's, serving sandwiches and salads. Sports events are aired on the TV.

Services: Room service from 5 to 10pm, complimentary grocery-shopping service, free newspapers daily.

Facilities: Coin-op washers and dryers, rooftop Jacuzzi, complimentary membership at the nearby Colony Square Health Club.

INEXPENSIVE

BILTMORE INN, 30 Fifth St. NE, at West Peachtree St., Atlanta, GA 30308. Tel. 404/874-0824 or toll free 800/822-0824. Fax 404/874-2913. 61 suites. A/C TV TEL **MARTA:** North Avenue.

$ Rates (including continental breakfast): $65–$95 single or double; 1,000-square-foot suite (sleeps four) $95–$125; executive suite (sleeps five) $125–$165; duplex townhouse (sleeps six) $135–$175; triplex penthouse (sleeps six) $175–$250. AE, DC, MC, V. **Parking:** Free.

⑤ A majestic 10-story brick building with a white-columned facade, its courtyard entrance shaded by stately oaks and magnolias, the Biltmore has a rich and glamorous history. Built in 1924 (as a hotel-cum-luxury apartment complex) by Coca-Cola heir William Candler, it played host in its heyday to everyone from *GWTW* stars Vivien Leigh and Olivia de Havilland to Presidents Franklin Roosevelt and Eisenhower. Closed in 1982, its apartment section was refurbished as an elegant all-suite hotel in 1986. The property is on the National Register of Historic Places.

A mahogany-paneled elevator whisks guests to opulent suites, each featuring 10-foot ceilings (many with skylights), hand-carved crown moldings, and an overhead fan, plus a fully equipped kitchen, dining area, and living room (except in studios). Very residential in feel, they're furnished in cherrywood antique reproductions, with area rugs strewn on glossy oak floors and gilt-framed Chinese art and botanical prints adorning cream walls. Lion-head door knockers, multipaned windows, brass bathroom fixtures, and French doors are additional enhancements. All accommodations are spacious. In-room amenities include clock radios and color cable TVs with movie stations. All but studios feature extra TVs and phones in the living rooms, and many rooms have private terraces or balconies. Duplex and triplex suites offer Jacuzzis.

Dining/Entertainment: Complimentary continental breakfast is served daily in a comfortably furnished 10th-floor lounge.

Services: Room service from dozens of area restaurants, free local calls, airport shuttle, complimentary shuttle from 7:30 to 10:30am and 4:30 to 7:30pm to anywhere within a 5-mile radius of the inn.

Facilities: Limousine rental; health-club privileges ($5 fee) at the state-of-the-art North Side Athletic Club, where facilities include an indoor/outdoor Olympic-size pool; complimentary washer/dryer for guest use.

DAYS INN PEACHTREE, 683 Peachtree St., between 3rd St. and Ponce de Leon Ave., Atlanta, GA 30308. Tel. 404/874-9200 or toll free 800/325-2525. 142 rms. A/C TV TEL **MARTA:** North Avenue.

$ Rates: $57–$60 single, $67–$72 double. Extra person $10. Children under 18 free. Weekend rates and packages available via the toll-free number, Super Saver rate of $39 a night may be available if you reserve at least 30 days in advance. AE, DC, DISC, MC, V. **Parking:** $2.

You'll realize this Days Inn is something special from the moment you enter its uniquely charming lobby with Persian rugs on Saltillo-tile floors and an 18th-century Georgian brass chandelier suspended from a lofty mahogany ceiling. The property occupies a 1924 building that was originally a select boarding house for young men. The hotel is across the street from the Fox Theatre, and since many of its entertainers (not the stars, but backup groups and musicians) stay here, it's not unusual to hear some pretty professional-sounding music emanating from the lobby's grand piano.

The rooms, decorated in teal, mauve, and burgundy, have handsome mahogany furnishings and grasspaper-covered walls hung with nautical- or equestrian-themed prints. All feature clock radios and remote-control color cable TVs with HBO movie channels, and some have comfortable, velvet-upholstered sofas.

Dining/Entertainment: Bridgetown Grill, a terrific Caribbean restaurant (see Chapter 6, "Atlanta Dining"), adjoins the property, as does a Wendy's. Complimentary wine, cheeses, and hot hors d'oeuvres are served at a cocktail party in the lobby every Thursday night; coffee is served in the lobby throughout the day.

Services: Complimentary newspapers daily at the front desk, airport shuttle.

LA QUINTA INN, 2115 Piedmont Rd. NE, between Lindbergh Dr. and Cheshire Bridge Rd., Atlanta, GA 30324. Tel. 404/876-4365 or toll free 800/531-5900. Fax 404/873-1007. 177 rms, 5 suites. A/C TV TEL **MARTA:** Lindbergh (about three-fourths of a mile north; a bus from there stops at the door).

$ Rates (including continental breakfast): $58 single; $63 double; King rooms $7 additional. Extra person $6. Children 17 and under free. Suites (for five to eight people) $90–$125. AE, CB, DC, DISC, MC, V. **Parking:** Free.

La Quinta, the Texas-based firm, took over this property in 1987 and redecorated in the southwestern style that characterizes its hotels nationwide—the two buildings have cream stucco exteriors and terra-cotta roofs. Rooms are decorated in teal and mauve, with color-coordinated drapes and bedspreads. Color cable TVs offer Showtime and pay movie (Satellite Cinema) stations, and you'll find a copy of the current *Newsweek* in your room. Another plus: local calls are free, and there's no service charge for credit-card calls. A complimentary continental breakfast (doughnuts, juice, fruit, tea or coffee) is served in a pleasant room off the lobby each morning. King rooms feature remote-control TVs, extra desk phones, clocks, recliners, and sofa beds.

Dining/Entertainment: Surprise, surprise! One of Atlanta's finest restaurants, the Chef's Café, leases space on the property. See details in Chapter 6, "Atlanta Dining."

Services: Coffee served in lobby all day.

Facilities: Small outdoor pool with sun deck.

QUALITY INN MIDTOWN, 1470 Spring St. NW, at 19th St., Atlanta, GA 30309. Tel. 404/872-5821 or toll free 800/221-2222. Fax 404/874-3602. 179 rms. A/C TV TEL **MARTA:** Memorial Arts Center.

$ Rates: $55–$75 single, $60–$80 double; Executive King rooms $80 single, $90 double; parlor suites $125–$175. Extra person $10. Children under 18 free. Weekend rates (Fri–Sun) $39–$59 per room per night. AE, CB, DC, DISC, ER, MC, V. **Parking:** Free.

The Quality welcomes guests in a large, inviting lobby with copper-mirrored columns. Rooms are clean, well-maintained, standard motel accommodations with new burgundy carpets and color-coordinated floral bedspreads. All offer dressing areas, remote-control cable TVs with HBO movies, and coffee makers. Rooms designated Executive Kings are larger and equipped with clock radios and sofas. There are also parlor suites—one- or two-bedroom accommodations whose adjoining parlors are equipped with sofa beds and their own TVs and phones; refrigerators are available on request.

Dining/Entertainment: The plant-filled Spring Street Café, overlooking the pool, serves breakfast, lunch, and dinner. In the comfortable adjoining Spirits lounge, sporting events are aired on a large-screen TV.

Services: Complimentary local paper delivered daily to your room, complimentary shuttle to MARTA and local attractions (daily 7am to 11pm).

Facilities: Exercise room, pool with two sun decks.

BUDGET

CHESHIRE MOTOR INN, 1865 Cheshire Bridge Rd. NE, between Wellborne Dr. NE and Manchester St. NE, Atlanta, GA 30324. Tel. 404/872-9628 or toll free 800/827-9628. 58 rms. A/C TV TEL **MARTA:** Lindbergh (about a mile away; you can catch a bus to the station in front of the hotel).

$ Rates: $29–$40 single, $6 each additional person. Children under 12 free. AE, DC, MC, V. **Parking:** Free.

This is my favorite kind of budget hotel, a small property run for decades by caring private owners (the Lacy family) who proffer homelike hospitality and many personal touches. On attractively landscaped, woodsy grounds, the Cheshire offers rooms that are spacious, immaculate, and cozy. Most have rust/brown color schemes, and all have one wood-paneled wall, 1950s-style furnishings, color cable TVs with HBO movies, dressing rooms, and in-room coffee makers. Some rooms have sofas. In the bath, you'll find shampoo, a toothbrush, toothpaste, and a razor. A big plus is a famous Atlanta restaurant, the Colonnade, on the premises, serving authentic southern food (see details in Chapter 6). Services include free newspapers (*USA Today* and the *Atlanta Journal-Constitution*) and coffee in the lobby each morning.

TRAVELODGE PEACHTREE, 1641 Peachtree St. NE, at I-85, Atlanta, GA 30309. Tel. 404/873-5731 or toll free 800/255-3050. 56 rms. A/C TV TEL **MARTA:** Arts Center.

$ Rates: $43–$48 single, $49–$59 double. Extra person $4. Children under 18 stay free. AE, CB, DC, DISC, ER, MC, V.

A small property housed in a 3-story yellow concrete building, the TraveLodge Peachtree offers a convenient location (the hotel is on the airport shuttle route) and low rates. The rooms, decorated in teal and mauve, with grasspaper-covered walls and mahogany furnishings, are equipped with color cable TVs offering HBO movies. There's no on-premises restaurant, but an International House of Pancakes is a block away, and coffee is served in the lobby throughout the day. There's a small pool and sundeck out back.

BED & BREAKFASTS

ANSLEY INN, 253 15th St. NE, at Lafayette Dr., Atlanta, GA 30309. Tel. 404/872-9000 or toll free 800/446-5416. Fax 404/892-2318. 33 rms, 1 cottage. A/C TV TEL **MARTA:** Arts Center.

$ Rates (including continental breakfast): $100–$250 single or double (average $150), two-bedroom cottage (sleeps six) $200. No charge for extra people in a room. AE, DC, DISC, ER, MC, V. **Parking:** Free.

Far and away my favorite accommodation in Atlanta, the Ansley Inn is in every way a delight. Occupying a 1907 yellow-brick Tudor mansion, this former estate of department-store magnate George Muse is located in one of the city's most beautiful and chic residential areas, Ansley Park. Ancient magnolias and white oaks shade the inn's front lawn.

The Persian-carpeted dining room, furnished with a long English Chippendale-style table and Victorian and Empire sideboards, has a beautiful arched ceiling carved with fruit motifs. It adjoins a handsomely furnished living room with Queen Anne–style wing chairs and plush Regency-style sofas in front of an 8-foot ceramic-tile fireplace. Pale peach walls in the Italian marble-floored hallways are hung with changing art exhibits, and lavish floral arrangements top antique tables. Classical music or traditional jazz played downstairs during the day further enhances the inn's ambience, which is refined but never haughty.

The rooms, all named for Ansley Park streets, also have oak floors strewn with Oriental rugs. Painted in pastel colors typical of the Tudor period, with glossy white trim, they're elegantly furnished in antique pieces and reproductions. Your accommodation might have a brass bed or an 18th-century four-poster, crystal lamps, swag-curtained windows, or a cushioned window seat overlooking the park. Some rooms have lofty cathedral ceilings and working fire-places, and all feature marble-topped oak wet bars, comfortable armchairs with hassocks, remote-control color TVs with just about every cable station, clock radios, and full baths with whirlpool tubs. You'll find a terry-cloth robe in the closet. The 1,300-square-foot cottage has a fully equipped kitchen, two bedrooms, and a living room with a working fireplace.

Most importantly, the Ansley Inn is more than just a beautiful stage set. Its charming staff offers warm hospitality and gracious service to guests, creating a friendly, homelike atmosphere that will make your stay a memorable experience.

Dining/Entertainment: Complimentary breakfast includes croissants, pastries, bagels, granola, fresh fruit, juices, hot chocolate, and tea or coffee.

Services: Newspaper of your choice delivered to your door daily; 24-hour concierge staff; room service from area restaurants; afternoon coffee, tea, cheeses, and cookies in the living room.

Facilities: Complimentary membership at Colony Square Athletic Club, one block away, offering a full complement of Nautilus equipment, Stairmasters, treadmills, Lifecycles, rowing machines, steam room, aerobics classes, and much more. The inn itself is building a large outdoor pool/sun deck at this writing.

SHELLMONT BED AND BREAKFAST LODGE, 821 Piedmont Ave. NE, at 6th St., Atlanta, GA 30308. Tel. 404/872-9290, 4 rms. A/C **MARTA:** North Avenue or Midtown.

$ Rates (including continental breakfast): $70 single, $80 double in main house; $85 single, $90 double in carriage house. Extra person $15. *Note:* children 12 and under allowed in the carriage house only. AE, MC, V. **Parking:** Free.

This charming 2-story Victorian mansion looks, from the outside, like a Wedgwood fairy-tale house embellished with cream-colored ribbons, bows, garlands, and shells. It was designed by noted Atlanta architect Walter T. Downing for Dr. W. P. Nicholson as a present for the doctor's new bride, hence the wedding-bell newel post on the stairway. The building dates to 1891 and is on the National Register of Historic Places. When innkeepers Ed and Debbie McCord purchased it in 1982, they were only the second owners. The property was, however, considerably down at the heels by that time. The McCords have done a superb job on its restoration, not only in repairing all the functional aspects, but in meticulously researching original paint colors, stencil designs, woodwork, and period furnishings and reproducing them with 100% accuracy.

Breakfast is served on fine china in a lovely dining room with a floor-to-ceiling mantel fireplace. Guests might while away an evening reading (the McCords keep a fairly extensive library) before a blazing fire in the oak-furnished living room. The walls of this room are covered in hand-printed silk-screen Victorian-reproduction wallpaper, the windows hung with lace curtains. There's also a downstairs parlor that was originally a music room (carved instruments adorning the mantelpiece honor the room's original function) and, Ed's favorite room, the Moorish-influenced, Kilim-carpeted "Turkish corner," with its inverted-dome ceiling.

Up the stairway (its landing graced by an exquisite five-paneled stained-glass window that the McCords believe is an authentic Tiffany) are the four guestrooms. They have gorgeous beds (perhaps you'll have an Eastlake or a bed with a 6-foot oak headboard embellished with carved ribbons and bows), leaded-glass or bay windows with floral-motif balloon curtains, Oriental rugs strewn on hand-oiled hard pine floors, and framed botanical prints on the walls. All have private baths, but no TVs or phones (local calls are free on the phone downstairs). The other accommodation, in an adjoining carriage house, offers a master bedroom, full modern bath, fully equipped kitchen, living room, and dressing area.

Fronted by a small garden, the Shellmont has both a front porch and a lovely veranda out back with wicker rocking chairs, the latter shaded by an ancient sycamore.

Dining/Entertainment: Daily breakfast, included in rates, of fresh-squeezed juice, fresh and dried fruits, homemade pastries, cereal, and tea or coffee.

Services: Ed and Debbie live on the premises and offer all the services of a hotel concierge, daily chamber service, and fruit and fresh flowers in your room daily.

Facilities: Garage.

WOODRUFF BED & BREAKFAST, 223 Ponce de Leon Ave. NE, at Myrtle St., Atlanta, GA 30308. Tel. 404/875-9449 or toll free 800/473-9449. 9 rms, 3 suites. A/C TV (on request) TEL **MARTA:** North Avenue.

$ Rates (including full breakfast): $65 single, $75 double; $100 for two rooms with a shared bath (for up to four people); $125 for a two-room suite with private phone and Jacuzzi. AE, DISC, MC, V. **Parking:** Free.

This 3-story white-brick Victorian house, built in 1906 by an Atlanta physician, went on to a more interesting incarnation in the 1950s when Miss Bessie Woodruff bought the property and turned it into a successful house of ill repute. Officially, it was a licensed massage facility (the "girls" actually wore white nurses' uniforms), and some of Atlanta's most prominent politicians came by frequently to relieve the tensions of public office. Current owners Dan and Doug Jones (they're cousins) not only honored Bessie by naming their bed and breakfast for her, they've displayed, in public areas, light boards that were used to keep track of the rooms in use, framed photographs of Bessie (she was a beauty), and her old love letters.

The first floor, entered via a foyer with beautiful beveled-glass doors, has a cozy plant-filled parlor with a bay window. Guests can relax here on a plush velvet sofa before a blazing fireplace or play the turn-of-the-century English piano. The dining room, with leaded-glass windows, features a massive oak table under a crystal chandelier. Oak floors, in rooms and public areas, are waxed and buffed to a high gloss and strewn with area rugs. The rooms, all but three with private baths, contain a mix of 19th- and early 20th-century English antiques, along with pieces one might categorize as "grandma's house" furnishings. Beds have ruffed comforters and lots of pillows. Your accommodation might have stained-glass or bay windows, an overhead fan, or French doors leading to a porch furnished with rocking chairs. The house itself also offers a large front porch overlooking the oak-shaded lawn.

Dining/Entertainment: Rates include a full southern breakfast—ham, eggs, biscuits, grits, fresh-ground coffee, fresh fruit, and fresh-squeezed orange juice, plus croissants, breads, and pastries. Complimentary cocktails, coffee, cookies, and popcorn are served in the parlor every afternoon.

Services: Newspapers, magazines, and books available.

Facilities: Color cable TV with VCR in the parlor, gorgeous latticed Jacuzzi room with stained-glass windows.

3. BUCKHEAD

Buckhead hotels combine the quiet residential appeal of midtown accommodations with the luxury of downtown properties. Many of Atlanta's best restaurants are close by. In my opinion, it's the optimum hotel location.

VERY EXPENSIVE

HOTEL NIKKO ATLANTA, 3300 Peachtree Rd., just east of Piedmont Rd., Atlanta, GA 30326. Tel. 404/365-8100 or toll free 800-NIKKO-US. Fax 404/233-5686. 418 rms, 22 suites. A/C MINIBAR TV TEL **MARTA:** Lenox.

$ Rates: Weekday $140–$185 single or double, Nikko floor $185–$215 single or double; weekend (Fri–Sun) $95 per room, Nikko floor $165–$185. Inquire about weekend packages. Extra person $25. Children under 16 stay free in parents' room. AE, CB, DC, DISC, ER, JCB, MC, V. **Parking:** $14.

The towering Hotel Nikko offers a winning combination of 18th-century American architecture and Japanese attention to aesthetic detail. An exquisite Japanese flower arrangement graces the entrance foyer, and the lobby is a sublime setting overlooking a 9,000-square-foot garden with traditional plantings, rock formations, and splashing waterfalls created by noted Kyoto landscape architects. A collection of museum-quality Japanese art, spanning four centuries, is displayed throughout the hotel.

Rooms, decorated in subtle hues (peach, teal, mocha, café-au-lait) are furnished in 18th-century mahogany reproductions, with crane-motif headboards, fresh orchids, and Japanese prints in black lacquer frames providing Eastern nuance. Every luxury is provided: three phones (bedside, bath, and desk), remote-control cable TVs with

Spectravision movie options, AM/FM clock radios, terry robes, and baths equipped with hair dryers, TV speakers, cosmetic mirrors, and scales. You'll even find an umbrella in your closet. The Nikko floors (23–25) comprise a concierge level where guests enjoy upgraded amenities, services of a private concierge, and use of a very elegant lounge (complete with working fireplace)—the setting for extended continental breakfasts, afternoon teas, a large array of cocktail-hour hors d'oeuvres, and evening desserts and cordials. Gratis use of a charming conference room off the lounge is an additional benefit.

Dining/Entertainment: Kamogawa, Atlanta's premier Japanese restaurant, offers a uniquely authentic dining experience (see Chapter 6, "Atlanta Dining"). The delightful Cassis, with soaring arched windows overlooking the Japanese garden, is also much acclaimed for its sophisticated and eclectic cuisine (entrées run the gamut from risotto of porcini mushrooms to Maryland crab cakes); all meals are served here, including a Japanese breakfast and lavish Sunday brunch. A pianist entertains daily from 5 to 8pm in the plush Lobby Bar, also the setting for English-style afternoon teas. Weather permitting, a Japanese tea is also served afternoons in a tranquil garden with pagoda seating on the third floor. And a jazz trio performs nightly in the Library Bar, a handsome mahogany-paneled setting with tapestried wing chairs and tufted-leather sofas before a blazing fireplace.

Services: Complimentary 1-hour clothes pressing and overnight shoeshine, 24-hour room service, 24-hour concierge, babysitting, toys/activities for children, massage, airport shuttle, complimentary shuttle within a 3-mile radius of the hotel.

Facilities: Comprehensive business center; fully equipped health club, with TVs and VCRs on the exercise bikes, Life Trim equipment, stair machines, aerobics videos, steam, and sauna; a lovely outdoor pool and sun deck. Lenox Square and Phipps Plaza shopping malls are two blocks away.

JW MARRIOTT AT LENOX, 3300 Lenox Rd. NE, at E. Paces Ferry Rd., Atlanta, GA 30326. Tel. 404/262-3344 or toll free 800/228-9290. Fax 404/262-8603. 323 rms, 48 suites. A/C MINIBAR TV TEL **MARTA:** Lenox.

$ Rates: $165–$175 single, $175–$185 double; Club Level rooms $185 single, $195 double. Extra person $10. Children under 18 stay free in parents' room. Weekend rate (Fri–Sun) $119 per room per night. AE, CB, DC, DISC, ER, MC, V. **Parking:** $8.

This luxurious Marriott, with an interior modeled after Atlanta's historic Swan House (see Chapter 7), is enchanting from the moment you step inside its elegant marble-floored entranceway under a silver-leafed coffered ceiling. The residential-style lobby divides into a series of beautifully appointed, cozy living rooms furnished with plush sofas and Chippendale pieces, its gracious ambience enhanced by classical music and exquisite flower arrangements.

Rooms are charmingly furnished with Chippendale-style mahogany pieces, the walls hung with gilt-framed watercolors of Buckhead mansions. Picture windows offer panoramic vistas. Handsome mahogany armoires house remote-control cable TVs with Spectravision movie channels, minibars, and AM/FM alarm clock radios. Each room has three phones (bath, bedside, and desk), and lavish marble baths are equipped with scales and hair dryers. Floors 23 to 25 comprise the Concierge Level, which features a gorgeous concierge-staffed private lounge, setting for a substantial buffet breakfast, afternoon cocktails and hors d'oeuvres, and late-night liqueurs and chocolates. The Marriott connects from an interior door to the Lenox Square Mall, and the even posher Phipps Plaza Mall is within walking distance.

Dining/Entertainment: The exquisite Swan Room is designed to suggest an 18th-century English garden, with pale-yellow walls, Chinese Chippendale-style chairs, and English Axminster carpeting. At night, special lighting creates a leaf design on the tablecloths, evoking an elegant dinner in the woods. Serving American/continental fare, The Swan Room is open for all meals; reasonably priced weekend buffet brunches are especially popular. The clubby Ottley's, with Persian runners on bare oak floors and mahogany-paneled walls hung with equestrian-themed art, offers piano bar entertainment Wednesday to Saturday evenings. Light fare is available. And yet another plush setting for cocktails/light fare is the cozy Lobby Lounge, with comfortable sofas and armchairs before a working pagoda-style fireplace backed by Brazilian marble.

Services: 24-hour room service, multilingual concierge staff, nightly bed turn down, complimentary overnight shoeshine, airport shuttle, 1-hour dry cleaning, *USA Today* delivered to your room each morning.

Facilities: Large indoor pool in a setting patterned after a Roman bath, fully equipped health club with steam and sauna, full business center, pastry shop, Lenox Square Mall (the largest in the Southeast) adjoining.

RITZ-CARLTON BUCKHEAD, 3434 Peachtree Rd. NE, at Phipps Dr., Atlanta, GA 30326. Tel. 404/237-2700 or toll free 800/241-3333. Fax 404/239-0078. 525 rms, 29 suites. A/C TV MINIBAR TEL **MARTA:** Lenox.

$ Rates: $149–$215 single or double; Club Floor rooms $249 single or double. Children under 12 stay free in parents' room. Weekend rate (Fri–Sun) $115 single or double; also inquire about packages. AE, CB, DC, DISC, ER, MC, V. **Parking:** $5 (self), $7 (valet).

From the mahogany-paneled lobby, with antique Oriental carpets on white marble floors and cut-crystal French chandeliers, to public areas graced with Regency and Georgian antiques and an outstanding collection of 18th- and 19th-century paintings and sculpture (some $4 million worth; an audio tour is available), every inch of this hotel bespeaks unexampled luxury. And the quality of service fully matches the sumptuous surroundings.

The exquisite rooms, all with large bay windows, are decorated in two color schemes: moss green/ecru and mauve/cream. Furnishings include a burled-walnut armoire (which houses a remote-control color cable TV with HBO), either a sofa or armchairs upholstered in raw silk, 18th-century-reproduction beds, beautiful Chinese lamps, and federalist mirrors. Framed botanical prints and historical lithographs adorn the walls; baths amply supplied with fine toiletries contain scales, phones, and makeup mirrors; and a fully stocked refrigerator/bar is concealed in a handsome cabinet. You'll find a terry robe in your closet.

Floors 18 and 19 are the hotel's Club Floors, with a deluxe private concierge-staffed lounge in which lavish complimentary buffets are served daily at breakfast and cocktail hour. Complimentary drinks and snacks are also available here throughout the day; a full English tea is served every afternoon, cordials and chocolates at night.

Dining/Entertainment: The Dining Room at the Ritz-Carlton Buckhead is Atlanta's premier restaurant; as such it is covered extensively in Chapter 6. The Lobby Lounge, its mahogany-paneled walls hung with 18th- and 19th-century portraits and sporting scenes, centers on a glowing oak-log fire. It is the setting for afternoon English-style teas. A classical pianist plays from 3 to 5pm daily. Also on the lobby floor is the Bar, another paneled, lamplit precinct with working fireplace. A pianist plays Cole Porter and other classic tunes in the Bar every afternoon at cocktail hour, and a jazz trio performs Monday to Saturday night from 8pm to midnight. Buffet lunches are served daily. The 3-tiered Café, an all-day dining room, its mahogany-paneled walls hung with equestrian-themed paintings, is also a repository of art and antiques. Its classic haute-cuisine menu includes a section labeled "fitness cuisine." A lavish buffet brunch is served here every Sunday, and late-night snacks and desserts are offered nightly. In the adjoining Café Bar, guests are invited to a meet-the-management cocktail party every Wednesday afternoon; there's dancing to the music of a five-piece orchestra Friday, Saturday, and Sunday night from 8pm to midnight, and ballroom-style tea dances take place every Friday from 5 to 8pm. Espresso, on the lower level, with indoor seating as well as outdoor umbrella tables on a poplar-shaded brick patio, serves full breakfasts and light luncheon fare weekdays from 7am to 4pm.

Services: Fresh flowers in your room daily, limousine on request, airport shuttle and shuttle to nearby malls, newspaper delivered to your door each morning, 24-hour room service, nightly bed turn down with gourmet chocolates, currency exchange, valet parking, concierge services, 1-hour pressing, on-premises seamstress, personalized shopping, complimentary shoeshine.

Facilities: Full business center, swimming and fitness center, steam and sauna rooms, Jacuzzi, gift shop, hair salon, tobacconist, fur boutique.

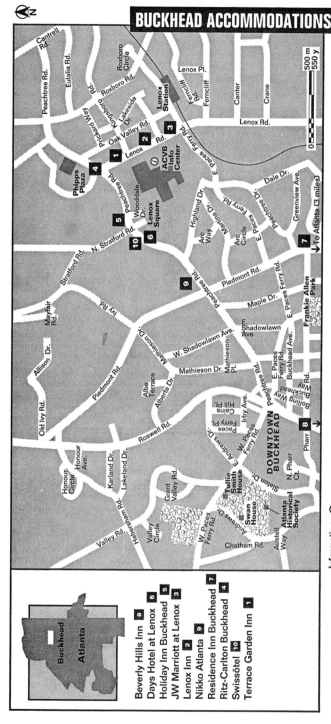

BUCKHEAD ACCOMMODATIONS

Information ⓘ

Beverly Hills Inn **8**
Days Hotel at Lenox **6**
Holiday Inn Buckhead **5**
JW Marriott at Lenox **3**
Lenox Inn **2**
Nikko Atlanta **9**
Residence Inn Buckhead **7**
Ritz-Carlton Buckhead **4**
Swissôtel **10**
Terrace Garden Inn **1**

Buckhead
Atlanta

SWISSÔTEL, 3391 Peachtree Rd. NE, between Lenox and Piedmont Rds., Atlanta, GA 30326. Tel. 404/365-0065 or toll free 800/63-SWISS. Fax 404/233-8786. 331 rms, 17 suites. A/C MINIBAR TV TEL **MARTA:** Lenox (complimentary transport to/from station).

$ Rates: $145–$195 single, $170–$220 double, suites $350–$900; Club level $205 single, $280 double. Each additional person $25. Children under 16 stay free. Weekend rate (available Fri-Sun) $99 per room, $165 Club level. AE, CB, DC, DISC, ER, JCB, MC, V. **Parking:** $9 valet, $6 self.

Opened in 1991, the Zurich-based Swissôtel (it's owned by Swissair) added a new aesthetic dimension to Atlanta's hotel scene. Its postmodern European architecture and interior spaces utilize Bauhaus elements, notably exemplified in the pristine white porcelainlike tile exterior with a graceful piano curve. An impressive lobby, with floor-to-45-foot-ceiling windows and a grand staircase, is warmed by the extensive use of reddish Australian lacewood paneling. Hallway carpets are designed after a Paul Klee painting, and original works by internationally known contemporary artists—Rauschenberg, Chagall, Schnabel, Stella, and many others—grace restaurants and public spaces. This is a visually exciting hotel.

Rooms are uniquely furnished in Biedermeier-style birds-eye maple pieces with black lacquer accents and capacious leather-topped desks. Color schemes—subtle tone-on-tone gray and lavender hues—are enhanced by interesting modernistic lamps and mirror frames and splash-of-color elements such as sienna velvet armchairs or chaise longues. Armoires house remote-control cable TVs with Spectravision/HBO movie options, and all rooms are equipped with terry robes, three phones (with call waiting), and AM/FM clock radios. Baths offer cosmetic mirrors, TV speakers, hair dryers, and Gucci toiletries. Especially nice are corner king rooms (ask for one when you reserve). The 21st and 22nd floors comprise a concierge-staffed Club level with a plush private lounge, the setting for gratis continental breakfasts, afternoon teas, cocktail hour hors d'oeuvres, and late-night pastries.

Dining/Entertainment: Opus, the hotel's acclaimed premier restaurant, is an elegant white-linened setting evocative of plush European resorts, with soaring ceilings and museum-quality photographs by Cartier-Bresson and Doisneau adorning Australian lacewood walls. *Esquire* magazine included Opus among its best new restaurants of 1991. New American cuisine is featured. The charming semicircular Café Gamay shares Opus's distinguished kitchen, offering its lunch menu throughout the day. In good weather, the café has patio dining. And sandwiched between these fine eateries is the posh art deco Lobby Bar, offering light fare and nightly piano entertainment.

Services: Concierge, complimentary shuttle to any destination in a 2-mile radius (including MARTA and the vast Lenox Square Mall), multilingual staff, airport shuttle, 24-hour room service, daily newspaper delivery.

Facilities: 24-hour business/communications center; a small but nicely equipped health club, including lap pool, sauna, steam room, and aerobics studio.

MODERATE

DAYS HOTEL AT LENOX, 3377 Peachtree Rd. NE, between Lenox and Piedmont Rds., Atlanta, GA 30326. Tel. 404/264-1111 or toll free 800/325-2525. Fax 404/231-3497. 295 rms, 5 suites. A/C TV TEL **MARTA:** Lenox.

$ Rates: $59–$89 single, $68–$99 double; rates vary with seasonal changes and/or convention activity. Extra person $10. Children under 12 free. Weekend rate (Fri–Sat) $49–$69 per room per night. Some money-saving packages available via the toll-free number. Super Saver rate may be available if you reserve 30 days in advance. AE, DC, DISC, MC, V. **Parking:** Free.

⑤ Not only is this hotel terrifically located (adjacent to the Lenox Square Mall), it's a special property in the Atlanta-based Days Inn chain. It was built in 1988 as a flagship for the new Days Hotel concept (an upgraded version of a Days Inn) and served as the prototype for the chain's expansion into Europe. It offers tremendous value. Its attractive rooms, on 11 stories, are decorated in earth tones, with grasspaper wall coverings; forest-green upholstered furnishings add a note of color. In-room amenities include remote-control color cable TVs with HBO and Spectravision movies, computer jacks, in-room safes, and AM/FM clock radios. Refrigerators and coffee makers are available on request, as are hairdryers.

Dining/Entertainment: The sunny, plant-filled Brentwood Café serves buffet and à la carte breakfast and lunch and a dinner that features steak, seafood, and poultry entrées, along with lighter fare. A cocktail lounge adjoins.

Services: Room service from 6am to 11pm, limousine rental, airport shuttle, free *USA Today* in the restaurant, free van transportation within 3 miles of the hotel.

Facilities: Outdoor pool (heated), coin-op washer and dryer; ice, snack, and soda machines on most floors; workout room; business center.

HOLIDAY INN BUCKHEAD, 3340 Peachtree Rd. NE, between Piedmont and Lenox Rds., Atlanta, GA 30326. Tel. 404/231-1234 or toll free 800/241-7078 or 800/HOLIDAY. Fax 404/231-5236. 221 rms. A/C TV TEL **MARTA:** Lenox.

$ Rates: $72–$78 single, $82–$88 double. Extra person $10. Children under 18 free. Weekend rate (Fri–Sat) $59 per room per night. AE, CB, DC, DISC, MC, V. **Parking:** Free.

Conveniently located in the Tower Place complex of restaurants, nightclubs, and movie theaters, this is a very pleasant Holiday Inn with a resortlike white stucco facade, an effect enhanced by awninged windows. A cozy, residential lobby is the prelude to attractively furnished rooms decorated in ecru/mauve/teal color schemes with burgundy carpets, prints of birds and flowers on the walls, and floral-motif bedspreads. In-room amenities include full-length mirrors and color TVs with HBO.

Dining/Entertainment: The Savannah Room, open for breakfast and dinner daily, lunch during the week, and Sunday brunch, specializes in steak and seafood at night, salads and sandwiches at lunch. A spacious lounge, Beauregard's, adjoins.

Services: Room service from 6am to 11pm, airport shuttle, complimentary van transport to Lenox Square and Phipps Plaza malls and the nearest MARTA station.

Facilities: Pleasantly secluded pool and sun deck, complimentary use of Sportslife, a fully equipped health club in the Tower Place complex.

RESIDENCE INN BUCKHEAD, 2960 Piedmont Rd. NE, between Pharr Rd. and Lindbergh Dr., Atlanta, GA 30305. Tel. 404/239-0677 or toll free **800/331-3131.** Fax 404/239-0677. 136 suites. A/C TV TEL **MARTA:** Lindbergh or Lenox (each about a mile away); buses stop half a block away.

$ Rates: Studio suites for up to four people, $96–$109; penthouse suites for up to six, $126–$139. Weekend rate (Fri–Sat) $79 studio, $128 penthouse. Reductions are available for stays of seven nights or longer. AE, DC, DISC, MC, V. **Parking:** Free.

This home-away-from-home was designed to meet the needs of travelers making extended visits, but it's marvelous even if you're only spending a single night. It's like having your own luxurious apartment, with a private entrance and a large, fully equipped kitchen containing a refrigerator (it makes ice), dishwasher (the maid does your dishes), sink, stove, microwave oven, toaster, coffee maker, and quality table settings for four. The kitchen is stocked with complimentary tea and coffee, sugar, cream, and microwave popcorn, and there's plenty of counter space for preparing meals.

All accommodations have comfortable living-room areas with convertible sofas, coffee tables, and armchairs. They're decorated in mauve or smoky blue color schemes, with pretty floral-print bedspreads and very nice watercolors and botanical prints on the walls. In-room amenities include clocks, AM/FM radios, and remote-control color/cable TVs with HBO (VCRs and movies can be rented). About half the suites have working fireplaces (during winter, logs are available from the front desk). The most luxurious accommodations are duplex penthouse suites with vaulted ceilings, full dining-room/office areas, two baths, and living-room fireplaces.

The Residence Inn is located on five attractively landscaped acres backed by woods, and the suites are in 2-story cream stucco chalets. You can park right outside your door.

Dining/Entertainment: One of the most salient features here is the cathedral-ceilinged Gatehouse Lounge. A color TV, small library, a stereo, and a big sectional sofa facing a blazing fireplace are among its amenities. The Gatehouse provides many opportunities to mingle with fellow guests over breakfast (a big buffet of fresh fruits, cereals, yogurt, pastries, muffins, and hot items like blintzes or pancakes) and at cocktail-hour parties on Monday, Tuesday, and Thursday from 5 to 7:30pm (featuring gratis beer, wine, and hot and cold hors d'oeuvres); Wednesday a full barbecue or buffet dinner is served during those hours. Big parties are also thrown on all major holidays, and guests receive little holiday gifts. In addition, there are outdoor barbecue grills and picnic tables, and food ranging from Lean Cuisine dinners to Dove bars is available at the front desk.

Services: Airport shuttle, babysitting, complimentary shuttle service within a 3-mile radius of the property, complimentary grocery shopping, free daily newspapers in lounge.

Facilities: Outdoor pool and sun deck with adjoining whirlpool; coin-op washers and dryers; on-premises basketball, volleyball, and paddle-tennis courts; and complimentary membership at an extensively equipped health club nearby.

TERRACE GARDEN INN, 3405 Lenox Rd. NE, between Peachtree and E. Paces Ferry Rds., Atlanta, GA 30326. Tel. 404/261-9250 or toll free 800/GETS-TGI. Fax 404/848-7301. 357 rms, 7 suites. A/C TV TEL **MARTA:** Lenox.

$ Rates: $95–$105 single, $105–$115 double. Club Level $125 single, $135 double. Extra person $10. Children under 18 free. Weekend rates (Fri–Sun) begin at $69–$109 per room per night. AE, DC, DISC, MC, V. **Parking:** Free (covered garage).

This is an especially lovely hotel that offers abundant services and facilities plus a great location (the Lenox Square Mall is just across the street)—all at very moderate rates. Antique furnishings, exquisite flower arrangements, ficus trees, and planters of greenery grace the public areas, and sprightly classical music replaces the usual din of Muzak. Rooms are elegantly residential in decor, furnished with French country and 18th-century Georgian-reproduction mahogany pieces (some have four-poster or brass beds); they're decorated in three attractive earth-toned color schemes with accents of moss green, sienna/cream, or mauve. Most rooms have balconies, and all offer extra phones in the bath, clock radios, and remote-control color TVs with HBO and Spectravision movies, plus other cable stations. Rooms with king-size beds have plush armchairs with ottomans.

Guests on Club floors enjoy additional amenities: a bilevel lounge with a concierge on duty; complimentary continental breakfast, cocktails, and hors d'oeuvres; free pressing and shoeshine services; upgraded in-room toiletries, terry robes, umbrellas, and nightly bed turn down with gourmet chocolates and liqueurs. The Terrace Garden's charm and graciousness have attracted numerous celebrity guests, from Presidents Carter, Nixon, and Reagan, to tennis star Andre Agassi and show-biz luminaries Elizabeth Taylor, Red Skelton, and Willie Nelson.

Dining/Entertainment: On two levels, Lillie's, one of Atlanta's prettiest hotel dining rooms, is garden-themed, with gilt-framed botanical prints on white-trimmed mauve walls, tapestried bamboo chairs at flower-bedecked tables, and lots of leafy greenery. A window wall on the upper level overlooks the pool. The fare is American/continental. Open daily from 6:30am to 11pm. The cozy, equestrian-themed Corner Hearth Lounge offers seating in plush chairs and sofas around a vast stone-walled, copper-hooded fireplace (ablaze in winter) and weeknight piano-bar entertainment. The equally delightful Cascades Lounge overlooks a series of small pools with waterfalls cascading over bronze dolphins.

Services: Room service from 6:30am to 11pm, free daily newspaper, free local calls, airport shuttle, concierge.

Facilities: Extensive Health & Racquet Center offers indoor tennis and racquetball, indoor jogging track, indoor pool, outdoor pool with waterfalls, Nautilus equipment, Lifecycles, stair machines, steam, sauna, and Jacuzzi.

INEXPENSIVE

LENOX INN, 3387 Lenox Rd. NE, between Peachtree and E. Paces Ferry Rds., Atlanta, GA 30326. Tel. 404/261-5500 or toll free 800/241-0200. Fax 404/262-1761. 180 rms. A/C TV TEL **MARTA:** Lenox.

$ Rates: $62 single; $67 double. Extra person $5. Children under 18 stay free. Weekend rate (Fri–Sat) $49.95 per room per night for up to four people. AE, CB, DC, MC, V. **Parking:** Free.

Considering all you get here, in a great location just across the street from Lenox Square Mall, the Lenox Inn is a great bargain. Under the same ownership as the adjacent Terrace Garden Inn and sharing many of its facilities, the Lenox offers accommodations in four 2- and 3-story cream-trimmed brick buildings with shuttered windows. They have a kind of quaint colonial look. Rooms are pristinely charming, decorated in mauve and forest green, with cherry-wood doors, Georgian-reproduction mahogany furnishings, cream-colored walls, and drapes in a pretty floral pattern. Amenities include a color cable TV with Spectravision and HBO movies and a full complement of toiletries in the bath. Some baths have extra sinks in dressing rooms, and rooms with king-size beds offer steambaths. Only one building has an elevator, by the way; ask for it, or a first-floor room elsewhere, if stairs are a problem.

Dining/Entertainment: A choice of a complimentary continental breakfast (homemade muffins, juice, and tea or coffee) or a large buffet breakfast ($6.25) is offered in a cozy, cherry-paneled restaurant with a working fireplace. Guests also gather here for complimentary cocktails and hors d'oeuvres nightly from 5:30 to 6:30pm. In summer there are occasionally gratis poolside cookouts/buffets with an open bar. And guests can charge meals at the Terrace Garden (see listing above) to their rooms at the Lenox.

Services: Airport shuttle, complimentary newspapers at front desk, free local calls.

Facilities: Two outdoor swimming pools, extensive health-club facilities of the Terrace Garden Inn next door at no charge.

BED & BREAKFASTS

BEVERLY HILLS INN, 65 Sheridan Dr. NE, just off Peachtree Rd., Atlanta, GA 30305. Tel. 404/233-8520 or toll free 800/331-8520. 18 suites. A/C TV TEL **MARTA bus:** No. 23 at the corner.

$ Rates (including continental breakfast): $65–$74 single, $74–$120 double for a one-bedroom suite; $90–$120 for a two-bedroom suite accommodating up to four people. Extra person $7. Children under 12 free. Reductions available for stays of a week or more. AE, CB, DC, DISC, ER, JCB, MC, V. **Parking:** Free.

Housed in a Wedgwood green 1920s California-style building, with forest-green shutters and window awnings, this charming B&B is located on a sedately residential tree-lined street. British owner/host Mit Amin offers warm hospitality to guests. On the first floor is a cozy parlor/library where a decanter of port is available all day. Another library is downstairs in the sunny garden room, which has a skylit conservatory area filled with plants.

Rooms are cheerful and attractive, decorated in an eclectic period mix of antiques (many of them English pieces) and collectibles, with very pretty floral fabric bedspreads and curtains, oak floors strewn with area rugs, and framed botanical prints on the walls. Some have canopied beds. All are equipped with kitchenettes (the maid does your dishes) and clock radios. Private balconies are entered via French doors. Several supermarkets are within easy walking distance, should you want to cook in your room, but the area also abounds with good restaurants. Classical music played in public areas enhances the residential ambience, as do dozens of flourishing plants.

Dining/Entertainment: An extended continental breakfast is served in the garden room. Or, in good weather, you can enjoy the morning meal at umbrella tables on the front lawn.

Services: You'll find a half bottle of burgundy in your room on arrival; four daily newspapers are complimentary; free local calls.

Facilities: Lounge with large-screen TV and VCR, Xerox and FAX machines, complimentary washer/dryer, complimentary membership privileges at the nearby Buckhead Towne Club, a state-of-the-art facility offering two outdoor swimming pools, Lifecycles, Stairmasters, saunas, Jacuzzi, a full complement of Nautilus equipment, racquetball, and squash.

4. GEORGIA TECH

INEXPENSIVE

COMFORT INN, 120 North Ave. NW, at I-75, Atlanta, GA 30313. Tel. 404/881-6788 or toll free 800/221-2222. 63 rms. A/C TV TEL **MARTA:** North Avenue.

$ Rates: $54–$62 single, $62–$68 double. Extra person $7. Children under 18 stay free. Reduced rates available for stays of a week or more. AE, CB, DC, DISC, MC, V. **Parking:** Free.

This small property, just across from Georgia Tech, opened in 1984 and was completely refurbished in 1990. Its cheerful rooms are decorated in a rose/blue/ivory color scheme, with dark walnut-look Formica furnishings and watercolors of beach scenes adorning white-papered walls. All have color cable TVs with HBO movie channels. A Wendy's adjoins, and Junior's, a very inexpensive cafeteria, is just next door. Complimentary coffee and doughnuts are served in the lobby each morning.

5. GEORGIA'S STONE MOUNTAIN

Georgia's Stone Mountain Park, just 16 miles east of downtown Atlanta, is a recreation area with 3,200 acres of lakes and wooded parkland. It is, in itself, a major travel destination, visited by over six million tourists annually. *Note:* There's a one-time $5 parking fee to enter the park.

EXPENSIVE

EVERGREEN CONFERENCE CENTER AND RESORT, One Lakeview Dr., Stone Mountain Park, Stone Mountain, GA 30086. Tel. 404/879-9900 or toll free 800/722-1000. Fax 404/469-9013. 220 rms. 29 suites. A/C TV TEL

$ Rates: $100–$140 single, $125–$160 double; rates depend on view. Extra person $20. Children under 18 free. Inquire about packages when you reserve. AE, CB, DC, MC, V. **Parking:** Free.

Geared primarily to business travel, the Evergreen is also a good choice for vacationers. Its three-turreted stucco buildings make up a lakefront "castle" nestled in a fragrant forest of pine. The lodgelike lobby centers on a massive stone fireplace, backed by cherry paneling. Rooms are large and luxuriously appointed, decorated in neutral tones and furnished with floral-tapestried armchairs and 18th-century American reproduction mahogany pieces. Each contains a remote-control color TV (concealed in a handsome armoire) and a clock radio.

Dining/Entertainment: The stunning Waterside Restaurant, under a 35-foot rotunda, offers lake, mountain, and treetop views. Buffets are offered at all meals in addition to à la carte regional American fare. Even breakfast can get fancy here, with entrées such as quail eggs and sautéed quail with grits. It's open daily from 6:30am to 11:30pm. Both Ivy's, a plush window-walled lounge offering complimentary cocktail-hour hors d'oeuvres, and Vista, a wicker-furnished lobby lounge, overlook the pool. Classical music is played in all public areas and restaurants here. The poolside snack bar is called Splash.

Services: 24-hour room service, airport limo, concierge; tickets for all park attractions sold at the concierge desk.

Facilities: Two nightlit tennis courts; full business/meeting facilities; health club, with indoor swimming pool, whirlpool, and workout rooms; large outdoor pool with whirlpool, baby wading pool, and sun deck.

INEXPENSIVE

STONE MOUNTAIN INN, Stone Mountain Park, Stone Mountain, GA 30086 (tel. 404/469-3311 or toll free 800/277-0007. Fax 404/498-5691. 89 rms, 3 suites. A/C TV TEL

$ Rates: May 22–Sept 13, $60–$85 single; $70–$95 double. Mar 1–May 21 and Sept 14–Oct 31, $50–$75 single; $60–$85 double. Nov 1–Feb 28, $50–$55 single; $60–$65 double. Honeymoon suites $155, including a bottle of champagne and breakfast. Many packages available. AE, CB, DC, MC, V. **Parking:** Free.

This charming inn, built in 1965, is housed in a 2-story white-colonnaded brick building that wraps around a central courtyard. Rooms, decorated in taupe and Williamsburg blue, are lovely, featuring Chippendale-reproduction walnut and mahogany furnishings, turn-of-the-century-style ceiling fan/ lighting fixtures, large vanity/dressing room areas, and spacious parlors with comfortable sofas and armchairs. Walls are covered in pretty floral-motif papers and hung with framed Williamsburg sampler embroideries. Honeymoon suites offer king-size, four-poster canopied beds. Color TVs are equipped with HBO and other cable stations. Almost all accommodations have courtyard-facing balconies or patios with rocking chairs. The inn prides itself on offering warm southern hospitality.

Dining/Entertainment: Confederate flags are the backdrop to a winding staircase that leads from the lobby to the inn's attractive dining room. Its floor-to-ceiling windows overlook verdant scenery, and there's balcony seating facing the mountain sculptures. All meals here are buffets (very reasonably priced) featuring southern fare.

Services: Room service during restaurant hours, airport limo; tickets for all park attractions sold at the front desk.

Facilities: The park itself offers everything in the way of recreational activities (see Chapter 7 for details). On the premises: coin-op laundry, business services, very large outdoor pool/sun deck in a woodsy setting.

A CAMPGROUND

FAMILY CAMPGROUND, Stone Mountain Park, P.O. Box 778, Stone Mountain, GA 30086. Tel. 404/498-5710.

$ Rates: $12 for a tent site; $13 for site with water and electricity; $14 for full hookup. Rates cover two people; additional people pay $2 per night. Children 11 and under stay free. AE, DISC, MC, V.

A very large campground, with sections for pop-ups, RVs, and tents, this is a great place to stay. Nestled in the woods, the area has many sites overlooking the lake, especially in the tent section. All have barbecue grills; picnic tables are scattered throughout. Public facilities include a dining pavilion, playgrounds, laundries, and showers. The park's beach is close by.

---

6. DRUID HILLS/EMORY UNIVERSITY/BROOKHAVEN

Though not a happening section of town in terms of restaurants or attractions, this area, east of midtown and Buckhead, offers good value for your hotel dollar. And if you have a car, the properties listed below are only about a 10-minute drive from the center of things.

MODERATE

COURTYARD BY MARRIOTT, 1236 Executive Park Dr., off N. Druid Hills Rd., Atlanta, GA 30329. Tel. 404/728-0708 or toll free 800/321-2211. Fax 404/636-4019. 133 rms, 12 suites. A/C TV TEL **MARTA bus:** in front of the hotel.

$ Rates: $83 single, $93 double; suites $96 single, $106 double. Extra person $10. Children under 18 free. Weekend rate (Fri–Sat) $59 per room per night. Reduced rates offered for stays of five days or more. AE, CB, DC, DISC, MC, V. **Parking:** Free.

Housed in a 4-story cream stucco building, in an attractively landscaped setting of trees, shrubbery, and well-tended flower beds, the Courtyard represents yet another kind of link in the Marriott chain. It's a limited-service (no bellmen, though you can get a luggage cart), moderately priced lodging. But don't picture a spartan, no-frills atmosphere. This is a beautiful property with a pleasant, plant-filled lobby and very nice rooms indeed.

Furnished with substantial oak pieces, the rooms have ecru walls hung with gilt-framed floral prints, brass lighting fixtures, and pretty print bedspreads. They're decorated in two color schemes—muted green or mocha-and-mauve, both with sienna accents. All rooms feature large desks, nice-size dressing-room areas, full-length folding-mirror closet doors, 25-foot phone cords, remote-control color cable TVs with HBO and Spectravision movie channels, bedside clock radios, and hot-water dispensers to you can make tea or coffee (both available free at the front desk) in your room. Suites—a good bet for families—have full sofa-bedded living rooms with extra phones and TVs plus wet bars with small refrigerators.

Dining/Entertainment: A delightful lobby restaurant, with seating around a fireplace and overlooking a verdant garden, serves breakfast, lunch, and dinner daily. Prices are very low. A comfortable lounge adjoins.

Services: Airport shuttle, room service at dinner.

Facilities: Medium-size outdoor pool, indoor whirlpool, poolside gazebo (nice for picnicking), lobby vending machines which supply necessaries, workout room, coin-op washers and dryers.

EMORY INN, 1641 Clifton Rd. NE, between Briarcliff and N. Decatur Rds., Atlanta, GA 30329. Tel. 404/712-6700 or toll free 800/933-6679. Fax 404/712-6701. 107 rms. A/C TV TEL. **MARTA bus:** In front of the hotel.

$ Rates: $84–$98 single; $10 each additional person. Weekend rate (Fri–Sat) $59–$64 per room for up to four people. Children under 12 stay free. AE, CB, DC, DISC, MC, V. **Parking:** Free.

Owned by Emory University, this totally delightful hotel is bordered by 14 acres of woodland property. Though it's quite centrally located—just six miles from downtown—it's peaceful out here; you'll wake to birds singing every morning. This sense of tranquillity is enhanced by classical music played in public areas which include a charming lobby and a cozy living room/lounge with a working fireplace. Rooms, furnished in Early American–style knotty-pine pieces, are attractively decorated in pale peach or apricot color schemes with teal accents. Many overlook the woods. Amenities include cable TVs, AM/FM clock radios, and telephone answering machines.

Dining/Entertainment: The lovely Emory Café, with bamboo and wicker garden furnishings and fresh flowers on every table, serves buffet and à la carte American/continental fare at all meals. There's also outdoor seating for dining or cocktails in a beautiful flower garden.

Services: Airport shuttle, room service during restaurant hours, complimentary shuttle service to Lenox Square Mall and local MARTA stations.

Facilities: Coin-op washers and dryers, medium-sized L-shaped swimming pool/sun deck bordered by flower beds, Jacuzzi, exercise room with Universal equipment, stair machine, and exercise bike.

BUDGET

BUDGETEL INN, 2535 Chantilly Dr. NE, just off Cheshire Bridge Rd., Atlanta, GA 30324. Tel. 404/321-0999 or toll free 800/428-3438. Fax 404/634-3884. 102 rms. A/C TV TEL **MARTA bus:** At the corner.

$ Rates: $34.95–$43.95 single; each additional person pays $6. Children 18 and under stay free. AE, CB, DC, DISC, MC, V. **Parking:** Free.

This hotel, part of a Milwaukee-based chain, offers great value to price-conscious travelers. Its small lobby is clean and cozy; its rooms are immaculate and well tended. Furnished in oak pieces, with attractive teal carpets, mauve bedspreads, and nicely chosen prints adorning ecru walls, all rooms have recessed windows (with screens) that can actually be opened—a welcome alternative to air conditioning. In-room amenities include dressing areas, coffee makers, 25-foot phone cords, computer jacks, and remote-control color TVs with Spectravision and Showtime movie stations. Ten larger rooms, called leisure suites, offer refrigerators, microwave ovens, hairdryers, and sofa beds. Coin-op washers and dryers are on the premises. There's no restaurant, but a sweet roll, juice, and coffee are delivered to your room gratis each morning.

7. OFF I-20

Though fairly far out east of town, these two properties are located right off I-20, allowing you to zip into downtown Atlanta in about 10 to 15 minutes by car.

BUDGET

ECONO LODGE, 2574 Candler Rd., just off I-20 at exit 33, Atlanta, GA 30032. Tel. 404/243-4422 or toll free 800/424-4777. 60 rms. A/C TV TEL **MARTA bus:** In front of hotel.
$ Rates: $32–$36 single, $36–$45 double. Extra person $4. Children under 12 free. AE, DC, MC, V. **Parking:** Free.
The Econo Lodge slogan is "spend a night, not a fortune," and that's just what you can do very happily here. The property opened in 1989, so its oak-furnished rooms are spiffy-looking and attractive, with plum carpeting and curtains and color-coordinated mauve-and-green floral-design bedspreads. You get a remote-control, 25-inch color TV with HBO, and some rooms with king-size beds even have wet bars with sinks and cabinets. The property is just a 10-minute drive from downtown. A Long John Silver's and a Wendy's adjoin the Lodge, numerous other eateries are close by, and free coffee, juice, and doughnuts are served in the lobby all day.

MOTEL 6, 2565 Wesley Chapel Rd., off I-20, Atlanta, GA 30035. Tel. 404/288-6911. 100 rms. A/C TV TEL
$ Rates: $26.95 single; each additional person $6. Children under 18 stay free. AE, CB, DC, DISC, MC, V. **Parking:** Free.
Located in Decatur, Motel 6 offers all you *really* need in the way of accommodations at a very low cost. And it has a swimming pool. Most of the rooms have two double beds (10 have one double bed), and all offer color TVs with free movie channels. They have brown carpeting and forest-green bedspreads. Dudley's, a western-style restaurant and lounge on the premises (it's like a cowboy version of "Cheers"), serves up steaks, salads, burgers, and sandwiches. It also has an oyster bar. Open till 3 or 4am every night, its entertainment options include three pool tables, a large-screen TV on which sports events are aired, and friendly conversation with locals.

CHAPTER 6

ATLANTA DINING

1. DOWNTOWN
- **FROMMER'S SMART TRAVELER: RESTAURANTS**

2. MIDTOWN
- **FROMMER'S COOL FOR KIDS: RESTAURANTS**

3. BUCKHEAD

4. VIRGINIA-HIGHLAND

5. SWEET AUBURN

6. DECATUR

7. CHAMBLEE

8. SPECIALTY DINING

Although I live in one of the nation's top restaurant towns—New York—most of the year, believe it or not I have occasional cravings for various only-in-Atlanta culinary creations—soft-shell crab in lemony red-pepper coulis at Pano and Paul's, parchment-baked fish in five-citrus sauce at Indigo Coastal Grill, Rocky's baked pasta balsamico, macaroni and cheese at the OK Cafe, Oreo cheesecake (the world's best) at Mick's . . . and many delectable others. This is a town that has gastronomically arrived while continuing to nurture its grits-and-greens roots. Atlanta dining options run the gamut from superb ethnic dishes (Chinese, Thai, and Cajun, to name a few) to the most sophisticated nouvelle and traditional haute-cuisine fare. All that and sugar-cured smoked ham with redeye gravy, too!

Atlantans love to dine out. Reservations, where accepted, are always a good idea—in some places, imperative. You're also expected to dress up a bit in all but the most casual eateries. Men generally wear suits and ties at dinner, and the women are plenty chic.

HOW TO READ THE LISTINGS

Listings are divided first by location, then alphabetically by price. I've used the following price categories: **very expensive** (dinner is over $45 per person for a full meal, including a glass of wine, tip, and tax), **expensive** ($35 to $45), **moderate** ($25 to $35), **inexpensive** ($15 to $25), and **budget** (under $15).

Keep in mind that the above categories refer to dinner prices, and some very expensive restaurants offer more affordable lunches or early-bird dinners. Also, I'm going under the assumption that you're not stinting when you order. Some restaurants, for instance, have entrées ranging from $12 to $20. In most cases, you can dine for less if you order carefully.

Note: MARTA stations are listed where they are within walking distance. If you need bus-routing information, call 848-4711.

1. DOWNTOWN

Your choices here range from the ultra-elegant (City Grill and Nikolai, which, along with the Dining Room in Buckhead, are the city's top restaurants) to the world's largest drive-in.

VERY EXPENSIVE

CITY GRILL, 50 Hurt Plaza, at Edgewood Ave. Tel. 524-2489.
Cuisine: CONTEMPORARY AMERICAN. **Reservations:** Required. **MARTA:** Peachtree Center. **Parking:** Complimentary valet parking.

$ Prices: Appetizers $6.75–$8 at lunch, $6.50–$11 at dinner; entrées $9–$16 at lunch, $18–$28.50 at dinner. AE, CB, DC, MC, V.

Open: Lunch Mon–Fri 11:30am–2:30pm; dinner nightly 5:30–10pm.

Atlanta's most opulent restaurant, City Grill opened in 1988 and immediately became a mecca for downtown power-lunchers and a high-society enclave at dinner. For openers, no dining room in town can match its architectural splendor. Ensconced in the lavishly refurbished Hurt Building, designed in 1912 to be the largest and most magnificent office building in the South, it is entered via a marble-walled Rotunda with a rosette- and gold-leaf-adorned dome. Highly polished black marble and custom-woven carpets extend the hues of the Rotunda into the Grand Lobby. Downstairs seating, amid potted palms, is in upholstered teal or moss-green neoclassical Georgian-, Sheraton-, and Queen Anne–style chairs at oversized tables covered in white linen. Murals of misty pastoral scenes adorn the walls, graceful European candelabra chandeliers glitter overhead, and floor-to-ceiling windows are framed by gold draperies. An aisle flanked by lofty gilt-topped columns and a staircase with an oak banister lead to balcony seating.

City Grill's setting is resplendent, and no less dazzling is the haute-cuisine fare whipped up in the kitchen by award-winning executive chef Martin Gagne (*Food & Wine* magazine calls him one of America's "top young culinarians"). Your dinner might begin with plump hickory-grilled shrimp served around a mound of potato mousseline and garnished with beautiful herbed potato chips (the herb leaves create a stained-glass effect). Also excellent, on my last visit, was a blini stuffed with lime-flavored avocado and blue crab served with pico de gallo on spicy gazpacho. The menu highlights such fresh fish and seafood entrées as rare peppered tuna medallions on grilled bok choy in a citrusy ginger-soy sauce. Crisp-roasted juicy duck was served with a delicate sweet potato latke in a piquant plum sauce flavored with cassis and candied ginger. And hickory-roasted loin of venison, redolent of garlic, sage, and rosemary, was perfectly complemented by a tartly sweet wine-flavored wild blueberry sauce and batonets (little sticks) of beets. Desserts are sumptuous and sizable—for example, a refreshing finale of chilled passion-fruit mousse around a scoop of passion-fruit sorbet, garnished by a medley of intricately carved fresh fruits. City Grill's extensive cellar is stocked with over 400 (mostly French and Californian) wines in all price ranges, 21 selections of which are available by the glass and several of which are exclusive to the restaurant. Do consult the sommelier.

MORTON'S OF CHICAGO, 245 Peachtree Center Ave., at Harris St. Tel. 577-4366.

Cuisine: STEAK AND SEAFOOD **Reservations:** Required.
MARTA: Peachtree Center. **Parking:** Free valet parking at dinner on Harris Street, between Peachtree Center Avenue and Courtland Street.

$ Prices: Entrées $7–$12 at lunch, $14–$25 at dinner. AE, CB, DC, MC, V.

Open: Lunch Mon–Fri 11:30am–2:30pm; dinner Mon–Sat 5:30–11pm, Sun 5–10pm.

The Morton's chain of gourmet steak houses was founded in 1976 by one-time Playboy executive vice-president Arnie Morton, who was also instrumental in developing the Playboy Club concept. His restaurant empire has been as successful as his bunny business, and it's no wonder: These are truly great steak houses. A keynote of every Morton's is a star-studded clientele. Here the cream stucco walls are lined with photos of famous beef eaters like Bob Hope, Ringo Starr, and Frank Sinatra. One night, 15 Atlanta Falcons descended on the restaurant like a swarm of locusts and consumed 56 appetizers in five minutes prior to double and even quadruple steak orders. They worked up a tab of $3,000! As for the Braves, they always order up 24-ounce steaks all around, even at lunch.

But it's not just the food that's appealing at Morton's. Few restaurants offer more in the way of solid comfort. Much of the seating is in roomy horseshoe-shaped cream leather booths at tables adorned with white linen and fresh flowers. Bronze pig-motif candle lamps (Mr. Morton's whimsical encouragement to make a pig of yourself) cast a soft glow. An exhibition kitchen is hung with copper pots, and wines are stored in a brick-walled rack.

There's no printed menu. Waiters in flowing white aprons roll up service carts laden with several cuts of meat, a cooked chicken, and a frisky live lobster. What you see is what you get. Do start off with an appetizer—perhaps lump crabmeat cocktail, smoked salmon, or a Caesar salad. Entrée choices include succulent prime midwestern beefsteaks—porterhouse, sirloin, rib eye, or double filet—prepared to your exact specifications—plus lemon oregano chicken, lamb chops, Sicilian veal, grilled swordfish, and prime rib. Side orders such as flavorfully fresh al dente asparagus, sautéed spinach with mushrooms, or hash browns are highly recommended, and portions are huge, so you can share. A loaf of onion bread on every table is complimentary.

Leave room for dessert—perhaps a lemon, Grand Marnier, or chocolate soufflé. There is, of course, an extensive wine list. At lunch you can opt for lighter entrées like omelets and burgers.

EXPENSIVE

DAILEY'S, 17 International Blvd., just east of Peachtree St. Tel. 681-3303.
Cuisine: CONTEMPORARY AMERICAN **Reservations:** Not accepted; arrive off-peak hours. **MARTA:** Peachtree Center. **Parking:** Street only, which is difficult in the heart of downtown.
$ Prices: Appetizers $3.95–$5.95 at lunch, $3.95–$6.75 at dinner; entrées $7–$9 at lunch, $12–$21 at dinner. AE, CB, DC, MC, V.
Open: Lunch Mon–Fri 11am–2:30pm; dinner Sun–Thurs 5:30–11pm, Fri–Sat 5:30pm–midnight.

Entered via a cozy bar, Dailey's is one flight up a majestic staircase reached via a lushly planted walkway. It's a beautiful room, a former warehouse with a 20-foot peaked ceiling crisscrossed with dark wooden beams, exposed brick walls, and pine-plank floors. Two immense brass and fluted-glass train-station lamps are hung on chains from the beams, but they cast little light; Dailey's is romantically dim, with candles aglow on tables covered in white linen. English carousel horses on brass poles are centerpieces, but attention tends to be riveted on a spotlit stage—the marble-topped dessert bar (more about that later).

Waiters, all very efficient and gracious, elucidate the blackboard menu. And a wonderful menu it is, highly original and frequently changing to include new creations and market-fresh specialties. Both appetizers and entrées run a wide gamut. On my last visit the former included escargots baked in garlic butter; flaky strudel stuffed with cheeses, artichoke hearts, and prosciuttini ham, topped with basil-garlic butter; and a signature dish—steamed broccoli dipped in parmesan-cheese batter and deep-fried. An entrée of swordfish steak was marinated in mustard sauce, rolled in cracked black peppercorns, grilled, and served with mustard-cognac sauce. Other excellent choices for the main course were large grilled Gulf shrimp dredged in grated coconut and served in tangy sweet-and-sour sauce, and fresh salmon filet wrapped in edible rice paper in soy balsamic sauce. Portions are huge and accompanied by a choice of fresh vegetables or new potatoes roasted in garlic-parsley butter; doughnutlike deep-fried yeast rolls served with whipped herb butter; and a large salad. There's a small but well-chosen wine list.

You simply mustn't pass up the above-mentioned dessert bar,

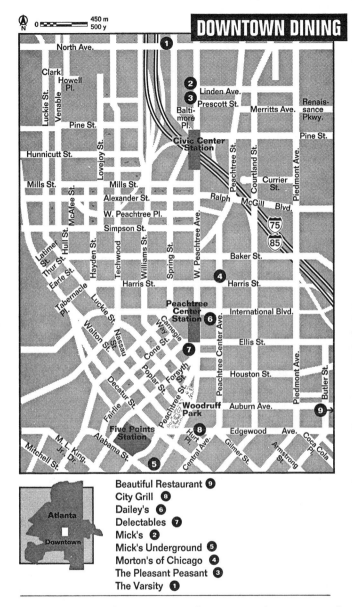

DOWNTOWN DINING

Beautiful Restaurant **9**
City Grill **8**
Dailey's **6**
Delectables **7**
Mick's **2**
Mick's Underground **5**
Morton's of Chicago **4**
The Pleasant Peasant **3**
The Varsity **1**

where a pastry chef is stationed at all times to explain an array of irresistible oven-fresh temptations. My favorite is the delectable apple caramel pie—cinnamon apples on a walnut crust, topped with brown-sugary streusel, vanilla ice cream, and ginger-caramel sauce. You can also opt for dessert and after-dinner drinks in the downstairs bar, where a pianist plays nightly. At lunch, similar entrées are supplemented by burgers, omelets, salads, and sandwiches.

FROMMER'S SMART TRAVELER:
RESTAURANTS

1. Eat your main meal at lunch; prices are lower then and you can enjoy gourmet entrées for much less than they'd cost at dinner.
2. Hotel breakfasts tend to be very pricey. Consider a hotel or B&B accommodation where rates include breakfast.
3. Some accommodations listed in this book have fully equipped kitchens; for families, especially, these can represent substantial savings.
4. Atlanta has many lovely parks. Occasionally buying picnic food and lunching alfresco will save money as well as affording you a relaxing break from sightseeing.

MODERATE

MICK'S, in Underground Atlanta, at the corner of Pryor and Alabama Sts. Tel. 525-2825.
   Cuisine: AMERICAN **Reservations:** Not accepted. **MARTA:** Five Points.
$ Prices: Appetizers $1.95–$6.95; entrées $6–$7.25; steak/seafood/prime rib $12–$i4.25. AE, CB, DC, MC, V.
   Open: Daily 11am–1am.

My favorite of the Underground eateries is Mick's, an imposing turn-of-the-century-themed 2-story restaurant in Humbug Square. It's fronted by a gaslit wraparound porch enclosed by black wrought-iron fencing, a marvelous venue for viewing indoor "street" action while sipping vodka-spiked pink lemonade. The main dining room, done up in Victorian-saloon red and black, has whitewashed brick walls hung with Early American patchwork quilts. It's a casual but very simpatico setting with candlelit tables and large candelabra chandeliers overhead. Upstairs is a cozy bar, furnished with cushioned wicker chairs amid potted palms. There's also café seating on both levels, the upper actually outdoors on a patio overlooking the fountain plaza.

Mick's is great for anything from a snack to a full meal. Nachos here are as good as nachos get—piled high with melted Monterey Jack cheese, jalapeños, sliced chicken breast, and/or chopped beef flavorfully spiced with cumin, cayenne, and chili powder. Hand-mixed guacamole and homemade chili are also excellent. A superb house specialty is char-grilled shrimp in lemon-garlic-herb butter served with salad, garlic bread, and delicious, slightly chunky mashed potatoes with mushroom gravy. Yet another option is chicken marinated in mustard sauce, dredged in cracked black peppercorns, hickory-grilled, and served on a whole-grain bun with mustard-cognac sauce; it comes with fries or pasta salad. Whatever you order, do leave room for dessert—perhaps the rich, silky-smooth chocolate-cream pie topped with whipped cream, or the buttery, brown-sugary fruit cobbler crowned with vanilla ice cream.

THE PLEASANT PEASANT, 555 Peachtree St., between Linden and Merritts Aves. Tel. 874-3223.
  Cuisine: CONTINENTAL **Reservations:** Not accepted.
  MARTA: North Avenue. **Parking:** Free self and valet parking.
$ **Prices:** Appetizers $3.75–$4.50 at lunch, $3.75–$6.50 at dinner; entrées $6–$9 at lunch, $10–$19 at dinner. AE, CB, DC, DISC, MC, V.
  Open: Lunch Mon–Fri 11:30am–2:30pm, dinner nightly 5:30pm–midnight.

Housed in a former drugstore, the Pleasant Peasant has all the elements of a typical New York Soho pub—exposed brick walls, white-tile floors, and a cream-colored pressed-tin ceiling. At night, the dining room is subtly (let's say romantically) lit by hurricane lamps on white-linen-covered tables. During the day, you can see that a large ficus and other greenery thrives in the sunshine streaming through a large skylight.

The menu, presented at your table on a blackboard, changes daily. At a recent dinner, there were appetizers of shrimp southwestern (five large Gulf shrimp baked in phyllo pastry with cumin/cayenne/chili-flavored cream cheese, served with piquant salsa) and homemade fettuccine tossed with fresh basil, spinach, tomatoes, parmesan cheese, garlic butter, and toasted almonds. Among the entrées: honey-sweetened duck in cilantro/jalapeño/lime sauce with macadamia nuts; char-grilled rack of lamb sliced into chops and served with spicy apple-butter barbecue sauce; and baked corn husks stuffed with thick fresh salmon filets. Sound good? You better believe it. All entrées include a big salad served with cheese toast and two vegetables—perhaps fresh asparagus and roasted red potatoes.

Lunch offers similar fare, along with fabulous soups (for example, classic French onion or creamy mushroom-hazelnut), omelets, and sandwiches. At either meal, do order a dessert such as apple-walnut pie with a brown-sugary crust, served warm and topped with cinnamon ice cream.

INEXPENSIVE

MICK'S, 557 Peachtree St., at Linden Ave. Tel. 875-6425.
  Cuisine: AMERICAN **Reservations:** Not accepted. **MARTA:** North Avenue. **Parking:** Free with validation.
$ **Prices:** Entrées $5–$8; children's menu under $3. AE, CB, DC, DISC, MC, V.
  Open: Sun–Thurs 11am–midnight, Fri–Sat 11am–1am; breakfast Sat–Sun 9am–noon.

Just next door to the Pleasant Peasant, and under the same ownership, Mick's was originally part of the same old-fashioned drugstore. Here, the interior evokes a classic American luncheonette. Nostalgic touches abound—neon clocks and signs, windows with

Venetian blinds, 1950s-style chrome lighting fixtures, and so on. Seating is in leather booths and banquettes at chrome-banded, black laminate tables or, of course, on counter stools. Just about everyone loves Mick's, including kids, who are handed their own low-priced menus designed in crayon by local schoolchildren.

Though the menu honors the Americana-luncheonette theme with items such as authentic cherry and vanilla Cokes, chili dogs, and meat loaf, most of the fare indicates a kitchen well versed in current culinary trends. Even those hot dogs are made with kosher all-beef franks. Among the specialties are calzones—for example, the empanada, which is stuffed with spicy Mexican beef, mozzarella and ricotta cheeses, and tomatoes in a crusty herb dough pocket, topped with fresh-lime-and-cilantro-flavored guacamole. Steamed broccoli and walnuts in a parmesan cream sauce over broccoli linguine is another dish I don't quite remember from childhood, but who cares. It's great. I also love Mick's hickory-grilled pork chops with fresh sage butter served with yummy homemade mashed potatoes. The best old-fashioned treats are extra-thick milk shakes and malts, banana splits, hot-fudge sundaes, cream pies, and strawberry shortcakes.

All portions are immense. And don't forget Mick's at breakfast on the weekend, when choices range from a lox-and-bagel platter to a spinach and bacon omelet with cheese grits. Fresh-squeezed orange juice, too. Other Mick's locations include Underground Atlanta (detailed above), the Lenox Square Mall (tel. 262-6425), and 2110 Peachtree Road (tel. 351-6425).

BUDGET

DELECTABLES, 1 Margaret Mitchell Sq., at the corner of Carnegie Way and Fairlie St. Tel. 681-2909.
   Cuisine: AMERICAN **Reservations:** For large parties only.
   MARTA: Peachtree Center. **Parking:** In nearby lots only, not validated.
$ Prices: Entrées $3.50–$7.25. No credit cards.
   Open: Mon–Fri 11am–2:30pm.

Down a flight of steps from the Atlanta-Fulton Public Library, Delectables is the charming domain of society caterers Cary and Nancy Smith. Though service is cafeteria-style, the setting is elegant. Pale peach walls are hung with photographs of Atlanta's original library, built in 1890; menus are propped on music stands; and tables, amid potted ficus trees, are covered in floral chintz and adorned by sprigs of flowers in bud vases. Food is served on quality china, and silver cutlery comes wrapped in thick white linen napkins. There's also a patio landscaped with terra-cotta planters of foster holly, kale, and ferns. Soft jazz or classical music plays in the background.

As for the fare, Delectables is not a misnomer. Everything here is made from fresh, first-quality ingredients. There's a scrumptious chili, with chunks of coarse-ground-beef tenderloin and beans, served with a cheddar corn muffin, grated cheese, and chopped onion. A popular item is the 12-layer salad of lettuce, cheddar, black olives, radishes, string beans, bell peppers, hard-boiled egg, and celery tossed in dilled mayonnaise. Want something heartier? Try tenderloin of beef with horseradish sauce and a salad of ziti tossed with Gouda cheese and broccoli. There are terrific sandwiches, too, like lemon tarragon chicken salad on whole wheat. Homemade desserts include a fabulous raspberry-almond tart topped with powdered sugar. Iced tea is served with fresh mint, and coffee is brewed from freshly ground beans. No alcoholic beverages are served.

THE VARSITY, 61 North Ave., at Spring St. Tel. 881-1706.
Cuisine: AMERICAN **Reservations:** Not accepted. **Parking:** Free.
$ Prices: Everything is under $2. No credit cards.
Open: Sun–Thurs 7am–12:30am, Fri–Sat 7am–2am.

Atlanta grew up around the Varsity, the world's largest drive-in restaurant, opened in 1928 by Frank Gordy and today run by his daughter Nancy. It's de rigueur to visit this fast-food mecca—its greasy feasts are an essential element of the Atlanta experience. A 150-foot stainless-steel counter is the hub of the operation, behind which red-shirted cooks and counterpeople rush out thousands of orders. It's a constant chorus of "What'll ya have?" with customer responses translated into such esoteric orders as "walk a dog sideways, bag of rags" (a hot dog with onions on the side and potato chips). It takes 200 employees to process the ton of onions, 2,500 pounds of potatoes, 2 miles of hot dogs, and 300 gallons of chili consumed here by some 16,000 hungry customers each day. Much of the help has been here for decades, and some, like carhop John Wesley Reiford, put on quite a show; he wears his own version of Carmen Miranda hats and sings the menu. The Varsity's interior is spartan, with tiered seating consisting in the main of large, windowed rooms with Formica tables. Five big color TVs are always on.

Order up a chili dog or a couple of chili burgers (they're only two ounces each), with fries, onion rings, and a frosted orange (it's a creamy frozen orange drink). Barbecued pork, homemade chicken or ham salad, and deviled-egg sandwiches are other options. And since none of this is health food (though it's all fresh and made from scratch), don't resist the fried apple or peach pie for dessert.

2. MIDTOWN

Midtown restaurants tend to be a little less flashy than those in downtown or Buckhead, perhaps because they're primarily patro-

FROMMER'S COOL FOR KIDS:
RESTAURANTS

The Varsity *(see p. 99)* The greasy feasts of the world's largest drive-in restaurant are of course big kid-pleasers.

Gorin's *(see p. 110)* This place offers the best kind of fast food—everything is homemade and fresh, prices are low, you can have quiche while the kids eat grilled cheese, and there are yummy ice-cream sundaes for dessert.

Fellini's *(see p. 124)* The New York–style pizza Fellini's serves is a treat that will please everyone. There's an outdoor patio upstairs.

Mick's *(see pp. 96, 97)* If you're looking for real sit-down meals in pleasant surroundings, the four locations of this excellent chain all serve the simple foods kids love at moderate to budget prices.

The OK Cafe *(see p. 123)* This casual, low-priced restaurant serves excellent home cooking–style food, and has a special brunch menu Saturday and Sunday.

nized by local people rather than tourists. An exception to this rule is the first listing below.

VERY EXPENSIVE

BICE RISTORANTE, 1100 Peachtree St. NE, between 12th and 13th Sts. Tel. 874-4445.
 Cuisine: "NEW AGE" ITALIAN **Reservations:** Required. **MARTA:** Midtown. **Parking:** Complimentary valet parking.
$ Prices: Appetizers $5–$8 at lunch, $6–$9 at dinner; entrées $9–$16 at lunch, $12–$22 at dinner. AE, CB, DC, MC, V.
 Open: Lunch Mon–Fri 11:30am–3pm; dinner Mon–Thurs 6–11pm, Fri–Sat 6pm–midnight, Sun 6–10:30pm.

Bice originated as a Tuscany trattoria in 1926, and over the ensuing decades expanded operations to other parts of Italy, to Paris, and, in recent years, to haute-hungry American cities like New York, Palm Beach, Beverly Hills—and now Atlanta.

Entered via an elegant bar/lounge (the perfect venue for posttheater cocktails/antipasti), the dining room is a glamorous contemporary setting. Under a 35-foot octagonal skylit dome, it has an airy, cathedral-like spaciousness—an effect enhanced by diaphanously curtained floor-to-ceiling windows and large white-linen-covered tables luxuriously spaced. Cherry-wood furnishings (complemented by cherry wainscoting) are in Milano-modern styles, whereas potted palms and a massive floral centerpiece strike a more traditional note. There's additional seating on an outdoor terrace, warmed by space heaters in winter.

Chef Paolo Luna has a light hand, so much so that waiters do not offer the pepper grinder with each course. We're not in Sicily here—this is delicate dining, involving the savoring of subtle nuances. His "new age" philosophy of Italian cuisine involves utilizing only market-fresh fare and preparing it in such a way as to optimize intrinsic flavor. "I probe each food for its treasures," says Luna. Dinner might begin with charcoal-seared Georgia foie gras in aged sherry-shallot vinaigrette, with garnishes of shaved Granny Smith apples and sweet-potato chips. Or perhaps with yellowfin-tuna carpaccio in truffle olive oil vinaigrette, topped with sliced fennel and shreds of eggplant. Do order Luna's unique signature salad comprised of four "smoked" organic lettuces in a light tomato/virgin olive oil dressing. Primi piatti include risottos and pastas, among the latter delicious spinach- and ricotta-stuffed raviolis in a mixed mushroom (portabello, shiitake, porcini) sauce. Piatti del giornio (main courses) are served on large white platters. Highly recommended in this category: seared, smoked Norwegian salmon in a buttery ginger crust, served with lightly sautéed cucumber in a slightly mustardy citrus sauce. Luna also does a noteworthy seared lamb chop, presented pinkly rare in Barolo red wine sauce with a warm bean salad (lima, black, and kidney) topped with wild mushrooms. For dessert, the Misto Plate allows diners to sample tasting portions of six confections. Go for it. An extensive wine list—mostly Italian and Californian—changes weekly with the availability of given vintages.

MODERATE

CHEF'S CAFÉ, 2115 Piedmont Rd., between Lindbergh Dr. and Cheshire Bridge Rd. Tel. 872-2284.
Cuisine: CONTEMPORARY AMERICAN **Reservations:** Recommended. **MARTA:** Lindbergh.

$ Prices: Appetizers $4.50–$7.50 at dinner, $2.95–$5.95 at brunch; entrées $10.95–$16.95 at dinner, $4.95–$10.95 at brunch. AE, CB, DC, MC, V.
Open: Sun–Thurs 6–10pm, Fri–Sat 6–11pm, Sun brunch 10am–2:30pm.

Though unpretentiously located adjacent to a La Quinta hotel, this charming café lacks nothing in the way of culinary sophistication. Chef Justin Ward creates entrées that are both innovative and tantalizing, using only the finest and freshest of ingredients. Menus change frequently to take advantage of seasonal specialties: All fish is fresh and local farmers grow specialty greens and produce to the restaurant's specifications. Bread is baked on the premises. The setting is lovely—textured peach walls are hung with

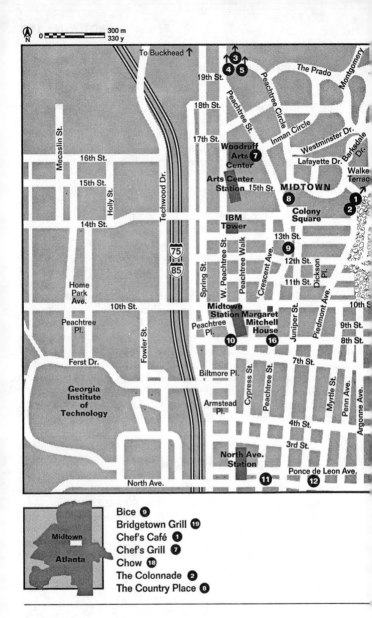

Bice **9**
Bridgetown Grill **19**
Chef's Café **1**
Chef's Grill **7**
Chow **18**
The Colonnade **2**
The Country Place **8**

whimsical oil paintings of rotund chefs pursuing crabs and other would-be food sources, soft lighting emanates from candles and faux-stone wall sconces, and flower-bedecked tables are covered in crisp white linen.

On recent visits, I've enjoyed appetizers of grilled pancetta-wrapped oysters on a bed of orange salsa cruda, and exquisitely light Gulf Coast crab cakes served with tomato butter. As for entrées, the

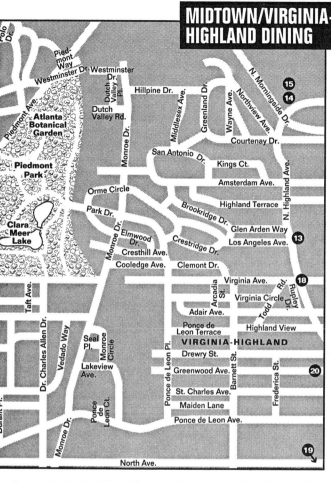

French Quarter Food Shop **16**
Gorin's **11**
Houston's **3**
Indigo Coastal Grill **14**
Mary Mac's Tearoom **12**
Murphy's **13**
Partner's Morningside Café **15**

Rocky's Brick Oven Pizzeria **5**
R. Thomas **4**
Surin of Thailand **20**
Taste of New Orleans **10**

Chef's Café makes a superb paella of scallops, shrimp, littleneck clams, saffron rice, and mushrooms, spiced with thyme. Grilled lamb loin is served with rosemary aioli chilled white bean salad, and ratatouille. And steamed salmon topped with julienned butterfly leeks, sautéed crisp vegetables, and grilled new potatoes is served with fresh tarragon-and-saffron-flavored sauce. Beautiful plate presentations further enhance your meal, as does a carefully constructed (mostly Californian) wine list, with 35 premium wines available by the glass.

Do not pass up the delectable desserts, such as a classic tarte Tatin topped with cinnamon ice cream, the lightest-and-creamiest-ever lemon cheesecake, brioche bread pudding in bourbon-caramel sauce, and rich Frangelico-flavored Belgian chocolate pâté studded with pistachios and served afloat an espresso crème anglaise. Brunch entrées range from crab cakes Benedict to smoked Irish salmon on a toasted bagel with herbed cream cheese and capers.

CHEF'S GRILL, in the lobby of the Woodruff Arts Center, 1280 Peachtree St. Tel. 881-0652.

Cuisine: CONTEMPORARY AMERICAN **Reservations:** Essential, especially for pretheater dinner. **MARTA:** Arts Center. **Parking:** Woodruff Arts Center garage on Lombardy Way between 15th and 16th streets.

$ Prices: Appetizers $3.50–$6.95 at lunch, $3.50–$7.50 at dinner; entrées $5.95–$9.95 at lunch, $12.95–$18.50 at dinner. AE, CB, DC, MC, V.

Open: Lunch Mon–Fri 11:30am–2:30pm; dinner Tues–Wed 5:30–8pm, Thurs–Sat 5:30–11pm.

Lucky theater patrons and concertgoers in Atlanta have a restaurant in Woodruff Arts Center that is unequaled in any other major city. Noted Atlanta restaurateur Mike Tuohy (he also owns Chef's Café) has created a gorgeous setting for his second venture—a restaurant offering all the heady excitement and glamour one could wish as the prelude or conclusion to an elegant evening on the town. Pale peach walls with deep teal accents are adorned with a mural in the style of Henri Rousseau, depicting creative geniuses in all spheres of art—Picasso, Duke Ellington, Chaplin, Shakespeare, Mozart, even John Lennon—lunching in an exotic garden. Soft lighting, white linen tablecloths, deft service, and taped light jazz or classical music all combine to create a most simpatico ambience. I particularly like a glassed-in café area called the Greenhouse.

Postperformance, you might want to make a light meal of an appetizer or two—perhaps fried calamari with lemon-caper mayonnaise, gravlax with Dijon-dill sour cream, or grilled Anaheim chili stuffed with goat cheese and chorizo sausage, served with green-pepper salsa. For a full meal, consider free-range grilled rosemary-lemon chicken, garnished with roasted pine nuts in garlic butter sauce; it's served with parmesan mashed potatoes and a medley of fresh vegetables.

Desserts are well worth the caloric intake—from a classic tiramisu to superb lemon meringue pie on a buttery tart crust. The wine list highlights American selections, with many by-the-glass options. Bravo to Mike Tuohy!

THE COUNTRY PLACE, 1197 Peachtree St. NE, between 14th and 15th Sts. in the Colony Square complex. Tel. 881-0144.

Cuisine: CONTEMPORARY AMERICAN **Reservations:** Accepted lunch only; dinner arrive off-peak hours to avoid lines. **MARTA:** Arts Center. **Parking:** Free validated parking in the Colony Square lot.

$ **Prices:** Appetizers $5.95–$7.95; entrées $7–$9 at lunch, $11–$16 at dinner. AE, CB, DC, MC, V.

Open: Lunch Mon–Fri 11am–3pm; dinner Sun–Wed 5:30–11pm, Thurs–Sat 5:30pm–midnight; Sunday brunch 11am–3pm.

Atlanta residents have voted the Country Place the city's most romantic restaurant. It is just lovely, with seating amid lush tropical greenery, ferns, arrangements of fresh flowers, and big pots of bright yellow chrysanthemums. Colorful flower arrangements also adorn tables covered in white linen, floors are terracotta, and walls are covered in beautiful blue-and-white Portuguese tiles. During the day, sunshine streams in through windowed walls, while at night, tables are softly lit by shaded pewter candle lamps. The perfect way to complete an evening is over cognac or dessert in the cozy canopied lounge, where a pianist plays light classical music and show tunes on a black baby grand.

Menu items are listed on a blackboard, with tantalizing details supplied by well-versed and friendly waiters. The kitchen is ever innovative and exciting, predictable only in its commitment to quality. A Country Place dinner might begin with an appetizer of spicy crab cakes (seasoned with cumin and chili powder, topped with dilled sour cream, and served with fresh salsa) or roasted chunks of elephant garlic with Montrachet cheese, roasted tomatoes, and toasted French bread. Fondly remembered entrées include a char-grilled chicken breast, marinated in extra virgin olive oil with fresh basil and topped with artichoke hearts, black olives, capers, onions, and roasted red peppers; a half duck cooked in vegetables for extra flavor, roasted crisp, and served with an orange/ginger/plum reduction sauce; and large Gulf shrimp scampi served over French bread toast saturated in garlic butter and sprinkled with fresh parsley. A beautifully presented mélange of vegetables—perhaps yellow squash, red potatoes, and broccoli—accompanies all entrées, as do deep-fried yeast rolls and salad.

Desserts are of the not-to-be-missed variety: for example, milk-chocolate/butter-pecan sour-cream cheesecake on a chocolate wafer crust, topped with whipped cream and roasted pecans. At lunch there are great salads, burgers, and homemade soups in addition to regular entrées. The wine list features many premium selections by the glass.

TASTE OF NEW ORLEANS, 889 West Peachtree St., at 8th St. Tel. 874-5535.

Cuisine: NEW AMERICAN CREOLE **Reservations:** Recommended at dinner. **MARTA:** Midtown. **Parking:** Free in adjoining lot.

$ **Prices:** Appetizers $2.95–$4.95; entrées $5.95–$6.95 at lunch, $8.95–$14.95 at dinner. AE, CB, DC, MC, V.

Open: Lunch Mon–Fri 11:30am–2pm; dinner Mon–Thurs 6–10pm, Fri–Sat 5:30–11pm.

Taste of New Orleans offers a comfortable setting for owner/chef John Beck's lighter version of creole cookery. A slightly austere gray and burgundy interior, with vertical aluminum blinds and glass-brick partitions, is warmed by soft sconce lighting and candlelight. Whimsical New Orleans–themed paintings and posters adorn pale gray walls, and an actual street lamp fronting a mural of a French Quarter brick-walled garden creates a trompe l'oeil effect.

Begin with an appetizer of delicious Long Island oysters en brochette; lightly battered, they're wrapped in bacon, deep-fried, and served on a piquant remoulade. Seafood gumbo and oyster/andouille sausage soup are also first rate here. Delicate, fluffy crawfish cakes (available as an appetizer or entrée) are seasoned with garlic, hot sauce, fresh basil, and romano cheese and served with jalapeño tartar sauce on tomato buerre blanc. When crawfish are out of season, Beck offers crab/shrimp seafood cakes. The same applies to his superb seafood etouffée. Blackened grouper (crispy here, not charred) is dusted with creole spices and lightly brushed with Dijon mustard, topped with hollandaise and toasted almonds, and served with a boiled red potato and a medley of fresh vegetables. And though fresh seafood is featured, you can also opt for tender Long Island duck, deboned, roasted, and glazed with a semisweet Grand Marnier orange sauce on a bed of pecan rice. The restaurant's velvet pies and classic bread pudding are renowned, but I like to check the dessert specials, which often include lighter options. The wine list is reasonably priced, with many by-the-glass offerings. Luncheon fare includes chicken andouille po-boys and Cajun meat pies.

INEXPENSIVE

THE COLONNADE, 1879 Cheshire Bridge Rd. NE, between Wellborne Dr. and Manchester St. Tel. 874-5642.

Cuisine: SOUTHERN **Reservations:** Not accepted. **Parking:** Free.

$ Prices: Entrées $6–$9 at lunch, $8–$14 at dinner. No credit cards.

Open: Lunch Mon–Sat 11am–2:30pm; dinner Mon–Sat 5–9pm, Sun 11am–8:30pm. **Closed:** Dec 24–25.

This Atlanta institution, established in 1927, offers some of the most authentic and savory southern specialties in town. It has an enormous local clientele of devoted regulars—many of whom look like they might enjoy a birthday greeting from Willard Scott any day—and some of the waiters have worked here for decades. Though comfortable, the Colonnade is totally unpretentious, a vast room with English prints on charcoal-slate walls and seating at butcher-block tables. A cozy bar with a working fireplace adjoins, a nice place to sit if you have to wait for a table.

At lunch or dinner, you might order fresh-from-the-oven turkey with dressing (they roast about a dozen a day), sugar-cured ham in redeye gravy, country-fried steak, or roast leg of lamb, all of which are served with a choice of two vegetables—you may choose from among homemade whipped potatoes, black-eyed peas, macaroni and cheese, sweet-potato soufflé, lima beans, greens, fried okra, and others. Homemade cornbread and yeast rolls accompany all entrées. In addition to menu listings, there are fancy specials ranging from Cornish game hens to frog legs and low-priced blue-plate specials. Everything is fresh and made from scratch, including desserts like the yellow cake topped with ice cream and drenched in semisweet hot fudge. Portions are very large.

FRENCH QUARTER FOOD SHOP, 923 Peachtree St. NE, just north of 8th St. Tel. 875-2489.

Cuisine: CAJUN **Reservations:** Not accepted. **MARTA:** Midtown. **Parking:** Free. Near Comedy Act Theater at lunch; between Franklin Printing and Stein Club, just north of the restaurant, at dinner.

$ Prices: Po-boy sandwiches $4.95–$5.95; entrées $4.95–$8.95 at lunch, $4.95–$12.95 at dinner. AE, MC, V.

Open: Lunch Mon–Fri 11am–2pm, Sat 11:30am–2:30pm; dinner Tues–Sat 6–10pm.

This little eatery is so 100% authentic that I rank it among Atlanta's best restaurants. Cajun owners Tony and Missy Privat (they met in a Louisiana cooking school) grew up on this cuisine and know its every nuance. Their restaurant is small and unpretentious (almost a joint), with black and white checkerboard tile floors and gray walls hung with French Quarter–themed art and Mardi Gras beads. An on-premises shop sells Louisiana products. In good weather, there are a handful of patio tables out front. The clientele ranges from folks in jeans to well-dressed Buckhead matrons and conservatively suited businessmen. Arrive early to avoid a wait for seating.

Everything here is just scrumptious. Gumbo is dark, rich, and spicy, thickened with roux and replete with savory chunks of andouille sausage. Velvety oyster-andouille bisque is another superb soup. Traditional red beans and rice are slow-simmered in andouille and hamhock stock, and two other Cajun signature dishes—crawfish etouffée and jambalaya—reach their culinary apogee here. Lightly battered fried oysters, plump and juicy, with a choice of two remoulade sauces, one hot, one cold (ask for both), are in the not-to-be-missed category. Oyster po-boys are also great, as is the muffaletta—a grilled sandwich on sesame boule stuffed with ham, Genoa salami, provolone, Swiss cheese, and a relish of coarsely chopped black and green olives, marinated mushrooms, and artichoke hearts. And one of the best things I ever tasted was a special here of fried soft-shell crab stuffed with bechamel-sauced crawfish in a roasted garlic cream sauce. For dessert, there's excellent crème caramel, but the pièce de résistance is nutmeg/cinnamon-flavored bread pudding. Studded with crushed pineapple, pecans, and raisins, it's smothered in fresh whipped cream and buttery bourbon sauce. The French Quarter doesn't have a liquor license; bring your own beer or wine.

HOUSTON'S, 2166 Peachtree Rd., at Colonial Homes Dr. in the Brookwood Square Shopping Center. Tel. 351-2442.

Cuisine: AMERICAN **Reservations:** Not accepted; arrive off-peak hours. **Parking:** Free.

$ Prices: Appetizers $4–$5, burgers and salads $6–$7, entrées $7–$15. AE, CB, DC, MC, V.

Open: Sun–Thurs 11am–11pm, Fri–Sat 11am–midnight.

Part of an Atlanta-based chain with restaurants throughout the country, Houston's has created an immensely popular dining format. It's a simple approach: They serve lavish portions of fresh, first-quality fare in very simpatico surroundings. The spacious dining room has a rustic ambience, with exposed brick walls and a crisscross of rough-hewn rafters under a skylight ceiling. Seating is in roomy burgundy leather booths at bare oak tables, with cozy lighting emanating from shaded table lamps. If you're in a rush, there's counter seating; and weather permitting, you can dine on the patio at tables with red umbrellas.

Thick, hickory-grilled burgers, made from choice chuck meat, are served with skillet beans, fries, or coleslaw. The same fixings come with barbecued chicken or tender, meaty ribs. But my favorite entrée is the salad of sliced grilled chicken (big chunks), tossed with chopped greens and julienned tortilla strips in a honey-lime vinaigrette, garnished with a light peanut sauce. Marvelous too are appetizers such as creamed spinach and artichoke hearts in parmesan cream sauce. Beverages range from premium wines by the glass to mixed drinks made with premium liquors, fresh-squeezed juices, and natural spring water—not to mention old-fashioned, extra-thick milk shakes. For dessert you can indulge in a huge, chewy brownie topped with vanilla ice cream and Kahlúa. A second location is in Buckhead at 3321 Lenox Rd. (tel. 237-7534).

MARY MAC'S TEAROOM, 224 Ponce de Leon Ave. NE, at Myrtle St. Tel. 876-6604.

Cuisine: SOUTHERN **Reservations:** Not accepted. **MARTA:** North Avenue. **Parking:** Easy on nearby streets.

$ Prices: Entrées $5–$6.25 at lunch, $6–$10 at dinner; junior plates (you can order them if you're 9 or 90) $3. No credit cards.

Open: Lunch Mon–Fri 11am–4pm, dinner Mon–Fri 5–8pm.

In business for many decades, Mary Mac's is a quaint and colorful Atlanta institution, a bastion of classic southern cuisine that is patronized by everyone from truck drivers to bank presidents. Jimmy Carter often came by for lunch when he was governor, and the state legislature can almost be said to meet here. Cream-colored walls in the four dining rooms are covered with photos of famous clients, along with murals of the Carter Center and the city skyline. The ambience is unpretentious; you dine off plastic dishes at Formica-topped tables set with terry-cloth napkins. You'll find a glass of pencils on your table; check off menu items (they change daily) and hand your selections to one of the waiters. Owner Margaret Lupo, her daughter Genie, and son Andy are always on hand welcoming diners and overseeing the kitchen.

Among the famous entrées are fried chicken dredged in buttermilk and flour, fried rainbow trout from the North Georgia mountains, and chicken pan pie topped with thick giblet gravy. All entrées come with a choice of side dishes. You might select corn bread with pot likker (a scrumptious broth made with chicken drippings and turnip greens), black-eyed peas, whipped potatoes, steamed okra, macaroni and cheese, or sweet-potato soufflé. Fresh-from-the-oven corn and bran muffins and yeast rolls are served with all meals. Desserts include fresh-baked pineapple pecan cake. There's a full bar.

R. THOMAS, 1812 Peachtree St. NW, between Collier Rd. and 26th St. Tel. 872-2942 or 885-9249.

Cuisine: AMERICAN **Reservations:** Not accepted.

$ Prices: $5–$9 for entrées, sandwiches, salads, omelets, and burgers. AE, MC, V.

Open: Daily 24 hours.

Owner Richard Thomas is king of late-night Atlanta, his 24-hour eatery a mecca for postdisco/posttheater crowds and actors unwinding after performances. Tom Cruise, Morgan Fairchild, Paul Newman, Joel Grey, and Raquel Welch have all dined here after hours. They come, like everyone else, to relax on the beautiful patio, lushly planted (Thomas is an avid gardener) and festively lit by candles and paper lanterns with multicolored lights. Open year round, the patio is especially cozy in winter when warmed by 12 heaters. Don't get the idea this is a fancy place, however. It's super-casual, and the interior is on the funky/rustic side, with a gold cupid overhead and tinsel hanging from the rafters. Comfort is the keynote, enhanced by good music—light jazz or rock—and friendly waiters.

Everything is made from scratch, and there's a slight California health-food overtone to the menu. You can even order an avocado-and-sprouts sandwich on nine-grain bread. All sandwiches are served with fries, baked potato, or acorn squash. Other choices—also served on nine-grain bread—include juicy 8-ounce burgers and citrus-marinated grilled chicken. Come by for breakfast at any time—perhaps eggs Benedict served with freshly made home fries or a quesadilla stuffed with eggs, cheese, and bacon and served with mango salsa. There are pasta dishes (for example, lemon and herb cream linguine), terrific salads, and baked potatoes stuffed with fillings such as portabello mushrooms, roasted peppers, and cheddar. For dessert, order up the delicious cinnamon-flavored apple pie in

Jack Daniel's whiskey sauce or a slab of homemade white chocolate cake. There's a full bar.

ROCKY'S BRICK OVEN PIZZERIA, 1770 Peachtree St. NE, at 26th St. Tel. 876-1111.

Cuisine: ITALIAN/PIZZA **Reservations:** Not accepted. **Parking:** Free.

$ Prices: $7.95 for an individual pizza; $14.95 for a pie serving two to three people; $17.95 for a pie serving four; $9.50 for pasta dishes; $6.95 for lunch specials. AE, MC, V.

Open: Sat–Mon 4pm–midnight, Tues–Thurs 11am–10:30pm, Fri 11am–midnight.

When I want pizza I want to be in Atlanta—at Rocky's— where irrepressible ex-Brooklynite Bob Russo (his father was Rocky) creates the best pies I've ever had. He makes his own mozzarella fresh every day, grows his own herbs and tomatoes, uses garlic lavishly, and bakes the pies in a hickory- and oakwood-burning oven from Milan, but none of that explains the culinary magic here. Let's just say, when it comes to pizza, Bob is Escoffier.

Rocky's is comfortable and candlelit, with seating in black tufted-leather booths at red-and-white checker-clothed tables. Archways are hung with cheeses, sausages, and strings of garlic. Opera and classical music enhance the atmosphere; it's not unusual for local opera singers to stand up and belt out arias. In fact, Rocky's attracts a lot of media people and celebrities, including Bob's pal Vincent Gardenia, who guest-chefs when in town. In addition to its cozy interior, the restaurant has a rustic open-air patio with umbrella tables that is heated in winter by a fireplace.

Bob specializes in pizzas from various provinces of Italy. My favorites are the chicken bianca oreganato (topped with sautéed chicken breast, virgin olive oil, fresh oregano, white wine, garlic, lemon juice, red onions, mozzarella, and rosemary) and the Rudolph Valentino, made with sweet-onion sauce and rosemary-seasoned roasted new potatoes. The perfect accompaniment is homemade zinfandel (Bob's grandfather's recipe) served with a slice of fresh peach. Rocky's baked pasta balsamico is another unforgettable dish—pasta baked with five cheeses and Pastore Italian sausage in a white-wine sauce flavored with chicken broth and balsamic vinegar. And the tricolor tortoloni Gorby (honoring Gorbachev), in a tomato-Stolichnaya cream sauce, is divine. Terrific salads here, too. Lunch-time options include calzones and sandwiches.

BUDGET

GORIN'S, 620 Peachtree St., between Ponce de Leon and North Aves. Tel. 874-0550.

Cuisine: AMERICAN/ICE CREAM **Reservations:** Not accepted. **MARTA:** North Avenue. **Parking:** Difficult on street; a parking lot is nearby.

$ Prices: Everything under $5. No credit cards.

Open: Mon–Fri 9:30am–6pm, Sat–Sun 10am–6pm.

Gorin's homemade ice cream is Atlanta's answer to Häagen-Dazs. And Gorin's locations, which also serve food in an ice-cream-parlor setting, are a great choice for casual meals with the kids. Not only is the ice cream homemade, sandwich meats and salads are also freshly prepared on the premises. Menu selections include a classic Reuben sandwich with Thousand Island dressing, ham and cheese with honey mustard on grilled egg bread, an almond chicken salad platter served with potato salad, and homemade soups. For dessert there are oven-fresh cakes and, of course, ice cream, over 200 flavors— everything from amaretto almond to peach cobbler. Light ice creams, frozen yogurts, sherbets, and sorbets are also served, as, of course, are milk shakes, malts, ice-cream sodas, and sundaes. In nice weather you can indulge at umbrella tables on the front patio.

A few blocks from this location is **Gorin's Diner,** at 1170 Peachtree St. (tel. 892-2500). Similar fare is served here in a re-creation of a classic American diner, complete with stainless-steel facade, gleaming neon, and checkerboard-tile floors. Check your phone book for other locations.

3. BUCKHEAD

Buckhead contains the majority of Atlanta's posh dining venues.

VERY EXPENSIVE

BONE'S, 3130 Piedmont Rd. NE, a half-block below Peachtree Rd. Tel. 237-2663.
   Cuisine: STEAK AND SEAFOOD **Reservations:** Essential.
   Parking: Complimentary valet parking.
$ Prices: Appetizers $8.95–$9.95; entrées $10.95–$23.95 at lunch, $19.95–$26.95 at dinner. AE, CB, DC, MC, V.
   Open: Lunch Mon–Fri 11:30am–2:30pm; dinner Sun–Thurs 6–11pm, Fri–Sat 6pm–midnight. **Closed:** Most major holidays.

Atlanta's most famous steak house, Bone's receives great reviews not only at home ("best steaks," raves *Atlanta* magazine) but in countless national publications, including the *New York Times, Esquire,* and *GQ.* It's a top power-lunch venue for the expense-account crowd (as many deals as steaks are cut here), which is provided with notepads and phones at the midday meal. And celebrity stories abound. When Bob Hope dined here, everyone respected his privacy until he rose to leave; then the entire dining room stood up and gave him a standing ovation. George Bush came in for dinner one night, booking six surrounding tables for Secret Service men (they ate, too). Ted Turner conducted his *Fortune* magazine cover-story interview here over lobster. And Chuck Mangione once gave an impromptu concert in the lounge.

The setting is traditional masculine-clubby, with bentwood chairs at tables covered in crisp white-linen, wide-plank oak floors, and globe-light fans overhead. Patinated wainscoted walls are covered with vintage museum-quality photographs depicting the history of Atlanta (do take a tour after you dine; it's a fascinating display), and caricatures of local personalities. Sports events are aired on the TV in the comfortable lounge.

As noted for its seafood as for its steaks and chops, Bone's flies Maine lobster in daily and serves fresh Gulf Coast crabmeat and shrimp. As for the steak, it's prime aged, corn-fed Iowa beef, butchered on the premises. A good beginning here is a salad of crabmeat, romaine and iceberg lettuce, chunks of avocado, mushrooms, and hearts of palm in a classic vinaigrette. Thick, juicy lamb chops (two 9-ounce chops, served with mint jelly) and tender char-grilled steak and prime-rib entrées are prepared to your exact specification and served in more-than-ample portions. Lobster is a specialty; request a steak-lobster combo if you so desire. Other seafood dishes range from grilled swordfish with roasted pepper butter sauce to grilled tuna with mint vinaigrette. Of the side dishes, I like the sea-breeze baked potato, brushed with egg and rolled in kosher salt to seal in moistness. Sautéed snow peas and fried onion rings are also great.

The wine gallery at Bone's houses over 500 selections; international in scope, it highlights California wines. There are rich desserts like mountain-high pie—layers of chocolate chocolate chip, rum raisin, and vanilla ice cream on a crème-de-menthe-soaked brownie, topped with chocolate sauce, whipped cream, and meringue. And finally, at this unabashedly macho enclave, a cigar humidor is brought to your table on request after dinner.

CHOPS, 70 W. Paces Ferry Rd., at Peachtree Rd. Tel. 262-2675.

Cuisine: STEAK AND SEAFOOD **Reservations:** Essential.
Parking: Complimentary valet parking at W. Paces Ferry entrance.
$ Prices: Appetizers $3.50–$7.95 at lunch, $3.75–$8.50 at dinner; entrées $8.50–$13.95 at lunch, $14.75–$28.50 at dinner. AE, CB, DC, DISC, MC, V.
Open: Lunch Mon–Fri 11:30am–2:30pm; dinner Mon–Thurs 5:30–11pm, Fri–Sat 5:30pm–midnight, Sun 5:30–10pm.

This very popular Atlanta steak house is an extremely elegant version of its clubby genre. Soft lighting emanates from art deco alabaster chandeliers. A coffered ceiling and columns are handsomely paneled in California redwood, as is the retro-look marble-topped bar. Trilevel seating is in comfortable upholstered redwood armchairs or roomy black leather semicircular banquettes at crisply white-linened tables. And moss green carpeting beautifully complements the redwood paneling and furnishings. USDA prime Chicago beef is aged in a glassed-in case, with additional cuts of meat displayed on a marble sideboard. And white-hatted chefs can be seen busily broiling, steaming, and sautéeing clams, oysters, and lobsters in an exhibition kitchen. Seafood is a real option here, not an afterthought as in most steak houses. Chops serves only the freshest fish and seafood, expertly and innovatively prepared.

A good beginning here, in fact, is seafood, perhaps Maryland soft-shell crab, lightly battered in seasoned flour and quick-fried crisp, served with lemon-mustard and red-pepper coulis. A recommended seafood entrée is boneless whole rainbow trout with diced lemon croutons, capers, and mushrooms. Meat entrées will require a hearty appetite (or doggy bags), for example, a 22-ounce portion of triple cut lamb loin chops, a 24-ounce porterhouse steak, or a hearty serving of roast prime rib of beef au jus in creamy horseradish sauce. All the meats are fork tender, juicy, and delicious, prepared exactly as ordered. Traditional à la carte side dishes like creamed spinach, jumbo asparagus hollandaise, cottage fries, or a skillet of steak mushrooms are a must. A large selection of wines is, of course, available, and if you have room for dessert the chocolate chip butterscotch pie is noteworthy. At lunch, delicious sandwiches are options.

THE DINING ROOM, at the Ritz-Carlton Buckhead, 3434 Peachtree Rd. NE, at Phipps Dr. Tel. 237-2700.
Cuisine: EUROPEAN HAUTE CUISINE **Reservations:** Essential, and as far in advance as possible. **MARTA:** Lenox. **Parking:** Complimentary valet parking.
$ Prices: Prix-fixe dinners only: $44 for three courses, including dessert; $56 for four; $78 for four with wines. AE, CB, DC, MC, V. **Open:** Mon–Sat 6:30–11pm.

Atlanta's most highly acclaimed restaurant, the Dining Room, is the domain of brilliantly talented Michelin-star chef Guenter Seeger. His traditional European haute-cuisine creations with American regional overtones are magical, drawing the maximum of flavor from the very freshest of ingredients. A network of Georgia farmers grow organic produce to his meticulous specifications; a San Antonio ranch does the same with venison; and fresh fish and seafood are flown in daily from Maine, Florida, and Louisiana waters.

Seeger's refined cuisine is a gem in a worthy setting. The Dining Room's mahogany-paneled walls are hung with a museum-quality collection of gilt-framed British hunt paintings. Diners sink into comfortable silk-upholstered armchairs and banquettes at elegantly appointed tables adorned with stunning arrangements of Hawaiian flowers—tropically hued orchids, birds of paradise, and anthurium. Shaded table lamps provide soft lighting, and background music is classical. Service is impeccable ("The waiters, the wine steward, all move in a well-orchestrated dance," raved one reviewer), but never haughty.

A four-course dinner here is as harmonious as a string-quartet concerto, each course complemented by appropriate wines and liqueurs. Menus change daily. On a recent visit, such a meal began with delicately cubed tuna ceviche with cilantro and osetra caviar garnish in extra-virgin olive oil. It was followed by grapefruit-garnished Gulf red snapper in a croustade of thinly sliced potatoes with citrus vinaigrette. Next came a crispy fan of rosemary-garnished duck breast with date purée in caramelized sherry-vinaigrette sauce. And dessert was a heavenly fig tart topped with vanilla ice cream and garnished with fresh mint and raspberries. Everything is sensational, and presentations, on white German Hutschenreuther china platters, are works of art. A very comprehensive list of over 350 wines is dominated by French and California selections, but also offers many German and Italian vintages.

THE HEDGEROSE HEIGHTS INN, 490 E. Paces Ferry Rd., at Maple Dr. Tel. 233-7673.

Cuisine: CLASSIC EUROPEAN **Reservations:** Essential. **Parking:** Free.

$ Prices: Appetizers $6.50–$8.75, entrées $17.25–$23.50. AE, CB, DC, MC, V.

Open: Tues–Sat 6:30–10pm, with two staggered seatings at 6:30, 7, and 7:30pm and 9, 9:30, and 10pm.

For over a decade a shining star in the galaxy of Atlanta's formal dining rooms, Hedgerose Heights is as charming as it is celebrated. Lilting classical music heralds your entrance to the gemlike little bar, where a hostess provides a warm welcome and escorts you to your table. Occupying a former Buckhead town house, the inn is living room–cozy, with pristine white wainscoting and intricately carved moldings framing peach and forest-green walls. Graceful arched niches contain exquisite flower arrangements, an ornate fireplace is filled with lush greenery, and the garden motif is further enhanced by botanical prints and ruffled floral chintz draperies. Crystal chandeliers glitter overhead, and seating is in comfortable armchairs at elegantly appointed white-linen-covered tables lit by shaded lamps.

Owner-chef Heinz Schwab, the son and grandson of chefs, trained in the classic European tradition, apprenticing from age 16 in the resort restaurants of his native Switzerland. His cooking garners only superlatives from food critics ("virtually flawless" raved New York's Mimi Sheraton). There are several wonderful appetizers. Delicate mousse of goose and duck liver is studded with grapes and green peppercorns, garnished with cornichons and cocktail onions, and served with crisp toast. Crabmeat-stuffed raviolis (plain and spinach) are glossed with noisette butter. And one of Schwab's unique creations is a tasty poached leek terrine served chilled with truffle vinaigrette. For your main course, there's lightly sautéed red snapper, Provence style, with red and yellow peppers, plump sundried tomatoes (made here, the best I've ever had), mushrooms, artichokes, and black olives. Game specials are superb. An entrée of medallions of venison with field mushrooms, sautéed spaetzle, lingonberries, chestnut purée, burgundy-poached pear, and white

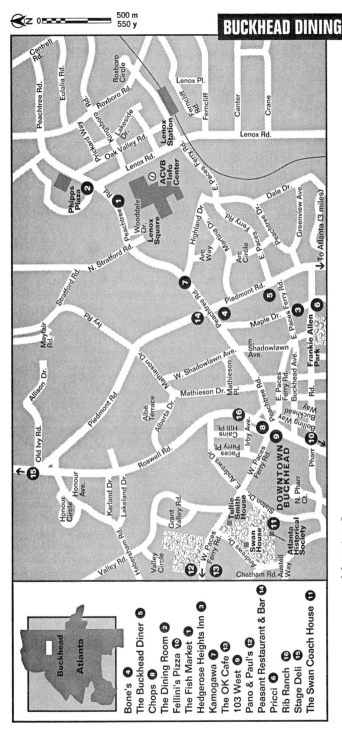

BUCKHEAD DINING

Information ⓘ

Bone's ❹
The Buckhead Diner ❺
Chops ❽
The Dining Room ❿
Fellini's Pizza ❷
The Fish Market ❶
Hedgerose Heights Inn ❸
Kamogawa ❼
The OK Cafe ❾
103 West ❾
Pano & Paul's ⓬
Peasant Restaurant & Bar ⓮
Pricci ❻
Rib Ranch ⓰
Stage Deli ⓯
The Swan Coach House ⑪

wine–poached apple seemed to combine the world's most ambrosial foods on a single plate. Also very memorable here: sautéed breast of pheasant with porcini mushroom sauce; roast duck, lushly prepared with apple, foie gras, and calvados sauce and served with lacy-crisp potato pancakes; and roast rack of lamb accompanied by fresh pasta. A very extensive wine list (over 300 selections) offers choices in several price ranges. For dessert, I never pass up the soufflé (flavors change nightly), which is all that a soufflé could ever aspire to. But there are sumptuous others such as a thin bittersweet chocolate cup filled with soft frozen cappuccino cream and Irish whiskey/hazelnut cream sauce dusted with powdered sugar. You can, by the way, come in for just dessert and cappuccino in the bar.

KAMOGAWA, in the Hotel Nikko, 3300 Peachtree Rd., just east of Piedmont Rd. Tel. 841-0314.
  Cuisine: JAPANESE **Reservations:** Highly recommended, especially for tatami rooms. **MARTA:** Lenox. **Parking:** Complimentary valet parking.
$ Prices: Appetizers $3.50–$6.50 at lunch, $6.50–$9.75 at dinner; entrées $7.75–$19.75 at lunch, $16.75–$24.50 at dinner; prix-fixe complete lunch $12.50, dinner $25–$35; kaiseki dinner $50, $70, or $100. AE, CB, DC, JCB, MC, V.
  Open: Lunch daily 11:30am–2pm, dinner nightly 6–10pm.

Built by temple craftsmen from Kyoto, Kamogawa has an understated decor authentically reflective of traditional Japanese interior design. Its clean lines derive from simple materials—rice paper, bamboo, pale cedar paneling, and granite pathways. And in lush contrast, large windows overlook a classic Japanese garden—a serene backdrop of waterfalls, carefully placed rocks and plants, and a "teahouse" structure meant for meditation. It's the perfect setting for a cuisine more subtle and refined than you're likely to have experienced at other Japanese restaurants in this country. If you have four or more in your party, I suggest reserving a tatami room for which you'll remove your shoes at the door and dine in luxurious privacy seated on floor cushions. It's less confining than a table and there's a pit for your legs, so you don't have to sit cross-legged. Flawless service is provided by graceful kimonoed waitresses. Other possibilities are regular table seating, a sushi bar, and teppanyaki grill tables.

Whichever dining venue you select, you'll experience exquisite nuances of food preparation and presentation. Every aesthetic element is considered. An appetizer of grilled salmon with shiitake mushrooms, for instance, comes wrapped in an artistically knotted leaf secured by a bamboo skewer; it's served on a lovely ceramic fan with a cherry blossom. And dobinmushi—an exotically herbed consommé infused with shrimp, chicken, oyster mushrooms, and gingko nuts—is served in a delicate ceramic spouted pot from which the soup is poured into a beautiful little dish and sipped. The visual and tactile elements of the pottery subtly heighten gustatory sensations. All entrées are served with chawanmushi (egg custard steamed with chicken, seafood, and herbs), steamed or herb rice, and marinated Japanese pickles. One of my favorites is filets of yellowtail tuna basted with teriyaki sauce and grilled to a crisp, aromatic flavor enhanced by ginger and shredded burdock root. A unique delicacy is nasu dengaku—a deep-fried eggplant dish; the cooked pulp is scooped out, mashed with sweet rice wine and a soupçon of miso sauce, stuffed into the shell, and served caramelized with ginger and shrimp garnishes. And a sushi course is *de rigueur*. Especially marvelous is the "dynamite" roll filled with avocado, yellowtail tuna, seaweed, scallion, and finely minced cucumber flavored with miso/mayonnaise/five-pepper sauce. Plum wines and sake are essential accompaniments to this sublime fare, though your server can also recommend appropriate French and California wines. Dessert is fresh fruit and green-tea ice cream. A specialty here is the prix-fixe kaiseki dinner, an esoteric ceremonial meal with multiple courses selected by the chef. I heartily recommend it to adventurous diners.

103 WEST, 103 W. Paces Ferry Rd., off Peachtree Rd. Tel. 233-5993.

Cuisine: FRENCH-INFLUENCED NEW AMERICAN **Reservations:** Highly recommended. **Parking:** Complimentary valet parking.

$ Prices: Appetizers $6.50–$8.50, entrées $14.95–$26.75. AE, CB, DC, DISC, MC, V.

Open: Mon–Sat 6–11pm.

Unrestrained Victorian opulence is the keynote of 103 West, from its porte-cochere entranceway lit by 19th-century coach lights to its posh interior with rose silk moiré wall coverings, Venetian sky-painted domes, Aubusson tapestries, and fleur-de-lis-patterned Axminster carpeting. Walls are hung with gilt-framed mirrors and oil paintings. Plants in ornately carved urns grace faux-marble columns, and arched windows are framed by heavy silk draperies. A pianist entertains during dinner.

This theatrical setting provides the perfect stage for chef Gerard Vullien's stellar performances. Under his auspices, 103 West has garnered dozens of awards for its excellent food, exquisite presentations, and extensive wine list (over 600 wines, 54 of them available by the glass).

Begin your meal with an appetizer of thick, scallion-studded crab cakes topped with a nest of sautéed shredded leeks, the cakes afloat on a basil-flavored beurre blanc sauce ringed with red-pepper rouille. Also superb are shrimp- and lobster-filled ravioli in lobster bisque garnished with cilantro and sour cream. Entrées—all accompanied by a beautiful bouquetière of vegetables—include roasted duck breast with peppered red wine sauce and a gratin of turnips and plums; Dover sole rolled with lemony garlic butter, dredged in brioche crumbs, and quickly deep-fried; and pinkly juicy roast rack of lamb seasoned with rosemary. The dessert menu offers many temptations—a luscious crème brûlée, hot soufflé Grand Marnier served with cold vanilla sauce, double-rich chocolate apricot cake with homemade ice cream, and baby chocolate truffles in a cookie basket, among others—but most tempting is the sampler of six desserts.

PANO & PAUL'S, 1232 W. Paces Ferry Rd. Tel. 261-3662.
    Cuisine: FRENCH-INFLUENCED AMERICAN **Reservations:** Essential. **Parking:** Free.

$ Prices: Appetizers $4.95–$8.75, entrées $14.50–$26.75. AE, CB, DC, DISC, MC, V.

    Open: Mon–Sat 6–11pm.

When Pano and Paul opened their deluxe dining emporium in 1979, they brought big-city sophistication to Atlanta's restaurant scene. For over a decade, they've continued to dazzle the dining public with dependable but ever-exciting French-influenced American cuisine, garnering countless awards, from Mobil's four stars to the International Wine Festival's Gold Medal for Best Restaurant Wine List. Well-heeled Atlanta business and society people consider the place a kind of posh private club.

And very posh it is, with intimate canopied booths framed by forest-green velvet curtains; delicate vases of fresh-cut flowers on rose damask-clothed tables lit by pink silk-shaded lamps; floral-patterned wall fabrics hung with ornate gilt-framed mirrors; and antique chandeliers and wall sconces. Tuxedoed waiters provide deft service, and a pianist entertains nightly in the opulent adjoining piano bar; consider adjourning to one of its plush burgundy velvet sofas for dessert or after-dinner drinks.

The kitchen, under executive chef Paul's expert direction, never rests on its laurels but stays apace—and ahead—of current culinary trends. Dinner here might begin with sautéed foie gras with apples and chives in a passion-fruit vinagrette, creamy cognac-laced lobster bisque with carrots and celery, or fresh beluga caviar mollasol, served with small whole-wheat pancakes and crème fraîche. In season, be sure to order an entrée of soft-shell crabs, lightly battered and sautéed crisp, a succulent treat served with potato soufflé, white lemon butter, and red-pepper coulis. Also highly recommendable is the grilled filet of lightly smoked salmon with Pommery honey cream on a bed of sesame spinach. Pano buys only whole fresh fish—never filets—and he has the best sources. Yet another entrée suggestion: sautéed duck breasts accompanied by wild rice in orange-ginger sauce tossed with fresh fruits and walnuts. The wine list is distinguished and the desserts are lush—from a classic crème brûlée to Kahlúa-flavored ice-cream pie with Oreo crust, topped with bourbon-flavored whipped cream, roasted pecans, and chocolate sauce.

EXPENSIVE

THE FISH MARKET, 3393 Peachtree Rd. NE, in the Lenox Square Mall. Tel. 262-3165.
    Cuisine: SEAFOOD **Reservations:** Highly recommended.
    MARTA: Lenox. **Parking:** Complimentary valet parking.

$ Prices: Appetizers $4.50–$7.50 at lunch, $5.50–$7.50 at dinner; entrées $6.95–$10.75 at lunch, $13.75–$21.50 at dinner. AE, CB, DC, DISC, MC, V.
Open: Lunch Mon–Sat 11:30am–2:30pm; dinner Mon–Sat 6–11pm.

A haven for weary shoppers because of its upscale mall location, the opulent Fish Market is also a power-lunch locale for Buckhead business execs and a romantic nighttime rendezvous. Owners Pano Karatassos and Paul Albrecht (see Pano & Paul's, above) have created an irreproachable gourmet continental/seafood establishment here, for which Pano personally selects fresh whole fish each morning from carefully chosen suppliers. In addition, the best international sources are tapped: Dover sole is flown in from Belgium, salmon from Galway, Ireland, orange roughy from New Zealand, lobsters from Boston, oysters from Maine. And the chef scours local farmer's markets for the finest fresh produce daily. The Fish Market's reputation is such that leading French chefs like Jacques Pepin and Roger Vergé have chosen to dine here when visiting Atlanta.

The setting is turn-of-the-century ornate, with faux-marble walls, domed skylights, an arbor of grape ivy overhead, lace-curtained windows, and seating in plush moss-green chairs. Shaded sconces and crystal chandeliers cast a rosy glow, enhanced at night by candles in pink, tulip-shaped holders. Sprays of fresh-cut flowers adorn each pink-clothed table.

In season, you can't do better than an appetizer of baby Maryland soft-shell crabs sautéed almondine in brown butter. And in-the-know diners always ask for the VIP salad of Bibb lettuce, hearts of palm, fresh mushrooms, artichoke hearts, and feta cheese in a tangy raspberry vinaigrette with a tiny jolt of jalapeño. Among entrées, a hearty bouillabaisse comes with chunks of Maine lobster, grouper, mussels, shrimps, and vegetables in an aromatic broth flavored with tomato, saffron, and Pernod. Louisiana oysters are also delicious, dredged in seasoned flour, crisp-fried, and served with honey-mustard sauce and matchstick potatoes. And blackened fish is done beautifully, served on a bed of spinach with chili hollandaise. All entrées come with a medley of crisp, al dente vegetables—an exquisite presentation that might include waffle-cut carrots, steamed red potatoes, snow peas, and haricots verts. The wine list, which has received dozens of awards, offers many moderately priced selections and wines by the glass. And for dessert, there's ultrarich chocolate pecan pie (like a fudge brownie on a higher plane) served with gobs of whipped cream.

PRICCI, 500 Pharr Rd., at Maple Dr. Tel. 237-2941.
Cuisine: ITALIAN REGIONAL **Reservations:** Recommended.
Parking: Valet parking is complimentary.
$ Prices: Appetizers $4.50–$6.50 at lunch, $4.50–$7.95 at dinner; pizzas $6.50–$8.50 at lunch or dinner; entrées $7.95–$12.50 at lunch, $10.50–$19.75 at dinner. AE, CB, DC, DISC, MC, V.

Open: Sun–Thurs 11am–11pm, Fri–Sat 11am–midnight.

One of Atlanta's hottest see-and-be-seen restaurants, Pricci is strikingly glamorous. Part of the drama ensues from an exhibition kitchen where a team of white-hatted chefs are engaged in culinary frenzy and a rosy glow emanates from the oak-fired pizza oven. A theatrical interior utilizes curved vaulted ceilings, gorgeous terrazzo marble floors, art deco–look chrome and brass dividers, rich decorative woods such as African turtle shell sapelle and East India rosewood, and stunning, whimsical hand-blown lighting fixtures. Crisply white-linen-covered tables, potted palms, and lavish floral arrangements add traditional panache. Sharing the premises is the Buckhead Bread Company, a state-of-the-art bakery that produces hearth-baked loaves of unbelievable goodness (you'll taste them during dinner, and you can buy them on the way out).

Pricci's fare is the hearty cuisine of Italy's Tuscan, Ligurian, and Milanese regions. Your meal might begin with a crisp mozzarella-filled pesto risotto on fresh tomatoes or, perhaps, beef tenderloin carpaccio drizzled with creamy mustard and served with shaved parmesan. My preference, though, is to begin with one of the thin-crusted oak-fired pizzas such as the rustica, topped with fresh-grilled tuna, thinly sliced grilled fennel, black olives, and provolone. Among the pasta dishes (available as appetizers or entrées) I love the bow ties in a slow-simmered sauce of coarsely chopped tomatoes, sautéed radicchio, smoked pancetta, and sweet onions, finished with pecorino romano cheese. Also noteworthy: homemade tortellini, filled with spinach, ricotta, and parmesan, and tossed in brown butter with toasted walnuts and fresh sage. More substantial entrées include spicy Tuscan seafood stew filled with chunks of fresh fish, shrimps, mussels, scallops, and tomatoes in herbed white wine broth; it's served with garlicky bruschetta. Or you could opt for juicy baby lamb shank in Barolo wine sauce, served with pastina, sliced artichokes, and roasted garlic. Two desserts were especially memorable—a caramelized upside-down apple tart with homemade vanilla ice cream and the most chocolaty ever flourless torte made with valrhona French cocoa and served with double-chocolate ice cream and whipped cream on crème anglaise. Get both; sharing is bliss. The lunch menu lists similar fare, plus focaccia sandwiches, and brunch here features family-style dining with food served from large platters and casseroles. The award-winning wine list highlights every wine-producing region of Italy and features a good selection of grappas—clear after-dinner wines made from distilled sediment of the wine-making process. Try one that is infused with macerated fruit.

MODERATE

THE BUCKHEAD DINER, 3073 Piedmont Rd., at E. Paces Ferry Rd. Tel. 262-3336.

Cuisine: AMERICAN **Reservations:** Not accepted; arrive off-peak hours. **Parking:** Complimentary valet parking.

$ Prices: Snacks, sandwiches, and salads $3.95–$10.95; entrées

$8–$11 at lunch, $9.25–$14.95 at dinner. AE, CB, DC, DISC, MC, V.

Open: Mon–Sat 11am–midnight; Sun (including brunch) 11am–10pm.

⭐ Nouvelle-diner chic has come to Atlanta in a big way, and no reconstructed roadhouse has more cachet than the Buckhead. It is *the* place in Atlanta to see and be seen, attracting a stream of celebrities, among them Princess Stephanie of Monaco, who stood patiently in line waiting for a table, then returned for another meal a few days later. As sleek as a Thunderbird convertible, the Buckhead was designed to the tune of $1.5 million by Pat Kuleto, who has also done interiors for noted California restaurateur Wolfgang Puck. Its exterior glitters with stainless-steel and neon tubing. Inside there's a trompe-l'oeil Italian marble floor, a "bar car" inspired by the opulence of the Orient Express, and a gorgeous counter of Honduran mahogany with ebony, cherry, and bird's-eye maple marquetry detail. Bustling white-hatted chefs behind the counter comprise an exhibition-kitchen area. Most diners, however, opt for the more intimate transom-windowed, upholstered mahogany booths. As in the bar, a vaulted ceiling evokes a luxury railroad dining car. Lighting emanates from beautiful art deco fixtures, and classic recorded jazz (Louis Armstrong, Ella Fitzgerald) creates an ambience evocative of an earlier era.

Charming young chef Gerry Klaskala has created a menu he describes as "new American cuisine with a Midwest solidity." That means entrées are a mix of Mom and modern: for example, grilled double-smoked pork chops with spinach, creamy polenta, and cranberry compote; batter-fried scallops with snow peas, red peppers, and honey-mustard sauce; and a grilled cheese sandwich of Jarlsberg and cheddar with plum tomato, scallions, and grainy mustard. Many low-priced little snack items—like crispy calamari and lamb enchiladas with yogurt and mint—make sampling possible. Both the menu and the wine list change seasonally, the latter always offering many selections by the glass. Desserts are great, ranging from peach bread pudding with Southern Comfort–flavored cream to upside-down apple pie topped with homemade cinnamon ice cream.

THE PEASANT RESTAURANT & BAR, 3402 Piedmont Rd. NE, a block north of Peachtree Rd. Tel. 231-8740.

Cuisine: CONTEMPORARY AMERICAN **Reservations:** Not accepted. **Parking:** Valet parking is complimentary.

$ **Prices:** Appetizers $3.75–$5.95 at lunch, $3.95–$6.95 at dinner; entrées $6.50–$8.95 at lunch, $9.95–$14.95 at dinner. AE, DC, DISC, MC, V.

Open: Lunch daily 11am–2:30pm; dinner Sun–Thurs 5:30–11pm, Fri–Sat 5:30pm–midnight.

The Peasant group owns 18 restaurants in Atlanta, many of which are described above (Mick's, A Country Place, Pleasant Peasant, Dailey's, even the trés haute City Grill). All of them offer marvelously unique menus and venues and waitstaff so gracious and efficient that I can spot a Peasant-trained waitperson at any Atlanta restaurant. This latest Peasant venture conforms to the same lofty standard. The setting is romantic, with candlelit tables amid potted palms. Walls, hung with large gilt-framed mirrors, alternate glossy black lacquer paneling with beautiful fleur-de-lis fabric. Shaded table lamps, English landscape paintings, French antiques, and lovely dried-flower arrangements add residential charm. There's an elegant bar area (come by some afternoon for hors d'oeuvres and cocktails), and a glass-walled conservatory section is verdant with lush plantings.

You might begin your meal here with a grilled quesadilla stuffed with shrimp, black beans, melted cheddar and Monterey Jack cheeses, and jalapeños, served with guacamole and sour cream. Another notable appetizer is sea scallops in a hot and spicy soy-chili sauce, with black beans on a bed of crisp-fried spinach leaves. Entrées come with delicious cheese toast and a huge salad. A good choice is pan-sautéed boneless chicken breast topped with Jarlsberg cheese sauce and accompanied by roasted tomatoes, hickory-grilled mushrooms, and savory onion-flavored homemade mashed potatoes. Grilled grouper (seafood is always fresh here) is served with avocado slices, roasted tomatoes, and butter-browned couscous tossed with mushrooms, macadamia nuts, and ginger. And extra-thick and juicy pork chops are stuffed with black beans, rice, and melted cheddar and garnished with avocado slices and fresh-fruit salsa. This is a sumptuous cuisine, and portions are huge. Desserts are no exception, with lavish offerings like caramel-butter pecan pie on pecan cookie crust, slathered with whipped cream, and topped with warm caramel and pecans. The wine list features California wines; about a dozen premium selections are offered by the glass.

STAGE DELI, 3850 Roswell Rd., a block north of Piedmont Rd. in the Buckhead Court Shopping Center. Tel. 233-DELI.

Cuisine: JEWISH DELI **Reservations:** For large parties only.
Parking: Free.
$ Prices: Sandwiches $5.95–$8.95 (to $12.95 for triple deckers); omelets, burgers, and salads $4.95–$7.50; entrées $9.95–$14.95. AE, MC, V.
Open: Mon–Thurs 7am–11pm, Fri 7am–1am, Sat 10am–1am, Sun 10am–11pm.

In 1991, Atlanta added a heretofore missing piece to its culinary jigsaw puzzle—a totally authentic transplanted New York deli. Gotham's Stage Deli—a legendary celebrity hangout for comedians (Shecky Greene, Bill Cosby, Alan King), not to mention athletes and politicians—has been slapping pastrami on rye for over half a century. The Atlanta branch is already creating a similar tradition. Mayor Maynard Jackson comes in frequently, as does the governor and local resident Fran Tarkenton. And when Democratic candidate for president Bill Clinton came to Atlanta, the Stage catered to his plane. The sleek setting is of the classic Broadway deli/pub genre—black and white small-tile flooring, schoolroom lights overhead, dark oak paneling and columns, and seating in roomy leather booths. Over the counter are paintings of famous New York theaters.

Most of the fare—including fresh-baked pumpernickel and rye breads, meats, chewy bagels, lox, spicy mustard, and pickles—comes in daily from the Big Apple. Hefty portions of food are served on colorful Fiestaware platters. Soups come in 16-ounce "cup" portions or 32-ounce "bowls." Opt for the mishmash, a chicken soup with the works—kreplach, matzo balls, and noodles. All the traditional Jewish soul foods are fabulous—thin-sliced hot pastrami or corned beef piled high on rye, potato pancakes with chunky homemade applesauce, delicious coarsely chopped liver mixed with hard-boiled egg, scrambled matzo brie, and the best-ever knishes—flaky croissantlike crusts filled with spicy spinach-flecked potatoes or a mix of potato with shredded deli meats. Thirty-one triple-decker sandwiches are named for New York and local celebrities—for example, the Jay Leno ("a little tongue, a lotta bologna, pastrami, cole slaw, and Russian dressing"). For dessert, the Stage torte, a very rich cheesecake topped with chocolate mousse and chocolate icing, should hold you for the next few mealtimes. There's a full bar, and a children's menu is a plus.

INEXPENSIVE

THE OK CAFE, 1284 W. Paces Ferry Rd., at Northside Dr. in the West Paces Ferry Shopping Center. Tel. 233-2888.

Cuisine: AMERICAN **Reservations:** Not accepted. **Parking:** Free.

$ Prices: Lunch and dinner burgers, salads, and sandwiches $4.50–$6.95; blue-plate specials $6.95–$7.95 at lunch, $7.95–$8.95 at dinner. AE, MC, V.

Open: 24 hours.

Though it was actually built in 1987, it's hard to believe this isn't an authentic 1950s rural Georgia roadhouse, transported "back to the future" by some magical force. A low yellow cement-block building, with striped aluminum awnings and a green shingled roof, it's heralded by the requisite neon roadhouse sign. Within, seating is in roomy leather booths at old-style Formica tables, windows are shaded with venetian blinds and framed by retro-look curtains, the jukebox is stocked with oldies, and waitresses are attired in white diner uniforms. Shaded table lamps further enhance the cozy ambience.

As for the food, it evokes memories of Mom, with blue-plate specials like meat loaf, fried catfish with Cajun ketchup, and roast turkey with dressing, all served with scrumptious homemade corn muffins and two side dishes—your choices including, among many others, creamy macaroni and cheese made with six cheeses (the best I've ever had), collard greens, lima beans, and sweet potatoes seasoned with nutmeg and cinnamon, studded with honeyed pecans, and topped with a cornflake crust. Excellent sandwiches, burgers, and salads are additional options, not to mention old-fashioned thick shakes and malteds served in the tumbler. And do leave room for dessert, be it homemade hot apple pie topped with brown sugar, pecans, cinnamon, and a scoop of vanilla ice cream, or hot-fudge cake—an ultramoist, ultrachocolaty brownie smothered in fresh whipped cream, nuts, strawberries, hot fudge, and vanilla ice cream. The OK is also a great place for country-style breakfasts and brunches.

THE SWAN COACH HOUSE, 3130 Slaton Dr. NW, at the Atlanta History Center. Tel. 261-0636.
   Cuisine: AMERICAN **Reservations:** Not accepted.
$ **Prices:** Entrées $6–$8. MC, V.
   Open: Mon–Sat 11:30am–2:30pm. **Closed:** Jan 1, Memorial Day, July 4, Thanksgiving, and Dec 25.

When you visit the Atlanta History Center in Buckhead (see Chapter 7, "What to See and Do in Atlanta," below), plan a lunch at this delightful restaurant. Tables are adorned with lovely flower arrangements, walls are covered in exquisite fruit-and-flower-motif fabric, crystal chandeliers glitter overhead, and multipaned windows overlook wooded grounds. A vast gift shop and art gallery adjoin the dining room.

The menu mirrors the ambience, featuring ladies' fork-luncheon fare such as salmon croquettes topped with white caper sauce and served with a spiced peach, vegetables, and congealed salad (chopped apples, pecans, and walnuts in a lime-jello mold). Or you might opt for chicken salad in pastry timbales served with cheese straws and creamy frozen fruit salad. There's even chicken à la king. Fresh muffins accompany all entrées. For dessert, order lemon chess pie or a French silk swan—a meringue base filled with frozen chocolate mousse and whipped cream, topped with slivered almonds, and garnished with a swan-shaped cracker. There's a full bar; drinks like peach fuzz and mint julep are featured. *Note:* You don't have to be visiting the AHC to dine here; it has a separate entrance.

BUDGET

FELLINI'S PIZZA, 2813 Peachtree Rd., between Rumson Rd. and Sheridan Dr. Tel. 266-0082.
   Cuisine: PIZZA **Reservations:** Not accepted. **Parking:** Free.
$ **Prices:** $1–$2.50 for a slice; $7.50–$9 for a pie, with additional toppings $1–$1.50; $4–$5 for calzones. No credit cards.
   Open: Mon–Sat 11:30am–2am, Sun noon–midnight.
You won't get chèvre or cilantro on your pies here, but you will get traditional toppings like anchovies, Italian sausage, meatballs, pepperoni, fresh mushrooms, and onions piled on cheesy New York-style pies with thin, doughy crusts that exude the heavenly aroma of fresh-baked bread. Fellini's is a classic pizza joint, and a darned good one. It's a wacky place, very untypical of Buckhead. A handful of

tables occupy the funky room downstairs, where the pizzas are made and rock music blares. Walls are plastered with antiestablishment cartoons and graffiti, rock posters, weird newspaper headlines (AFRICAN TRIBE WORSHIPS JOHN WAYNE AS GOD), and a painting of Elvis. When you order you'll be given a whimsical photo (perhaps a group of guys dressed as hens), so the waiter can identify you when he delivers your order. Unless you like a chaotic din, head upstairs to the open-air deck under a canvas tent top (it's enclosed by plastic flaps and heated in winter) or grab a café table out front.

The pizzas, regular and Sicilian, are made with only the freshest ingredients. Other options are immense crusty calzones stuffed with fillings like sausage and cheese and a tasty salad of lettuce, mushrooms, onions, green peppers, and olives in a creamy Italian dressing. Beer and wine are available.

There's another Fellini's at 422 Seminole Ave., at the junction of Euclid and Moreland avenues in Little Five Points (tel. 525-2530).

THE RIB RANCH, 25 Irby Ave. NW, just west of Roswell Rd. between W. Paces Ferry Rd. and E. Andrews Dr. Tel. 233-7644.
　　Cuisine: TEXAS BARBECUE **Reservations:** Not accepted.
　　Parking: Free in a few spaces here; paid parking down the street.
$ Prices: Barbecue sandwiches $3.15–$4.95, platters $6.25–$6.75, ribs $7.50–$11.50, children's plates $2.25. DC, MC, V.
　　Open: Mon–Sat 11am–11pm, Sun noon–10pm.

Fronted by a Texas flag awning shading a few picnic tables, the Rib Ranch is your archetypical Lone Star rib joint. The cozy interior, with dark-stained pine floors and café-curtained windows, is cluttered with mounted deer trophies, neon beer signs, license plates, and university football banners suspended from a low-beamed ceiling. Beer openers also hang from the ceiling over each red-and-white checker-clothed table. And, of course, the jukebox is stocked with country tunes.

Come here for fork-tender Texas-style ribs and barbecue that have been slow-cooked over hickory wood and basted with tangy sauce. The beef ribs are the most truly Texan, but the pork ribs are equally delicious. Don't bother with the chicken; it's undistinguished. There are all kinds of side dishes, the best being spicy Brunswick stew—a mix of tomato, shredded pork and beef, okra, onions, and lima beans. Also noteworthy: authentic all-beef chili, crisp fresh-made onion rings, and homemade sweet and creamy coleslaw. Beer is the beverage of choice, and you can have a brownie for dessert.

4. VIRGINIA-HIGHLAND

Make a meal in this charming district the occasion to see a nontouristy part of Atlanta. Come a little early, so you can browse in Virginia-Highland's great little shops and boutiques.

MODERATE

CHOW, 1026½ N. Highland Ave. NE, at Virginia Ave. Tel. 872-0869.

Cuisine: NEW AMERICAN **Reservations:** Not accepted.
Parking: Free behind restaurant on Highland, north of Virginia.
$ Prices: Appetizers $4.50–$7.95; entrées $5.95–$7.95 at lunch/brunch, mostly $9.95–$14.95 at dinner. AE, MC, V.
Open: Lunch Tues–Fri 11:30am–3pm; brunch Sat–Sun 11am–3pm; dinner Sun–Thurs 6–10:30pm, Fri–Sat 6–11:30pm.

At the very hub of Atlanta's arty Virginia-Highland area, Chow evokes the casual chic of New York's trendy Soho district. Glossy cream walls function as gallery space for quality artworks, large halaphane lamps are suspended from a high pressed-tin ceiling (very New York), and bare oak floors further an uncluttered less-is-more ambience. However, the setting is warmly inviting rather than stark. Highly polished black granite tables are candlelit and adorned by exquisite flower arrangements, the soft lighting is flattering, and a rough-hewn stone wall adds rustic charm. In good weather, outdoor balcony seating under a striped awning is very popular. Chow has always attracted a sophisticated clientele. Movie people tend to come by when they're doing films in town (Morgan Freeman was a regular during *Driving Miss Daisy*), and Atlanta's most famous couple, Jane and Ted, were having lunch (she ordered a salad, of course) last time I was in.

Dinner here might begin with rosemary- and thyme-marinated baked garlic cloves served with feta cheese spread and toasted French bread croutons; a plate of hummus dip with pita bread, plump black olives, and cucumber slices; or lightly battered fried calamari with a spicy chunky-tomato marinara sauce. Entrées include many pasta dishes such as Gulf shrimp and smoked salmon tossed with homemade fettuccine in a basil cream sauce. Also featured is fresh seafood (everything here is fresh and prepared from scratch)—for example, grilled tuna marinated in sherry, ginger, soy, and garlic, served with a medley of fresh vegetables. Then again, there's herb/parmesan-breaded chicken in lemon butter sauce with fresh basil, topped with roasted pine nuts. All entrées come with a salad. Desserts are lush; I like the homemade brown-sugary carrot cake, studded with raisins, pecans, and pineapple and slathered with creamy icing. The lunch menu features salads, overstuffed sandwiches, burgers, pasta dishes, and quesadillas. Brunch adds breakfasty fare like omelets, French toast, bagels with cream cheese and nova, and Belgian waffles. There's a full bar, and a large selection of wines and aperitifs are offered by the glass.

INDIGO COASTAL GRILL, 1397 N. Highland Ave. NE, between N. Morningside and University Drs. Tel. 876-0676.

Cuisine: COASTAL **Reservations:** Accepted Sun–Wed only; other nights arrive at off-peak hours to avoid a wait. **Parking:** Lot across the street.

$ Prices: Appetizers $3.95–$7.95, entrées $11–$15. AE, MC, V.
Open: Sun–Thurs 5:30–11pm, Fri–Sat 5:30–11:30pm.

Two of Atlanta's most popular restaurants, Indigo Coastal Grill and Partners (next door, details below), are run by Alix Kenagy (she's the culinary genius) and her husband, Dan Carson (he's the wine expert). I simply can't pile on enough accolades to the exquisite dining experience these restaurants offer. If I lived in Atlanta, I'd be such a regular patron they'd have to put up a brass plaque behind my seat. The Grill's decor has been variously described as "Caribbean camp" and "battered beach house." Fronted by a beautiful aquarium of tropical fish, it has walls the color of Bermuda sand hung with beach-themed paintings of tropical palms and opalescent ocean, a beamed turquoise ceiling, and touches of coral enhancing the island-holiday ambience. It's a casual setting: fans slowly whirr overhead, floors are planked with pine, and candlelit tables are covered with brown butcher paper. There's an exhibition kitchen hung with rolled-up bamboo matchstick shades and a screened-in back porch (heated in winter) under a striped canvas tent top. Christopher Reeve once threw a party on this porch; he's one of the numerous celebrities who've dined here and at Partner's.

The base menu, which changes every three weeks, focuses on coastal cuisines; specials are listed on a blackboard over the bar. There are always knockout appetizers—fried plaintains served with cayenne-spiced lime/avocado dip; Caribbean lamb turnovers, like doughy, crusty calzones stuffed with a savory filling of spiced sautéed ground lamb, red cabbage, and black beans, served with yogurt-mint sauce; or fresh, juicy lime- and tequila-basted oysters grilled with buttery leeks, poblano and Fresno peppers, and smoked jalapeños. Or you might begin with a creamy cayenne-spiced chowder containing big chunks of lobster, fresh corn, and poblano peppers, laced with sherry. Exquisite entrées usually include a fish baked in parchment, perhaps Hawaiian opah (a tender fish), cooked with sweet potato and pineapple slices, snowpeas, and red peppers in a buttery five-citrus sauce (grapefruit, tangerine, Key lime, orange, and lemon), served with black beans and saffron-flavored rice. Also frequently on the menu is grilled Jamaican-style chicken, marinated in jerk (an exotic spice mixture of pimiento seeds, Scotch bonnet peppers, Fresno peppers, garlic, and ground green scallions in olive oil) and served with rice and beans, cucumber salad, and a slice of grilled pineapple topped with sour cream.

The wine list is well researched by Dan, and desserts are ambrosial. The Key lime pie (Dan's Mom's recipe) is wonderfully light and tart with a scrumptious graham-cracker crust. Also memorable—Bahamian bananas, butter-fried and served with Key lime/cream sauce sweetened with raw sugar.

PARTNERS MORNINGSIDE CAFÉ, 1399 N. Highland Ave., between N. Morningside and University Drs. Tel. 876-8104.

Cuisine: CROSS-CULTURAL **Reservations:** Accepted Sun–Wed only; other nights arrive at off-peak hours to avoid a wait. **Parking:** Lot across the street.

$ Prices: Appetizers $4.50–$7.50, entrées $12–$16.95. AE, MC, V.

Open: Tues–Thurs 5:30–11pm, Fri–Sat 5:30–11:30pm.

Another fabulous Alix Kenagy/Dan Carson enterprise (see Indigo Coastal Grill above), Partners offers an internationally inspired menu. A former fashion editor, Alix has an artistic flair equal to her kitchen skills. She designed the restaurant's warmly intimate setting, with distressed-look faux-Tuscan walls and a terracotta ceiling. Bare yellow pine floors, Georgia hard-pine cabinets, candlelit tables, and big baskets of dried flowers add country coziness. It's all just funky and unserious enough to make for a lively ambience. Partners crackles with excitement every night, and Alix is always on hand to greet guests, a charming hostess at a great party.

Menus change frequently to reflect market specialties. A recent meal here began with an aromatic chowder of oysters, andouille sausage, and sliced new potatoes, spiced with cayenne and Thai peppers, in a creamy oyster-liquor/fish-stock base. A leek-ravioli appetizer was stuffed with finely chopped green onions and Bel Paese, ricotta, and fontina cheeses and served afloat chive-garnished sherried-cream/mushroom sauce. Other choices that evening included oysters on the barbie (in a smoky topping of grilled leeks, smoked jalapeños, and bacon, flecked with tomato) and scrumptious grilled Vietnamese chicken cakes studded with lemongrass and served on cilantro aioli. As for entrées, there's a pasta special every night, such as fresh linguine tossed with roughly diced tomatoes, fresh basil, sweet red onion, balsamic vinegar, and extra virgin olive oil, topped with Italian fennel sausage, roasted peppers, and shavings of parmesan. A chicken special might be a grilled double breast topped with melted Brie, fresh pears, and apricot butter, garnished with fresh basil and served with herbed linguine. A delicious light salad in Caesar dressing accompanies all entrées.

Do consider ordering half portions to experience a greater variety of dishes. Whatever you get, save room for Alix's extraordinary desserts, including chunky, tart apple cake, served warm, topped with buttery caramel sauce lavishly studded with pecans and a scoop of vanilla-bean ice cream. Dan's recherché wine list features many by-the-glass selections.

INEXPENSIVE

BRIDGETOWN GRILL, 1156 Euclid Ave. NE, between Moreland and Colquitt Aves. Tel. 653-0110.
Cuisine: CARIBBEAN **Reservations:** Not accepted. **MARTA:** Bus Nos. 6 and 48 stop here. **Parking:** Free in a lot on Seminole Ave. behind restaurant.

$ Prices: Appetizers $1.50–$4.50; entrées $4.50–$5.95 at lunch, $5.50–$12.95 at dinner. MC, V.

Open: Mon–Thurs 11:30am–10pm, Fri 11:30am–midnight, Sat noon–midnight, Sun noon–10pm. (Dinner menu begins at 5pm.)

I adore long, leisurely weekend brunches, comfortably ensconced in a roomy white wooden booth of Bridgetown's airy skylit patio. Lush tropical plantings and a Caribbean-style beach bar nestling in the corner further enhance the island ambience. And since it's heated in winter, this sun-dappled setting can be enjoyed year round. The interior is also simpatico, with saltillo-tile floors and exposed brick walls hung with Haitian folk art painted on oil drums. At night, candlelight sets the mood.

To get things going, order up delicious flaky-crust Jamaican patties stuffed with spicy ground beef or shredded vegetables. Bay scallops ceviche, marinated in lime, jalapeños, and cilantro, comes garnished with mandarin oranges, tomato wedges, and pineapple chunks. And you can't go wrong with a basket of jerk chicken wings. Jerk chicken is a specialty here, seasoned in a mix of spices that yield an explosion of subtle flavors with every bite. You can order it grilled in a sandwich, as an entrée served with raspberry-tamarind sauce (like all entrées here, it comes with salad, black beans, and rice), or in a terrific salad tossed with greens, grated Monterey Jack cheese, fresh mushrooms, tomatoes, pineapple chunks, oranges, and coconut with mango vinaigrette dressing. Also available jerk-seasoned are barbecued pork chops, sautéed plump Gulf shrimp served with mango-citrus sauce, and grilled filet of salmon in Scotch bonnet pepper butter. After such hearty fare, I think a light coconut flan is the best dessert choice, but there are richer options such as creamy key lime pie and chocolate cheesecake with raspberry sauce. Beverages (there's a full bar) include nonalcoholic ginger beer and DG grapefruit drink, both excellent foils for spicy fare. Pitcherfuls of rum-based tropical coolers are also available.

There's another Bridgetown Grill at 689 Peachtree St., at 3rd Street (tel. 873-5361). It's open Monday 11am to 10pm, Tuesday to Thursday 11am to 11pm, Friday to Saturday 11am to midnight, Sunday noon to 10pm. No patio here, but the menu is more extensive.

SURIN OF THAILAND, 810 N. Highland Ave., at Greenwood Ave. Tel. 892-7789.

Cuisine: THAI **Reservations:** Not accepted. **Parking:** Free in lot behind restaurant. If that's full there's paid parking across the street; get a receipt and the restaurant will reimburse you.

$ Prices: Appetizers $3–$5.95; lunch entrées $4–$6.50, dinner entrées $6.50–$8.95. AE, DISC, MC, V.

Open: Mon–Thurs 11:30am–10pm, Fri 11:30am–11:30pm, Sat noon–11:30pm, Sun noon–10pm.

This pristinely charming Thai restaurant opened in 1991 to rave reviews, and it has continued to enjoy hearty acclaim for its scrumptious and very authentic fare. It's a very comfortable setting, with bare oak floors and candlelit tables covered in royal blue linen cloths. Colorful Thai banners (depicting a golden Buddha, a

Thai dancer, and other familiar imagery) are suspended from a lofty pressed-tin ceiling, and cheerful yellow walls are hung with striking color photographs of Thailand taken by Caroline House (one of the owners). During the day, light streams in through a wall of windows overlooking the street.

The same menu is offered throughout the day, with specials at both meals. All sauces are made from scratch, and everything—including seafood—is fresh and delicious. There are many tempting appetizers, my favorite of which is chef Surin Techarukpong's perfectly crispy mee-krob—a pungent rice noodle dish sauced with tamarind and garnished with plump shrimp, egg, and bean sprouts. Other good choices are satays (kebabs) of chicken or beef in spicy peanut sauce served with cucumber salad; tender poached rice paper rolls, stuffed with minced pork, shrimp, bean sprouts, and fresh Thai basil, served with hot peppery plum sauce; and a subtly spiced yum yai salad of romaine lettuce, shredded carrot, hard-boiled egg, cucumber, shrimp, and chicken in a light sweet and sour peanut dressing. The rich chicken-coconut soup, flavored with kaffir lime leaf and replete with chunks of chicken, tiger shrimp, and fresh mushroom slices, is also excellent. Entrées include chicken panang in red curry paste—a savory mix of chili peppers, lemongrass, galingale (a gingerlike root), lime peel, fresh Thai basil, and other spices. And if it's on the specials menu, opt for neur nam tok—strips of grilled beef tenderloin seasoned with lime, hot serrano chili peppers, fresh basil, fish sauce, and green onion; it's eaten rolled in cabbage leaves. This is a complex cuisine in which each dish yields a kaleidoscopic spectrum of spicy flavors. Beverage choices include exotic drinks like mango daiquiris, sake, a small wine list, and creamy-sweet Thai herbal iced tea. For dessert there's homemade coconut ice cream as well as mango, green tea, and ginger versions—all fittingly light and cooling finales. On weekends, arrive early or late to avoid a wait for seating.

BUDGET

MURPHY'S, 1019 Los Angeles Ave. NE, at N. Highland Ave. Tel. 872-0904.
  Cuisine: AMERICAN **Reservations:** Not accepted. **Parking:** Street only.
$ Prices: Appetizers $2–$5 at lunch, $2–$6 at dinner; entrées $4.95–$6.95 at lunch, $6.95–$11.95 at dinner; breakfast fare $2–$6. AE, MC, V ($15 minimum).
  Open: Mon, Wed–Thurs 7:30am–10pm, Tues 11am–10pm, Fri 7:30am–11pm, Sat 8am–11pm, Sun 8am–10pm.

Murphy's, originally a wine-and-cheese shop that evolved into a restaurant and bakery, is as cozy as a cracker-barrel store. Its main dining area, under a low beamed ceiling, has yellow brick walls hung with copper pots, shuttered bay windows, and shelves aclutter with breadbaskets and ceramic jugs. There's additional seating on a patio under a green-and-white striped awning (open air in good weather, heated and enclosed by plastic in winter). Or you can sit at the counter and bask in the heavenly aroma of fresh coffee being ground. Classical music is played at all times.

Everything here is fresh. At lunch and dinner there are haute-deli sandwiches such as basil-flavored chicken salad tossed with mayo and sour cream and served with lettuce, tomato, and sprouts on whole wheat; deep-dish quiches served with salad; hearty homemade soups; and entrées running the gamut from rotini pasta tossed in a fresh-herb cream sauce with artichokes, peas, and julienned spinach to fresh Georgia trout, lightly battered, grilled, and topped with pecan butter. Breakfast/brunch items are also wide-ranging, including omelets, Mexican breakfasts rolled in tortillas, Belgian waffles, French toast, and bagel-and-lox platters. Irish potatoes—large chunks sautéed with onions, peppers, and zucchini, seasoned with Cajun spices—are a specialty. And luscious fresh-baked desserts include four-layer white-chocolate mousse cake and Bavarian raspberry cake frosted with lemon mousse. Beer and wine are available.

5. SWEET AUBURN

BUDGET

THE BEAUTIFUL RESTAURANT, 397 Auburn Ave., at Jackson St. Tel. 223-0800.
   Cuisine: SOUTHERN/SOUL FOOD **Reservations:** Not accepted. **MARTA:** King Memorial. **Parking:** Free.
$ Prices: Everything, except steaks, under $5. No credit cards.
   Open: Daily 7am–8:30pm.

It's not really all that beautiful, but this tiny eatery—one of a chain of soul-food cafeterias run by the Perfect Church—is a very good place for a lunch break when you're touring the Sweet Auburn district of Atlanta (see Chapter 8). There's seating in a few orange plastic booths and at long Formica tables; counterpersons are also attired in orange. A few hanging plants constitute the sole attempt at decoration. You don't come here for ambience but for hearty homemade southern fare. There's always a choice of meat dishes—baked pork chops, baked chicken in thick gravy, barbecued beef tips, meat loaf—plus a half dozen or so side dishes. These might include collard greens, candied yams, black-eyed peas, baked macaroni, lima beans, and spiced rice, all of them delicious. Fresh-baked corn bread is served with all entrées. And there are homemade desserts such as peach cobbler, sweet-potato pie, and banana pudding topped with vanilla wafers, along with an intriguing southern specialty called red velvet cake—a rich chocolate cake that is dyed red with food coloring! No alcoholic beverages are served. Good southern-style breakfasts here, too.

6. DECATUR

BUDGET

THUMBS UP, 254 W. Ponce de Leon Ave., near Commerce Dr. Tel. 377-5623.
    Cuisine: AMERICAN **Reservations:** Not accepted; arrive off-peak hours. **Parking:** Street only.
$ Prices: Appetizers $3.75–$5.25; entrées $3.75–$6.25 at breakfast and lunch, $4.25–$9.50 at dinner. No credit cards.
    Open: Breakfast Tues–Fri 7:30–10:45am, Sat–Sun 8am–2pm; lunch Tues–Fri 11am–3pm; dinner Tues–Sat 5:30–10pm.

This tiny, somewhat funky Decatur restaurant consists of 10 tables and a counter in a small front room and 5 additional tables and another counter in the high-ceilinged, raspberry-colored back room. In the front section, sunshine streams in through a café-curtained corner window, providing lots of light for hanging plants. The peach walls are plastered with framed rave reviews, and shelves are aclutter with knickknacks, old radios, and cameras. I prefer the back room, away from the hectic counter/grill activity.

Breakfast is the most popular meal here, featuring items like scrambled eggs with fresh herbs and cream cheese, homemade multigrain biscuits, and the house specialty, O'Brien spuds—baked potatoes chopped into large chunks, sautéed with onions, peppers, and spices, and topped with melted cheddar. Thick slabs of challah French toast served with powdered sugar, butter, and pure Vermont maple syrup are another tempting option. Ditto Belgian waffles and buckwheat cakes. But lunch and dinner also merit consideration. At lunch you might order sandwiches, salads, or entrées such as smoked barbecued chicken served with homemade potato salad and baked beans. Dinner features similar choices, along with some Mexican specialties and fancier entrées including a pinkly juicy 1½-inch thick blackened salmon steak. Owners Lou and Barbara Locricchio, always on hand to welcome diners, serve only fresh vegetables and organic meats from a North Georgia farm. Wine and beer are available, and the homemade Key lime pie and peanut-butter torte are delicious.

7. CHAMBLEE

INEXPENSIVE

HONTO, 3295 Chamblee-Dunwoody Rd., between Buford Hwy. and Peachtree Industrial Blvd. Tel. 458-8088.

Cuisine: CANTONESE **Reservations:** For large parties only.
Parking: Free.

$ Prices: Appetizers $1.60–$3.95; entrées mostly $6–$11,
$3.50–$4.50 for lunch specials, including soup, fried rice, and egg
rolls. AE, MC, V.

Open: Sun–Thurs 11:30am–10pm; Fri–Sat 11:30am–11pm;
special dim sum meals Sat–Mon 11am–2pm.

Almost all the restaurants listed in this book are very centrally
located, but this one's well worth an extra 10 minutes on the
road. *Atlanta* magazine calls it the city's best Chinese restaurant; I'd go even further and say it's on a par with the best Chinese
restaurants in New York and San Francisco. Honto isn't a fancy
place. Large and well lit, it has peach walls hung with Chinese art and
dining areas separated by carved golden arches. The most important
aspect of its decor, however, is a row of pink strips of paper marked
with Chinese characters that inform diners (those who can read
Chinese) of fresh seafood and other market specialties available on
any given day. Ignore the printed menu; instead, put yourself in the
expert hands of chef Johnny To, indicating the amount you wish to
spend and any food preferences (for shrimp, beef, lobster, or pork
dishes), and let him create a feast for you.

On a recent visit, seasonally fresh entrées included delectably
tender sautéed beef with snow peas, thinly sliced carrots, and oyster
mushrooms in a brown sauce; crispy fresh pan-fried pompano,
garnished with cilantro, in a delicately seasoned soy sauce; a superb
dish of clams steamed in garlic butter and served in a piquant
cilantro-flavored broth (it comes in a big cast-iron pot); and sautéed
soft-shell crab flavored with ginger and green onions, served with
black-bean sauce. Though these dishes may sound prosaic, you'll find
they are exquisitely flavored and very unique. Every morsel is a
delight, and many morsels there are—portions are vast. This is also a
great place for dim sum (Chinese tea lunch) meals consisting of
numerous appetizer-size dishes.

8. SPECIALTY DINING

All of the establishments listed in this section have been described in
detail elsewhere in this chapter. They're noted here for special
attributes and/or because they are the best in their category.

LOCAL FAVORITES

For authentic southern cooking, Atlanta residents flock to the
unpretentious **Colonnade,** 1879 Cheshire Bridge Road NE (tel.
874-5642).

If you grew up in Atlanta, chili dogs at the **Varsity,** 61 North

Ave. (tel. 881-1706), the world's largest drive-in restaurant, are as much a part of your heritage as *Gone With the Wind.*

And the "in" place to see and be seen is the **Buckhead Diner,** 3073 Piedmont Rd. (tel. 262-3336).

HOTEL DINING

Atlanta's premier restaurant is a hotel dining room—the ultraelegant **Dining Room** at the Ritz-Carlton Buckhead, 3434 Peachtree Rd. NE (tel. 237-2700). Its cuisine is renowned nationally.

HOTEL DINING WITH A VIEW

Nikolai's Roof, atop the Atlanta Hilton at 255 Courtland St. (tel. 659-2000), offers superb French/Russian cuisine and 30th-floor skyline views.

The **Sun Dial,** a revolving restaurant-cum-aerie on the 73rd floor of the Westin Peachtree Plaza, 210 Peachtree St. (tel. 589-7506), offers the most breathtaking city views in town. You can enjoy the panorama for very low prices at lunch Monday to Saturday (most entrées are $6 to $9). Sunday the Sun Dial sets out a lavish buffet brunch ($21.50 prix fixe).

THEATER DISTRICT DINING

Atlanta doesn't really have a theater district, but it does have a major performance facility for theater, concerts, and more called the Woodruff Arts Center. The Woodruff shelters one of the city's best restaurants, the marvelous **Chef's Grill,** 1280 Peachtree St. (tel. 881-0652). Even if you don't like the show, the Grill's nouvelle culinary creations will make your evening memorable.

LIGHT, CASUAL, AND FAST FOOD

You don't need a suit and tie at **Rocky's Brick Oven Pizzeria,** 1770 Peachtree St. (tel. 876-1111), but you won't get better food if you spend 10 times as much in the most plush surroundings. Jeans and such are also acceptable at **Houston's,** 2166 Peachtree Rd. (tel. 351-2442), specializing in hickory-grilled burgers, chicken, and ribs (great salads, too); **Thumbs Up,** 254 W. Ponce de Leon Ave. (tel. 377-5623), featuring immense pork chops with homemade O'Brien spuds; **Murphy's,** 1019 Los Angeles Ave. NE (tel. 872-0904), a cozy neighborhood hangout; **R. Thomas,** 1812 Peachtree St. NW (tel. 872-2942), offering hearty sandwiches on nine-grain bread in a simpatico setting; and all of the places specified for kids above.

BREAKFAST/BRUNCH

One of the best things in life has to be a leisurely Sunday brunch. You sip champagne, maybe read the funnies, and hang out for a couple of hours eating and schmoozing. Reservations are suggested at all the establishments listed below. Hotel dining options all feature validated free parking. *Note:* You won't get an alcoholic drink on Sunday until 12:30pm.

For laid-back sun-dappled brunches, you can't beat the patio at **Bridgetown Grill** (see listing above). A meal here is like a minivacation.

The **Ritz-Carlton Buckhead,** 3434 Peachtree Rd. (tel. 237-2700), serves an exquisite brunch in the 3-tiered **Café** on Sunday from 11:30am to 2:30pm. The buffet boasts a caviar station, no less, as well as a carving station, an array of smoked fish, entrées such as grilled chicken with wild mushrooms in a madeira sauce, fresh fruits and cheeses, salads, vegetables, egg dishes, breakfast meats, pâtés and terrines, fresh-baked breads, and over 30 cakes and pastries. A pianist entertains. Price is $32, $16 for children 12 and under.

The **Ritz-Carlton Atlanta,** 181 Peachtree St. (tel. 659-0400), offers an equally impressive buffet downtown ($28 for adults, $14 for children 12 and under) with an exquisite 100-item spread every Sunday from 10:30am to 2:30pm. A harpist and flutist entertain.

A delightful plan is to drive out to Stone Mountain for the day, eat yourself into oblivion at the **Evergreen Conference Center and Resort** in Georgia's Stone Mountain Park (tel. 879-9900), and then walk off a few thousand calories on the park's wooded paths. A bountiful buffet, served Sunday from 11:30am to 3pm, includes hot entrées, carved-meat stations, an omelet station, blintzes, eggs Benedict, Belgian waffles, homemade breads, fresh fruit and cheeses, vegetables, a complimentary glass of champagne, and a wide array of desserts. Adults pay $16.95, children 4 to 10 pay $8.95, under 4 free.

Chef's Café, 2115 Piedmont Rd. (tel. 872-2284), has a special brunch menu Sunday between 10am and 2:30pm. It features entrées ($5 to $10.95) like smoked Irish salmon on a toasted bagel with herbed cream cheese, red onion, chopped egg, and capers; crab cakes Benedict, topped with poached eggs in tomato hollandaise and served with hash browns; and brioche french toast with orange-pistachio butter and maple syrup.

The **OK Cafe,** 1284 W. Paces Ferry Rd. (tel. 233-2888), offers a special brunch menu Saturday and Sunday from 10am to 3pm. The setting is casual, prices are low (entrées $5 to $8), and the food is delicious. Options include: blue-plate specials such as roast turkey and dressing served with a fresh-baked corn muffin and two vegetables (perhaps sweet-potato soufflé and collard greens); sourdough french toast; and griddle cakes with Granny Smith apples and pecans. Wear your jeans.

JAPANESE BREAKFAST

Tired of the same old bacon and eggs? The **Westin Peachtree Plaza,** 210 Peachtree St. (tel. 659-1400), offers a traditional Japanese breakfast daily in its Café restaurant. Priced at $9.75, it consists of grilled salmon, rice, miso soup, pickled vegetables, roasted seaweed, rice, and green tea.

A very similar meal is offered daily at Cassis, a delightful restaurant overlooking a Japanese rock garden in the **Hotel Nikko,** 3300 Peachtree Rd. (tel. 365-8100). Price is $15.50.

AFTERNOON TEA

This gracious southern city is the perfect place to enjoy the very civilized custom of afternoon tea. The following hotels offer the most exquisite venues for this leisurely repast.

The **Ritz-Carlton Buckhead,** 3434 Peachtree Rd. NE (tel. 237-2700), serves tea in its lobby lounge from 3 to 5pm daily. A pot of freshly brewed tea (your choice of about 10 varieties) comes with traditional tea sandwiches (smoked salmon, chive and egg, cucumber and cream cheese, or ham and asparagus), fresh-baked scones with Devonshire cream and fruit preserves, English tea bread, and a miniature fruit tart. A classical pianist provides tranquil background music. Price is $12. Reservations recommended.

The **Ritz-Carlton Atlanta,** 181 Peachtree St. (tel. 659-0400), not to be outdone by its uptown relative, serves an identical tea in its mahogany-paneled, Persian-carpeted lobby lounge daily from 2:30 to 4:30pm. It, too, features a pianist. Price is $12. Another option here is a $7.50 minitea including tea, sandwiches as above, chocolate-dipped strawberries, and petits fours.

The **Hotel Nikko,** 3300 Peachtree Rd. (tel. 365-8100), also serves a traditional English tea daily from 3 to 5pm in its stunning Lobby Bar overlooking a Japanese rock garden. A full tea—including finger sandwiches, cakes, pastries, and scones with Devonshire cream—is $12.50.

LATE NIGHT/24-HOUR

R. Thomas, mentioned above under "Light, Casual, and Fast Food," is open 24 hours weekends and closed only between 6 and 11am weekdays. The plant-filled, candlelit patio, warmed by heaters in winter, is Atlanta's favorite late-night locale. And you can eat food like Mom's round the clock at the **OK Cafe,** also noted above.

PICNIC FARE AND WHERE TO EAT IT

Best choice is **Partner's Pantry,** 1395 N. Highland Ave. (tel. 873-5899), a take-out place nonpareil run by the owners of Indigo Coastal Grill and Partner's, two of my very favorite Atlanta restaurants. You can get anything from roast-duck salad to cumin-spiced couscous with pine nuts and raisins, not to mention Caribbean lamb patties, pasta salads, stuffed Brie, and goat-cheese/black-bean enchiladas. Luscious desserts, too. There is no better picnic fare anywhere.

Another possibility, though it's a little out of the way, is the **DeKalb Farmer's Market,** 3000 E. Ponce de Leon Ave. (tel. 277-6400)—with 450 varieties of cheese alone!

Good places to picnic: Georgia's Stone Mountain, Piedmont or Grant Park, Château Elan, and Yellow River Wildlife Game Ranch (all described in Chapter 7, "What to See and Do in Atlanta").

WHAT TO SEE & DO IN ATLANTA

- **SUGGESTED ITINERARIES**
- **DID YOU KNOW . . . ?**
1. **THE TOP ATTRACTIONS**
- **DID YOU KNOW . . . ?**
- **FROMMER'S FAVORITE ATLANTA EXPERIENCES**
2. **MORE ATTRACTIONS**
3. **COOL FOR KIDS**
4. **ORGANIZED TOURS**
5. **SPORTS & RECREATION**

People used to say Atlanta was a great place to live, but you wouldn't want to visit. I'm happy to report that this is no longer the case. Atlanta offers numerous attractions—from one of the nation's most scenic parks to important black history landmarks, from a presidential center to a puppetry center. The area is rich in Civil War sites, and, in a related area, in *Gone With the Wind* memorabilia.

The best way to tackle it all is to read the comprehensive descriptions below and plan a personalized itinerary for your trip, allowing ample time to experience your selected sights. It's much more satisfying to see a few things in depth than to race around helter-skelter trying to see everything. There is no ideal agenda for everyone. The optimum plan depends on your interests, the amount of time you have, and whether or not you're traveling with kids. (*Note:* Don't pass up the attractions listed below as being of special interest to kids because you've reached man's estate; most of them will appeal to all age groups.) Do be sure to dress comfortably; tight shoes could sour you on the Taj Mahal. Visiting places near one another on the same day conserves time and energy. And I think taking long breaks (perhaps a 2-hour lunch or a picnic in the park) adds a lot to one's enjoyment.

MARTA stops close to attractions are listed where applicable. If you need bus-routing information, call 848-4711.

SUGGESTED ITINERARIES

IF YOU HAVE ONE DAY Head up to Buckhead and visit the Atlanta History Center—pretty much a full day's activity with house tours, museum exhibits, and woodland trails to explore. Have lunch at the Swan Coach House on the premises. If you have extra time

DID YOU KNOW . . . ?

- Atlanta has the largest mall in the Southeast (Lenox Square).
- Atlanta has the tallest escalator in the Southeast (at MARTA's Peachtree Center station—192 feet).
- Atlanta has the tallest hotel in the Western Hemisphere—the 723-foot, 73-story Westin Peachtree Plaza.
- Not a single scene from the movie *Gone With the Wind* was filmed in Georgia, though a few bushels of Georgia red clay were transported to the Hollywood set to add verisimilitude.
- Hartsfield is the world's third-busiest airport and is consistently ranked among the best airports in the world. Eighty percent of the United States population is within a 2-hour flight of Atlanta.

(and energy) in the afternoon, take a stroll around this beautiful neighborhood where almost every home is a mansion. From the History Center go south on Andrews Drive and/or west on West Paces Ferry Road. If the weather is not right for a leisurely stroll, head downtown to Underground Atlanta, see the shops and sights, and have dinner at Mick's. Or, take the New Georgia Railroad dinner train.

IF YOU HAVE TWO DAYS Follow the suggestions above on the first day. On the second day, get up early, go over to Auburn Avenue (see walking tour in Chapter 8), and visit the Martin Luther King, Jr., National Historic Site and surrounding attractions. In the afternoon, time and energy permitting, head over to Grant Park and see Cyclorama and/or Zoo Atlanta.

IF YOU HAVE THREE DAYS On your first two days, you should see as many of the sights described above as a comfortable pace allows. If the weather is fine on the morning of your last day, nothing could be more pleasurable than a day at Georgia's Stone Mountain Park. There's much to do and see here. In summer, be sure to stay late and see Lasershow.

On the other hand, if it's cold or rainy, plan a morning tour of the Carter Presidential Center or CNN Center, possibly doing the other in the afternoon.

IF YOU HAVE FIVE DAYS OR MORE Take it easy. Over the first four days, juggle the above suggestions as you see fit. On the fifth day, if you have kids, or you just like this kind of thing, now's the time for a little R&R. Go to Six Flags Over Georgia, White Water, or the marvelous Yellow River Wildlife Game Ranch. Civil War buffs should take in the Big Shanty Museum and Kennesaw Mountain/National Battlefield Park (both can be done in one day). Or do the Day 3 activity you didn't choose.

1. THE TOP ATTRACTIONS

These may or may not be the top attractions to you, and nowhere is it written that you have to see them all. Give equal consideration to attractions listed elsewhere in this chapter when planning your itinerary.

ATLANTA HISTORY CENTER, 3101 Andrews Dr. NW, off W. Paces Ferry Rd. Tel. 261-1837.

Dedicated to "preserving, protecting, and displaying information on the history of Atlanta," the Atlanta History Center (operated by the Atlanta Historical Society) maintains a vast collection of relevant photographs, maps, books, newspaper accounts, furnishings, Civil War artifacts, decorative arts, Margaret Mitchell memorabilia, and more. It occupies 32 woodland acres, with self-guided walking trails and six gardens that are each done in the style of a different historical period. Plan to spend the better part of a day here; there's much to do. And do call ahead, or inquire on the premises, about the comprehensive schedule of lectures, storytelling festivals, book signings, gardening symposia, sheep-shearing demonstrations, workshops for adults and children, and other events that take place here on a regular basis. Also check tour time for the day of your visit. You can have lunch at the delightful **Swan Coach House** restaurant on the premises (details in Chapter 6, "Atlanta Dining").

Begin your visit at **McElreath Hall,** which houses the center's archives and library and serves as an information/orientation center for visitors. A major exhibit in the hall is "Atlanta and the War: 1861–1865," which documents events that led to Sherman's attack on the city and the tragic aftermath. Displays include flags carried by Confederate units in the Battle of Atlanta, medical artifacts illustrative of the grim fate faced by ill or wounded soldiers (among other things, a Confederate doctor's kit always included a saw!), uniforms, "Great Locomotive Chase" memorabilia, weaponry, letters, maps, communiqués, military documents, Confederate money, tableaux of camp life, and Sherman's war wagon. A slide show elucidates the exhibits.

Also on the center's grounds is the **Swan House,** the 1928 estate of Edward Hamilton Inman, scion of an old Atlanta family and owner of one of the world's largest cotton brokerages. The house and gardens were designed by renowned architect Philip Trammell Shutze and are considered his finest residential work. The "swan" motif originated with Mrs. Inman, inspired by a pair of 18th-century swan console tables that you'll see in the dining room. The house is interesting not only architecturally but for its eclectic contents and furnishings, which comprise a veritable museum of decorative arts. Mr. Inman died three years after the house was completed at the age of 49, but his wife, Emily, lived here until her death in 1965.

Swan House is fronted by a classical colonnaded porte cochere, leading to a circular entrance hall with lofty Ionic columns and a dramatic spiral stairway. The formal gardens include terraced lawns and waterfalls, retaining walls with recessed ivied arches, and fountain statuary. In the entrance hall, you'll notice that the fanlight over the door centers on a swan, announcing the theme of the house.

The grand stair hall is furnished with 18th- and 19th-century English console tables, needlework side chairs, and a Chinese lacquer coromandel screen, one of many chinoiserie touches in the house.

The wood-paneled library centers on a 17th-century lime wood overmantel intricately carved with swags of fruit and flowers. The red silk Scalamandré sofa is typical of the oversized pieces that were a hallmark of 1920s interior design. Nineteenth-century Federalist mirrors reflect Mr. Inman's taste (she liked swans, he liked eagles). The 18th-century Dutch tall case clock, ornamented with marquetry, plays excerpts from hymns every half hour.

A Tabriz carpet graces the walnut floor of the living room. The room is painted mint green, a popular 1920s color, and its ceiling and moldings display elaborate Georgian plasterwork. The mantel is flanked by columns with carved Corinthian swan capitals, while two Venetian blackamoor tables (held up by carved Nubian slaves) are surmounted by Federalist mirrors (swans and eagles again).

Family china (including a lavender Royal Doulton set custom made for Tiffany) is displayed in the Aubusson-carpeted dining room. Here walls are covered in hand-painted chinoiserie paper, windows draped in silk rainbow plaid taffeta silk. Note the rococo marble-topped swan tables. The Inmans took their morning meal in a charming octagonal breakfast room, with windows overlooking woodland scenery and a beautifully detailed vaulted ceiling.

Upstairs, Mrs. Inman's bedroom is furnished with a high-post bed and a silk-upholstered Sheraton settee. Her adjoining faux-marble bathroom has a toilet hidden in a rattan chair and a huge-headed shower which must have provided heavenly cascades of water.

As you tour the house, you'll also see many museum-quality 17th- and 18th-century English paintings. And on the upstairs level is the Philip Shutze Collection of Decorative Arts—a marvelous array of china, silver, furnishings, rugs, and other art objects ranging from Chinese export porcelain to George Washington memorabilia. A must for aficionados, it can be seen only on tours weekdays at 11am and 3pm or by appointment. Half-hour tours of the house itself take place throughout the day on a continual basis.

Another major exhibit is "Atlanta Resurgens," tracing the growth of the city from 1865 to the present. Among its displays: artifacts of bitter Reconstruction days (including an actual Yankee carpetbag); copies of Amendments 13 through 15 to the Constitution, abolishing slavery and guaranteeing basic rights of all citizens; artifacts from the Cotton States and International Exposition of 1895; memorabilia from segregation days such as "white" and "colored" restroom signs; early Coca-Cola bottles; Margaret Mitchell's writing board and a first edition of *GWTW;* and much more. One room is devoted to the civil rights movement and Martin Luther King, Jr., another focuses on the Cotton States Exposition of 1895. There are also temporary exhibits.

The **Tullie Smith Farm** depicts the life of Georgia's mid-19th-century farmers. A 2-story "plantation-plain" house built in the early 1840s, it was brought here along with period outbuildings in 1969. The farm was originally located outside 1864 city limits, so it survived Atlanta's destruction during the Civil War. This was no Tara-like colonnaded mansion—just an everyday farmhouse whose occupants lived in rustic simplicity. The "plantation-plain" style derives from English architecture. It features a gabled roof with twin chimneys and a full front porch with a room at one end to lodge travelers and itinerant parsons. In premedia days, travelers were an important source of news.

In the Hall Room (today set up as a dining room, though rooms in the 19th-century did not have such defined functions), the furnishings are handcrafted, some of them painted with pigments made of buttermilk and Georgia red clay. A pine cabinet decorated with punched-tin sand-dollar-motif panels served as a "pie safe" in which leftover food was stored. The dining room table is set with historic Staffordshire china commemorating the War of 1812. Some children's toys are displayed.

The master bedroom has a rope bed with a feather mattress and a crib which was always occupied by the youngest baby. Here, demonstrations are given on a spinning wheel, and you'll learn that the term *spinster* derives from the fact that unmarried women had so much time to spin. A basket of pomander balls was typical—the 19th-century answer to today's air fresheners.

In a back room, there are weaving demonstrations, and a display shows natural materials used to dye yarns. Demonstrations of 19th-century hearth cookery (Brunswick stew, corn bread) take place in the whitewashed log kitchen, where game and herbs hang from the rafters. Additional outbuildings are a barn, corncrib, root cellar, blacksmith shop, and smokehouse. The gardens and grounds are authentic to the period. Costumed docents give tours throughout the day, and there are frequent demonstrations of 19th-century farm activities.

Leave some time to stroll the grounds, most notably the forested mile-long **Swan Woods Trail.** It includes plants native to Georgia and the Garden for Peace where you will see a sculpture by noted Soviet artist Georgi Dzhaparidze and Atlanta artist Hans Godo Frabel.

As we go to press, the center is constructing an 83,000-square-foot **Museum of Atlanta History** on its premises, which may be open by the time you read this. Neoclassic in design, to harmonize with the elegant Swan House, it will become the new point of entry to the entire Atlanta History Center complex. The centerpiece will be a permanent exhibit telling Atlanta's history through four periods—rural origins, development in the late 19th century as an important transportation center, 20th-century rise to prominence as a commercial city, and recent history. Other sections will focus on volatile periods, most notably the Civil War. The museum will also house the extensive DuBose Civil War Collection of over 5,000 objects, along with the Thomas S. Dickey Civil War Ordnance Collection and other extensive Civil War–related holdings. These will be exhibited in a permanent Civil War Gallery scheduled to open by 1996. Gallery space will also be alloted for permanent Margaret Mitchell and *Gone With the Wind* exhibits, the John A. Burrison Folklife Collection, and a large collection of costumes and textiles. There will be two Discovery Rooms featuring hands-on activities for children.

Admission: $6 for adults, $4.50 for seniors and students 18 or older, $3 for children 6–17, under 6 free. Thursday afternoons, from 1pm on, admission is free to all.

Open: Mon–Sat 9am–5:30pm, Sun and some holidays noon–5pm. **Closed:** Thanksgiving, Christmas Eve, Christmas, and New Year's Day. *Note:* The tour schedule for various buildings is rather complex; call ahead to find out tour hours for each attraction on the day of your visit. **MARTA:** Take MARTA rail to Lenox station, from there bus no. 23 to Peachtree Street and West Paces Ferry Road, walk three blocks west to Andrews Drive.

BIRTH HOME OF MARTIN LUTHER KING, JR., 501 Auburn Ave., at Hogue St. Tel. 331-3920.

Note: Tickets for a tour of the house must be obtained at the Martin Luther King Center at 499 Auburn Ave.

Martin Luther King, Jr., was born in this 2-story Queen Anne–style house on January 15, 1929, the oldest son of a Baptist minister and an elementary-school music teacher. His childhood was a normal one. He preferred playing baseball to piano lessons, liked to play Monopoly (his old set is in the study), and got a kick out of tearing the heads off his older sister's dolls. Nonviolence came later. To quote his sister, Christine King Farris, "My brother was no saint ordained at birth, instead he was an average and ordinary man, called by . . . God . . . to perform extraordinary deeds."

King lived here through the age of 12, then moved with his family to a house a few blocks away. A visit provides many insights into the boyhood of, and formative influences on, one of the greatest leaders of our time. The house, built in 1894, was originally owned by a white family. The Rev. A. D. Williams, King's maternal grandfather and pastor of Ebenezer Baptist Church, bought it in 1909. Reverend Williams was active not only in the church, but in the community and in the early manifestations of the civil rights movement. He was a charter member of Atlanta's NAACP and led a series of black registration and voting drives as far back as 1917. Martin Luther King, Sr., moved in on Thanksgiving Day, 1926, when he married Williams's daughter Alberta. When Reverend Williams died in 1931, Martin's father became head of the household and also took over the pulpit at Ebenezer Church.

The King family retained ownership of the house at 501 Auburn even after they moved away. Martin's younger brother, Alfred Daniel, lived here with his family from 1954 to 1963. In 1971, King's mother deeded the home to the Martin Luther King, Jr., Center, and a still-ongoing process of restoration began to return the house to its appearance during the years of Martin's boyhood. The furnishings, wallpapers, linoleums, and paint colors are all originals or similar period reproductions, and many personal items belonging to the family are on display.

Tours begin in the downstairs parlor, where you'll see family photographs showing Martin Luther King, Jr., as a child. The parlor was also used for choir practice, for the dreaded piano lessons, and as a rec room where the family gathered around the radio to listen to shows like "The Shadow." In the dining room, world events were regularly discussed over meals, and every Sunday, before dinner, each child was required to recite a newly learned Bible verse from memory. You'll also see the coal cellar (stoking coal was one of Martin's childhood chores); the children's play area; the upstairs bedroom of King's parents in which Christine, Martin, and Alfred Daniel were born, with a family physician attending; Reverend Williams's den, where he prepared his sermons and the family gathered for nightly Bible study; the bedroom Martin shared with his brother ("always in disarray," says Christine); and Christine's bedroom.

Admission: Free.

Open: Daily Sept–May 10am–5pm, June–Aug 10am–7pm, with half-hour tours given on a continuing basis throughout the day. **Closed:** Christmas, New Year's Day. **MARTA:** King Memorial Station, about eight blocks away.

MARTIN LUTHER KING, JR., CENTER FOR NON-VIOLENT SOCIAL CHANGE, 449 Auburn Ave., between Boulevard and Jackson St. Tel. 524-1956.

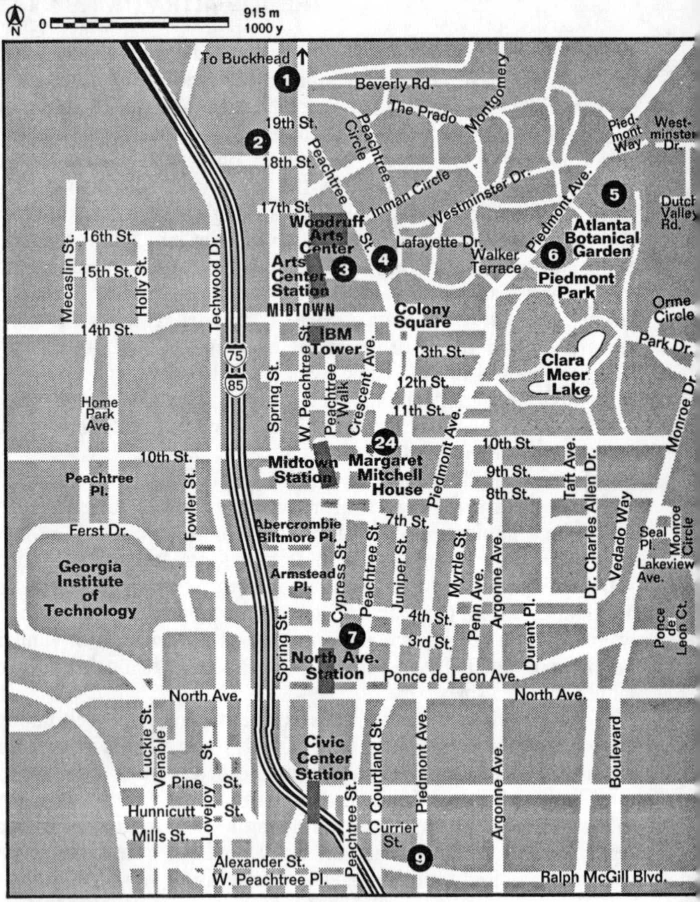

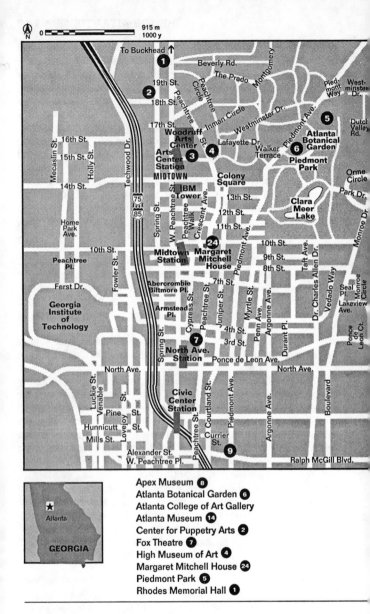

915 m
1000 y
N
0
To Buckhead
Beverly Rd.
The Prado
Montgomery
19th St.
18th St.
Peachtree Circle
Peachtree St.
17th St.
Inman Circle
Westminster Dr.
Piedmont Ave.
Pied-mont Way
West-minster Dr.
Dutch Valley Rd.
Woodruff Arts Center
Arts Center Station
Lafayette Dr.
Walker Terrace
Atlanta Botanical Garden
Piedmont Park
MIDTOWN
Colony Square
Orme Circle
Park Dr.
IBM Tower
13th St.
12th St.
11th St.
Clara Meer Lake
Monroe Dr.
16th St.
15th St.
14th St.
Mecaslin St.
Holly St.
Techwood Dr.
75
85
Spring St.
W. Peachtree St.
Peachtree Walk
Crescent Ave.
Home Park Ave.
10th St.
9th St.
8th St.
Midtown Station
Margaret Mitchell House
Peachtree Pl.
Fowler St.
Taft Ave.
Dr. Charles Allen Dr.
Vedado Way
Ferst Dr.
Abercrombie Biltmore Pl.
7th St.
Seal Pl.
Monroe Circle
Lakeview Ave.
Georgia Institute of Technology
Armstead Pl.
Cypress St.
Peachtree St.
Juniper St.
Myrtle St.
Penn Ave.
Argonne Ave.
Durant Pl.
4th St.
3rd St.
Ponce de Leon Ct.
North Ave. Station
Ponce de Leon Ave.
North Ave.
Luckie St.
Venable
Lovejoy St.
Pine St.
Hunnicutt St.
Mills St.
Civic Center Station
Courtland St.
Piedmont Ave.
Boulevard
Currier St.
Alexander St.
W. Peachtree Pl.
Ralph McGill Blvd.

Atlanta
GEORGIA

Apex Museum 8
Atlanta Botanical Garden 6
Atlanta College of Art Gallery
Atlanta Museum 14
Center for Puppetry Arts 2
Fox Theatre 7
High Museum of Art 4
Margaret Mitchell House 24
Piedmont Park 5
Rhodes Memorial Hall 1

★ Martin Luther King's commitment to nonviolent social change lives on at this memorial and educational center under the direction of Coretta Scott King. On the premises is an information counter where you can find out about all Auburn Avenue attractions and obtain tickets to tour the King birth home (details below). A nongovernmental member of the United Nations, the center works with government agencies and the private sector to

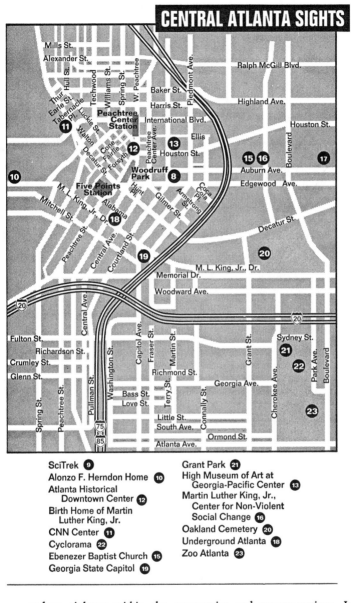

CENTRAL ATLANTA SIGHTS

SciTrek ❾

Alonzo F. Herndon Home ❿

Atlanta Historical
  Downtown Center ⓰⓶

Birth Home of Martin
  Luther King, Jr.

CNN Center ⓫

Cyclorama ⓶⓶

Ebenezer Baptist Church ⓯

Georgia State Capitol ⓲⓽

Grant Park ⓶⓵

High Museum of Art at
  Georgia-Pacific Center ⓭

Martin Luther King, Jr.,
  Center for Non-Violent
  Social Change ⓰

Oakland Cemetery ⓶⓪

Underground Atlanta ⓲⓭

Zoo Atlanta ⓶⓭

reduce violence within the community and among nations. It provides day care for low-income families, assists students in developing leadership skills in nonviolence, and holds workshops on topics like hunger and illiteracy. Its library and archives house the world's largest collection of books and other materials documenting the civil rights movement, including Dr. King's personal papers and a rare 87-volume edition of *The Collected Works of Mahatma Gandhi,* a

MARTIN LUTHER KING, JR., NATIONAL HISTORIC SITE

Under the auspices of the National Parks Service is an area of about 10 blocks around Auburn Avenue, established in 1980 to "preserve the birthplace and boyhood surroundings of the nation's foremost civil rights leader." It includes King's boyhood home and the Ebenezer Baptist Church, of which King, his father, and his grandfather were ministers. Other Auburn Avenue attractions, not under NPS auspices, include the Martin Luther King, Jr., Center for Non-Violent Social Change (where King is buried) and the APEX Museum.

The area is known as Sweet Auburn. John Wesley Dobbs, maternal grandfather of Atlanta mayor Maynard Jackson, is the person who first called it such, after Oliver Goldsmith's *The Deserted Village*, the first line of which reads, "Sweet Auburn! loveliest village of the plains." Mayor Jackson says his grandfather called the area "sweet" because the keys to black liberation existed here in the form of "the three b's—bucks, ballots, and books."

See Chapter 8, "Strolling Around Atlanta," for a walking tour of the area.

gift from the government of India. Equally important, it is Martin Luther King's final resting place, a living memorial to an inspiring leader which is visited by tens of thousands each year, including heads of foreign governments.

Visitors are given a self-guided tour brochure. The tour begins in the Exhibition Hall, where memorabilia of King and the civil rights movement are displayed in an exhibit called "King: Images of the Drum Major." Here you can see his Bible and clerical robe, a handwritten sermon, a photographic essay on his life and work, the Grammy Award King won for his "Why I Oppose the War in Vietnam" speech, and, on a grim note, the suit he was wearing when a deranged woman stabbed him in New York City and the key to his room at the Lorraine Motel in Memphis, Tennessee, where he was assassinated. In an alcove off the main exhibit area is a video display on Martin Luther King's life and works. Additional exhibits—including a room honoring Rosa Parks (whose refusal to give up her seat on a city bus led to the Montgomery bus boycott) and another honoring Gandhi—are in Freedom Hall.

Outside is Freedom Plaza, where Dr. King's white marble crypt rests on a beautiful 5-tiered Reflecting Pool, a symbol of the life-giving nature of water. The tomb is inscribed with his words: "Free at Last. Free at Last. Thank God Almighty I'm Free at Last." An eternal flame burns in a small circular pavilion directly fronting the crypt. The Freedom Walkway, a vaulted colonnade paralleling the pool, will eventually be painted with murals depicting the civil rights struggle. Located at the end of Freedom Walkway is the Chapel of All Faiths, symbolizing the ecumenical nature of Dr. King's work and the universality of the basic tenets of all the world's great religions.

A very important part of your visit is the Screening Room, where four excellent half-hour videos about Martin Luther King play continuously throughout the day. Enhanced by music that ranges from spirituals to rap, they show many of his most stirring sermons and speeches, including "I've Been to the Mountaintop" and "I Have a Dream"—speeches that are as much a part of America's heritage as the Gettysburg Address.

A store on the premises offers King memorabilia and a wide selection of books and cassettes. Inquire about events and workshops taking place during your stay. The annual Kingfest, from early June through mid-August, features music, theatrical performances, a kids' day, and many other events. And every October 2, Gandhi's birthday is celebrated with a party featuring Indian food. A very nice cafeteria is on the premises.

Admission: Free. To see the videos, adults pay $1, children 6–12 pay 50¢, under 6 free.

Open: Daily 9:30am–5:30pm. **Closed:** Thanksgiving, Christmas, New Year's Day. **MARTA:** Five Points.

APEX MUSEUM, 135 Auburn Ave., at Courtland St. Tel. 521-APEX.

Opened in 1985, the APEX (African-American Panoramic Experience) Museum both chronicles the history of Sweet Auburn,

---

 FROMMER'S FAVORITE ATLANTA EXPERIENCES

Afternoon Tea at the Ritz-Carlton Buckhead It's served in the lovely mahogany-paneled lobby lounge, where an oak-log fire crackles in the hearth and a classical pianist provides soothing background music. Fresh-baked scones with fruit preserves and Devonshire cream, finger sandwiches, English tea bread and tarts, and pots of your favorite tea.

Georgia's Stone Mountain Park A leisurely day spent seeing the sights, including lunch or bountiful buffet Sunday brunch at the Evergreen Conference Center and Resort.

Yellow River Wildlife Game Ranch A totally satisfying encounter of the four-legged kind. Bring a picnic lunch.

Atlanta's foremost black residential and business district, and serves as a national African American museum and cultural center. In the museum's Trolley Car Theater, a replica of a turn-of-the-century tram that ran on Auburn Avenue, you'll see a 12-minute multimedia presentation on the area's history narrated by Cicely Tyson and Julian Bond. Sweet Auburn history is also represented in tableaux such as a replica of the barbershop run by Alonzo Herndon and a re-creation of the Gate City Drugstore (Atlanta's first black pharmacy), including some original furnishings. There are also changing exhibits.

APEX is still in its infancy, but future plans call for its development into a major cultural force in the community, offering many programs for adults and children. Its aim is to "chronicle the history of the African American experience from early man in Africa to contemporary times." Do inquire about special events and workshops taking place during your visit to Atlanta.

Across the street from the APEX museum, at 100 Auburn Ave., is Herndon Plaza, where you can see a permanent exhibit on the Herndon family and changing shows of the works of African American artists.

Admission: $2 for adults, $1 for seniors and students, children under 5 free.

Open: Tues–Sat 10am–5pm, till 6pm Wed nights; also Sun 1–5pm Feb and June–Aug. **Closed:** Thanksgiving, Christmas, and New Year's Day. **MARTA:** Five Points.

EBENEZER BAPTIST CHURCH, 407–413 Auburn Ave. Tel. 688-7263.

Founded in 1886, Ebenezer was a spiritual center of the civil rights movement during the years 1960 to 1968, when Martin Luther King, Jr., served as copastor. His grandfather, the Rev. A. D. Williams, dedicated the church to "the advancement of black people and every righteous and social movement." Williams's activist example was followed by his son-in-law and successor, Martin Luther King, Sr., who worked for voting rights and other aspects of black civil and social advancement. Later, Martin Luther King, Jr., would join his forebears in pursuing justice for black Americans. You can listen to a taped message on the history of the church. An ecumenical service takes place here every year during King week.

Admission: Free.

Open: Mon–Fri 9:30am–noon and 1:30–4:30pm, Sun for services only at 7:45 and 10:45am. **MARTA:** King Memorial Station is about eight blocks away.

CYCLORAMA, 800 Cherokee Ave., in Grant Park. Tel. 624-1071 or 658-7625.

Though it sounds like something out of Disney World, this Cyclorama was created in the 1880s, and its concept—a huge, 360-degree cylindrical painting—dates back to a century earlier. Cycloramas were the rage of 18th- and 19th-century Europe, Russia, Japan, and later, the United States, depicting subject matter ranging from the splendors of Pompeii to Napoleonic battles. Enhanced by multimedia effects and faux-terrain dioramas extending 30 feet from the painting into the foreground, they were the forerunners of newsreels, travelogues, and TV war coverage.

The one you'll see here—a 42-foot-high cylindrical oil painting, 358 feet in circumference (on about 16,000 square feet of canvas)— depicts in meticulous detail the events of the Battle of Atlanta, July 22, 1864. It took 11 Eastern European artists, working in America in the studio of William Wehner, 22 months to complete. For 20th-century tourists, the concept itself is as interesting as the action depicted, and the restoration is incredibly impressive. Though painted on fine Belgian linen in the painstaking methodology of the 19th-century academies, the work suffered in moves from city to city, and later (when motion-picture epics made cycloramas passé) from neglect. Well-intentioned but incompetent attempts at restoration caused further damage, including the introduction of authentic Georgia red clay into the diorama battlefield area that brought in canvas-destroying beetles, vermin, and bacteria. In the 1970s, a severe storm waterlogged the painting, causing seemingly irreversible damage. But Mayor Maynard Jackson recognized the historic and artistic importance of Cyclorama; under his auspices $11 million was raised for its restoration. It took 2½ years for renowned conservator Gustav Berger and his crew to repair the damaged work, a process which included mending over 700 rips and tears in the canvas.

The fascinating story of Cyclorama's development and restoration is related in a video format near the auditorium entrance. After this orientation, visitors file into the auditorium, which has a rotating viewing platform, to view Cyclorama itself. Its central theme is General John B. Hood's desperate attempt to halt Sherman's inexorable advance into the city. Comprehensively narrated, and complete with music and sound effects including galloping horses and cannon fire, it vividly depicts the troop movements and battles of the day in which the Confederates lost 8,000 men, the Federals 3,722. A figure highlighted far beyond his historic importance is General John A. Logan of the Federal Army of Tennessee. He commissioned the painting at a cost of $42,000 as a campaign move in his bid for the vice presidency. He's shown gloriously galloping into the fray, bravely exposing himself and his men to enemy fire. The work was originally called *Logan's Great Battle.*

The building housing Cyclorama also comprises a museum of related artifacts, most importantly the steam locomotive Texas from the 1862 Great Locomotive Chase. Other exhibits include displays of Civil War arms and artillery, Civil War–themed paintings, portraits of Confederate and Union leaders, "life in camp" artifacts and photographs, and uniforms, as well as further elucidation of the Battle of Atlanta and Cyclorama. A bookstore on the premises is a repository of Civil War literature, including a sizable black history section.

Admission: $3.50 for adults, $3 for seniors, $2 for children 6–12, under 6 free (not recommended for very young children).

Open: Daily June–Sept 9:20am–5:30pm, Oct–May 9:20am–4:30pm. **Closed:** Thanksgiving, Christmas, New Year's Day, and Martin Luther King Day. **Bus:** Take Georgia Avenue bus No. 97 from Five Points Station.

OAKLAND CEMETERY, 248 Oakland Ave. SE; main entrance at Oakland Ave. and Martin Luther King Dr. Tel. 577-8163.

On the National Register of Historic Places, this outstanding 88-acre Victorian cemetery is one of the city's most important historic sites. Founded in 1850, it survived the Civil War and remained the only cemetery in Atlanta for 34 years. Among the over 48,000 people buried here are Confederate and Union soldiers (including five Southern generals), prominent families and paupers, governors and mayors, golfing great Bobby Jones, and Atlanta's most famous personage, Margaret Mitchell. There's a Jewish section (consecrated by a temple), a black section (dating from segregation days), and a potter's field. Two monuments honor the Confederate war dead. And standing at the marker that commemorates the Great Locomotive Chase, you can see the trees from which the Yankee raiders were hung (Confederate conductor Captain William Fuller is buried here).

Almost every grave has a story. Real-estate tycoon Jasper Newton Smith had a life-size statue of himself erected on his grave so he could watch the city's goings-on into eternity. The sculptor originally gave Smith a tie, but Smith, who never wore one, refused to pay for the piece until the tie was chiseled off. Dr. James Nissen, Oakland's first burial, feared being buried alive; his will stated that his jugular vein be severed prior to interment. And John Morgan Dye was a baby who died during the siege of Atlanta; his mother walked through the raging battle to the cemetery carrying the small corpse. The smallest grave, however, is that of "Tweet," a pet mockingbird buried in his family's lot. You'll also learn about graveyard symbolism on the tour: a lopped-tree-trunk marker indicates a life cut short or goals unachieved, rocks on a grave denote a life built on a solid foundation, a shell means resurrection, and so on.

The cemetery is renowned not only for historical reasons, but as an outdoor "museum" of Gothic and classical-revival mausolea, bronze urns, stained glass, and Victorian statuary. Atlanta residents also view Oakland's rolling terrain as parkland; dozens of people actually jog here every day, and picnickers are a common sight. Every October, there's a celebration to commemorate the cemetery's founding, with turn-of-the-century music, food, and storytelling. Though you can visit whenever the cemetery is open, do try to come when you can take a guided tour. It's fascinating.

Admission: Free.

Open: Daily sunrise to 7pm (6pm in winter); Visitor Center Mon–Fri 9am–5pm. Purchase an informative self-guide walking tour map/brochure at the Visitor Center for $1.25. **MARTA:** King Memorial. **Parking:** Inside the cemetery, near the Visitor Center.

GEORGIA'S STONE MOUNTAIN PARK, 16 miles east of downtown on U.S. 78. Tel. 498-5600.

✪ A monolithic gray granite outcropping (the world's largest), carved with a massive monument to the Confederacy, Stone Mountain is a distinctive landmark on Atlanta's horizon and the focal point of its major recreation area—3,200 acres of lakes and beautiful wooded parkland. It's Georgia's number-one tourist attraction.

Over half a century in the making, Stone Mountain's neoclassic carving is the world's largest piece of sculpture at 90 feet high and 190 feet wide. Originally conceived by Gutzon Borglum, it depicts Confederate leaders Jefferson Davis, Robert E. Lee, and Stonewall Jackson galloping on horseback throughout eternity. Borglum started work on the mountain sculpture in 1923; after 10 years he abandoned it, due to insurmountable technical problems and rifts with its sponsors. He went on to South Dakota, where he gained fame carving Mount Rushmore. No sign of his work remains at Stone Mountain, but it was his vision that inspired the project. Augustus Lukeman took over in 1925, but three years later, the work still far from complete, the family that owned the mountain lost patience and reclaimed the property. It wasn't until 1963, the state having purchased the mountain and surrounding property for a park, that work resumed under Walter Kirtland Hancock and Roy Faulkner. It was completed in 1970.

The best view of the mountain is from below, but you can ascend a walking trail up and down its moss-covered slopes, especially lovely in spring when they're blanketed in wildflowers, or take the narrated tram ride to the top. There are picnic tables at the summit, along with a snack bar and a gift shop. Trams run about every 20 minutes in both directions.

A highlight at Stone Mountain is **Lasershow,** a spectacular of laser lights and fireworks with animation and music. It begins in April (Friday, Saturday, and Sunday night at 9pm); from early May through Labor Day it can be seen nightly; then it resumes its Friday-through-Sunday schedule during September; Friday and Saturday night only in October. Don't miss it.

Other major park attractions include: the **Stone Mountain Scenic Railroad,** comprising three Civil War steam trains that chug around the 5-mile base of Stone Mountain. The ride takes 25 minutes. Trains depart from Memorial Depot, an old-fashioned train station with a very attractive restaurant on the premises serving chicken dinners with all the fixings; on its walls hang mural-size oil paintings of Native Americans and settlers done in the 1930s. Fronting the depot are a barbecue snack bar, lemonade and funnel-cake concessions, and the Ole Wood Cutter, an artist who makes handmade wood items.

The **Scarlett O'Hara,** a paddle-wheel riverboat, cruises the 363-acre Stone Mountain Lake.

The **Antique Auto & Music Museum** is a jumble of old radios, jukeboxes, working nickelodeons, pianos, Lionel trains, carousel horses, and clocks along with classic cars such as a 1925 Ford Model T truck, a 1948 Tucker, a 1928 Martin built for World War I ace General Billy Mitchell out of airplane parts, and an electric car.

The 19-building **Antebellum Plantation** offers self-guided tours assisted by hosts in period dress at each structure. Highlights include an authentic 1830s country store; the 1845 Kingston House (it represents a typical overseer's house); the clapboard slave cabins; the 1790s Thornton House, elegant home of a large landowner; the smokehouse and well; a doctor's office; a barn, a coach house, and crop-storage cribs; a necessary; a cook house; and the 1850 neoclassical Tara-like Dickey House. The grounds also contain formal gardens and a kitchen garden. It takes at least an hour to tour the entire complex (a map is provided at the entrance), really a major Atlanta sightseeing attraction in itself. Often (especially in summer), there are crafts and cooking demonstrations, medicine shows, storytellers, and balladeers on the premises. You can even take a 20-minute horse-drawn carriage ride around the area ($5 for adults, $3 for children 3 to 11; free for children under 3).

Confederate Hall, an information center, houses a large narrated exhibit called "The War in Georgia," a chronological picture story of the Civil War.

At **Memorial Hall,** another information center, a 9-minute tape on Stone Mountain history and geology is shown throughout the day. A Civil War museum is upstairs.

Additional activities: golf (on a top-rated 27-hole course designed by Robert Trent Jones), miniature golf, eight night-lighted Laykold tennis courts, an Olympic-size indoor skating rink (open year round), a sizable stretch of sandy lakefront beach with wonderful water slides, 20 acres of nature trails with natural animal habitats and a petting zoo, carillon concerts, boating (rowboats, canoes, sailboats, and paddleboats), bicycle rental, fishing, hiking, picnicking, and more.

Stone Mountain Park is one of the most beautiful parks in the nation. Consider spending a few days of your trip here; it's a great place for a romantic getaway or a family vacation. On-site accommodations are detailed in Chapter 5, "Atlanta Accommodations." If you can only spare a day, it's an easy drive (about 30 minutes) from downtown.

Admission: There's a parking charge of $5 a day, $20 annually (one-time-only charge if you stay on the grounds); major attractions are $2.50–$3 each for adults, $1.50–$2 for children 3–11, free for children under 3. A ticket for all six major attractions is $12.50 for adults, $7.50 for children.

Open: Year round, gates open 6am–midnight. Major attractions are open fall and winter 10am–5pm, spring and summer 10am–9pm. **Closed:** Attractions only are closed Christmas Day; park is open. **Train:** You can take the New Georgia Railroad from Underground Atlanta (90 Central Ave.). Departures every other Saturday at 10am and 2pm, returning at 3:15pm. For information call 404/656-0769.

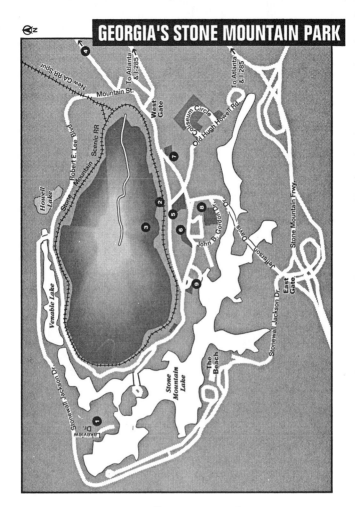

GEORGIA'S STONE MOUNTAIN PARK

Antebellum Plantation **8**
Antique Auto & Music Museum **7**
Confederate Hall **4**
Confederate Memorial Carving **3**
Evergreen Conference Center and Resort **1**
Lasershow **5**
Memorial Hall **6**
Scarlett O'Hara **9**
Stone Mountain Scenic Railroad **2**

THE CARTER PRESIDENTIAL CENTER AND LIBRARY, 1 Copenhill Ave., at N. Highland and Cleburne Aves. Tel. 331-3942.

Opened in October 1986, with four contemporary circular buildings on 30 acres of gardens, lakes, and waterfalls, this impressive presidential center includes a library housing some 27 million pages of documents, memoranda, and correspondence from Jimmy

Carter's White House years. There are also 1½ million photographs and hundreds of hours of audio- and videotapes, the latter documenting everything from meetings with world leaders to a footrace between the president and his daughter, Amy. However, Carter planned the facility as more than a repository for papers, books, and memorabilia. It is a place in which he continues to work on the agenda he began during his presidency. Under its auspices are the Carter Center of Emory University, an organization that conducts research and holds symposia on contemporary international issues; Global 2000, an organization that addresses international health and environmental issues; the Carter-Menil Human Rights Foundation; and the Task Force for Child Survival. The hilltop site of the Carter Center is a historic one, by the way; it was from this spot that Sherman watched the Battle of Atlanta.

In the facility's extensive museum, you'll see an exact replica of the Oval Office during Carter's presidency, an exhibit enhanced by a recording of Carter speaking about his experiences in that office. A large display of "gifts of state" runs the gamut from a Dresden figurine of George and Martha Washington (a gift from Ireland) to a bisque doll in a silk kimono given to Amy by the emperor of Japan. You'll see the table setting used when the Carters entertained Chinese vice premier Deng Xiaoping and his wife in the State Dining Room; a video of artists such as the late pianist Vladimir Horowitz performing in the East Room; campaign memorabilia; and a large display devoted to the activities of Rosalynn Carter. A changing exhibit area houses art shows.

Other exhibits focus on Carter's support of human rights (there's a letter from Soviet dissident Andrei Sakharov and Carter's reply); his boyhood (his sixth-grade report card and a photo of the Plains High baseball team are two of the items on display); and his prepresidential life as a peanut farmer, governor, and state senator. Of course, the major issues of his administration—the Middle East; the nuclear threat and SALT II talks; terrorism; the advent of formal diplomatic relations with China; and the environment—are featured in displays as well.

There are informative videos throughout, including an interactive "town meeting" format in which visitors can ask Carter questions on subjects ranging from world affairs to his personal life (and propose future questions for which he will tape answers). And a most interesting participatory video lets you choose your response to a terrorist crisis and learn the probable consequences of your choice.

Consider having lunch here. There's an attractive cafeteria on the premises with patio seating overlooking a Japanese garden and pond.

Admission: $2.50 for adults, $1.50 for seniors, free for children under 16.

Open: Mon–Sat 9am–4:45pm, Sun noon–4:45pm. **Closed:** New Year's Day, Thanksgiving, Christmas.

FERNBANK MUSEUM OF NATURAL HISTORY, 767 Clifton Rd., off Ponce de Leon Ave. Tel. 378-0127.

This brand-new $42.8 million museum (it actually opened after we went to press) is the largest museum of the natural sciences in the Southeast. It encompasses the 65-acre Fernbank Forest, the Fernbank Science Center (see details below under "Cool for Kids"), extensive gardens, greenhouses, and parklands. Be sure to see all these attractions when you visit.

In addition to its permanent exhibition area in a central Great Hall under a soaring 85-foot skylight, the museum has a 15,000-square-foot area for temporary traveling shows such as the Smithsonian's "Tropical Rainforest: A Disappearing Treasure." The major permanent exhibit, "A Walk Through Time in Georgia," uses the state as a microcosm to tell the story of the earth's development through time. Six regional galleries here re-create landform regions from the pine-forested Piedmont Plateau to the mossy Okefenokee Swamp.

In spacious discovery rooms children ages three to five can "pollinate" flowers and feed toy worms to mechanical baby birds. Older kids get to cast nets off a shrimp boat and sight birds from viewing platforms overlooking the "Blue Ridge Mountains." And, in the Robin Harris Naturalist Center, kids of all ages can watch scientists at work and categorize fossils, shells, and plant specimens they find along Fernbank's nature walks.

A highlight is an IMAX theater (the first in Georgia) which premiered the film *Mountain Gorillas,* shot in Rwanda, Africa. If you're not familiar with spectacular IMAX films (here shown on a screen measuring 52 feet by 70 feet), they're a not-to-be-missed attraction—a major thrill.

A pleasant dining room is on the premises, and a large museum shop focuses on educational merchandise.

Note: At presstime, hours of operation and admission prices are not yet established. Call before you go.

CNN CENTER, Marietta St. at Techwood Dr. Tel. 827-2300.

The CNN Center is headquarters for media magnate Ted Turner's 24-hour cable news networks, CNN and Headline News. During 45-minute guided tours, visitors get a behind-the-scenes look at the high-tech world of TV network news in action. You'll find the Tour Desk in the main lobby at the base of an 8-story escalator. While you're waiting for the tour to begin, have your photograph taken behind a CNN anchor desk replica.

Tours begin in an exhibit area where displays include MGM movie stills (Turner owns a portion of the MGM film library); a scaled-down model of the Galaxy One satellite that carries the signal for the company's networks; exhibits on Jacques Cousteau, John James Audubon, and *National Geographic* (all subjects of numerous specials on Turner-owned TBS); an exhibit on TBS sports (Turner owns the Atlanta Hawks and the Atlanta Braves); a duplicate of MGM's Oscar for *Gone With the Wind;* and items involved in CNN's much-lauded coverage of the Gulf War.

On another level, visitors observe the CNN newsroom from a glass-walled viewing station. You'll see the domestic and international desks, and writers in the process of composing news scripts. On a monitor, you can observe what newscasters are up to during their breaks (often chomping sandwiches). Tour guides are knowledgeable and can answer virtually any question.

There are over a dozen restaurants and fast-food outlets on the premises, a variety of shops, and a movie theater. The Turner Store on the premises carries network-logo clothing and gift items, along with MGM movie memorabilia (this is your chance to buy a Rhett Butler jack-in-the-box or a *Gone With The Wind* beach towel). There are frequent exhibits, concerts, crafts shows, and other special events in the atrium lobby; ask your tour guide what's on.

Admission: $5 for adults, $2.50 for seniors and children 6–12; under 5 free. *Note:* Tickets are available on a first-come, first-served basis on the day of the tour only. Arrive early for the tour you wish to take, since only 30 tickets are sold per tour, and they sometimes sell out.

Open: 45-minute tours are given on the hour Mon–Fri 10am–5pm, Sat–Sun 10am–4pm. **Closed:** New Year's Day, Easter, Memorial Day, July 4, Labor Day, Thanksgiving, and Dec 24–25. **MARTA:** Omni. **Parking:** Across the street in a lot.

HIGH MUSEUM OF ART, 1280 Peachtree St. NE, at 16th St. Tel. 892-3600 or 892-HIGH (24-hour information line).

The High Museum of Art, founded in 1926, opened its award-winning building in 1983. Designed by architect Richard Meier, this 135,000-square-foot, $20 million facility—part of the Woodruff Arts Center complex—is itself a work of art. A dazzling white porcelain-tiled edifice with an equally pristine white interior (the *New York Times* jokingly cautioned that visitors risk snow blindness on a sunny day), it houses four floors of galleries connected by semicircular pedestrian ramps girding a spacious, sun-filled, 4-story atrium. It's a very favorable setting in which to view art.

The permanent collection includes over 8,000 pieces, among them a significant group of 19th- and 20th-century American paintings. It features Hudson River school artists such as Thomas Cole and Frederic Church, as well as works by Thomas Sully, John Singer Sargent, and William Harnett. The Virginia Carroll Crawford Collection of American Decorative Arts comprehensively documents styles from 1825 to 1917. The Samuel H. Kress Foundation collection comprises Italian paintings and sculpture from the 14th through the 18th century. And the Uhry Print Collection contains important works by French impressionists and postimpressionists, German expressionists, and American 20th-century artists. Also notable are collections of sub-Saharan African art and works by noted 19th- and 20th-century American and European photographers.

In addition to its permanent collection, the museum hosts a

number of traveling exhibitions each year, complemented by films, lectures, workshops, gallery talks, concerts, and other cultural events. Recent temporary exhibits have focused on works of Edvard Munch, Rembrandt, Max Weber, landscape painters from Corot to Monet, and abstract expressionist drawings. Inquire at the desk about happenings during your stay, and call in advance to find out when you can take a free gallery tour (they're offered September through May only). When you visit, plan to have lunch at the superb Woodruff Arts Center restaurant, Chef's Grill (details in Chapter 6, "Atlanta Dining"). *Note:* There is a smaller branch of this museum at the Georgia-Pacific Center downtown (see "More Attractions," below).

Admission: $4 for adults, $2 for seniors and students with ID, $1 for children 6–17, children under 6 free. Free to all on Thurs 1–5pm.

Open: Tues–Sat 10am–5pm, Fri till 9pm, Sun noon–5pm. **Closed:** Mon, July 4, Thanksgiving, Christmas, and New Year's Day. **MARTA:** Arts Center. A parking garage is located on Lombardy Way between 15th and 16th Streets.

FOX THEATRE, 660 Peachtree St. NE, at Ponce de Leon Ave. Tel. 881-1977 for box office, 876-2040 for tours.

Originally conceived as a Shriners' temple in 1916, this lavish, block-long Moorish-Egyptian fantasyland ended up as a movie theater when the Shriners realized their grandiose conception had far exceeded their budget. In 1927, they sold the "temple" to movie magnate William Fox, who amended their plans and created a peerless pleasure palace. The building was designed by French architect Oliver J. Vinour (he trained at the Ecole des Beaux Arts in Paris), who utilized design motifs of the Middle East in his creation, including replicas of art and furnishings from King Tut's tomb.

Atlanta's new theater opened in 1929 as a masterpiece of Oriental splendor, its Moorish facade, onion domes, and minarets an exotic contrast to the surrounding Victorian boardinghouses. Brass-trimmed marble kiosks imported from France served as ticket booths. The 140-foot entrance arcade led to a lushly carpeted lobby with blue-tiled goldfish pools. And the auditorium was an Arabian courtyard under a twinkling starlit sky that could, with state-of-the-art technology, be transformed to a sunrise or sunset sky and produce rain, fog, and snow. A striped bedouin canopy sheltered the balcony, and sequin- and rhinestone-studded stage curtains depicted mosques and Moorish horsemen. As the show began, a gigantic gilded 3,610-pipe Möller organ rose majestically from its vault, its rich chords accompanied by a full orchestra. A medley of popular songs, cartoons, a follow-the-bouncing-ball sing-along, a stage-show extravaganza by a bevy of Rockette-like chorines called the Fanchon and Marco Sunkist Beauties, and a newsreel preceded every main feature. At night there were dances in the Egyptian Ballroom, designed to replicate King Solomon's temple. And even the men's lounge was exotically appointed with hieroglyphic adornments, winged scarab-motif friezes, bas reliefs of royal figures, and throne chairs.

Unfortunately, the Fox's opening coincided with the Great Depression, and it proved impossible to maintain its unstinting opulence. In 1932 the company declared bankruptcy and closed its doors. The theater reopened three years later for occasional concerts featuring cultural superstars such as Leopold Stokowski and Yehudi Menuhin. By the forties, it was a viable concern once more, and in 1947 the Metropolitan Opera began a 20-year stint of week-long performances here. An oversize panoramic screen was installed in the 1950s, along with a 26-speaker stereophonic system. But like monumental movie palaces nationwide, the Fox inevitably declined in the age of television. In 1975 its doors were padlocked once again.

An organization of concerned citizens calling themselves Atlanta Landmarks raised $1.8 million and saved the Fox from the wrecking ball in 1978, foiling Southern Bell's plans to purchase and demolish it to make way for a regional headquarters building. Ever since, it's been a thriving entity, featuring Broadway shows, headliners (Ray Charles, Liza Minelli, Ben Vereen), dance companies such as Alvin Ailey, and comedy stars such as Jay Leno and Whoopi Goldberg. A big event every summer is the Fox Summer Film Festival, which features organ concerts, sing-alongs, and cartoons with classic and current blockbuster movies (see the "Calendar of Events" in Chapter 2 for details). Best of all, the theater has been restored to its former glory, its fabulous furnishings and fixtures, terrazzo-tile floors and elaborately stenciled ceilings, gilded columns and velvet draperies all refurbished or replaced with replicas.

To tour the Fox is to enter the fantasy world of Hollywood's heyday—a world in which dreams usually do come true and adventures abound. I highly recommend the tour, but perhaps the best way to experience the Fox is to attend a show. I guarantee you'll be caught up in its glamorous mystique.

Admission: Tours cost $5 for adults, $3 for seniors and students.

Open: The Atlanta Preservation Center conducts walking tours of the Fox Theatre and its surrounding area Mon and Thurs at 10am and Sat at 10 and 11:30am. **MARTA:** North Avenue.

ATLANTA BOTANICAL GARDEN, in Piedmont Park, at Piedmont Ave. and the Prado. Tel. 876-5858.

This delightful botanical garden, occupying 30 acres in Piedmont Park, was founded in 1977 and has since expanded considerably. It consists of three main sections. **The Gardens,** designed to be an inspiration to the local horticultural set, highlight plants that flourish in North Georgia's extended growing season. Displays in this section include an ivy collection, a group of grass plots (a helpful exhibit for Georgian homeowners choosing lawn grass), an English knot-designed Herb Garden, a tranquil moongated Japanese Garden, a Rose Garden, and a Fragrance Garden built for the blind. These lovely gardens are enhanced by fountains, stone statuary, benches, and pagodas. Lunch is served Tuesday to Sunday from April through October on Lanier Terrace, overlooking the Rose Garden.

Two natural arboretum settings comprising 15 acres of hardwood forest are the **Upper Woodlands,** with a paved path, a fern glade and camellia garden, and beautiful statuary, and the still more rustic **Storza Woods,** with an unpaved path. Both make for easy and very pleasant walks.

Most exciting is the 16,000-square-foot, glass-walled **Dorothy Chapman Fuqua Conservatory,** opened in 1989 to house rare and endangered plants from exotic climes. With 54 acres of irreplaceable rain forest being bulldozed every minute, facilities such as this provide a much-needed haven for technology-threatened plant species. Approached via an arbored promenade and fronted by a lotus pond, the conservatory has a revolving globe outside its entrance showing the many regions worldwide where plant life is endangered. An interactive video display enhances visitor understanding of exhibits.

The focal point of the conservatory is the misty Tropical Rotunda, housing fern collections, old-world succulents, cycads (the most primitive seed-bearing plants known), epiphytes (plants that don't require soil to grow), gorgeous orchids, carnivorous plants (always intriguing), a wide variety of begonias, and towering tropical palms. Its a lush and humid jungle, with brightly hued native birds warbling overhead, a splashing waterfall, and winding pathways lined with fragrant hibiscus, gardenias, and flowering jasmine vines. Of special interest is a double coconut palm seed from the Seychelles, the largest and heaviest seed in the plant kingdom. Its first 12-foot leaves have already begun to grow, but it will be 100 years before the tree reaches its full height.

The arid Mediterranean/Desert House displays Madagascar succulents such as a unique family of spiky plants called Didieriaceae. Here, too, are "living stones" (desert succulents that nature designed to look like pebbles to protect them from being eaten by animals), tree aloes, Caudiciforms (with swollen stems and roots for storing water), eucalyptus trees from Australia, and conifers from Africa and the Canary Islands. Adjoining is an area for special exhibits.

The building also houses an orangery of rare tropical mango, papaya, star fruit, lychee, coffee, and citrus trees.

There are flower shows throughout the year, along with lectures and other activities. Call to find out what's on during your stay. A marvelous gift shop is on the premises; your purchases help support the garden.

Admission: $4.50 for adults, $2.25 for seniors and children 6–12, children under 6 free. Admission is free every Thurs 1pm to closing. Parking is free on the premises.

Open: Tues–Sun 9am–6pm, till 8pm during daylight savings time.

GEORGIA STATE CAPITOL, Capitol Hill at Washington St. Tel. 656-2844.

After the Revolutionary War, Georgia's capital, first situated in Louisville, rotated for many years between Augusta and Savannah. In

1807, westward expansion of the state caused the capital to be moved to Milledgeville, a more central location, which remained the seat of Georgia government for 61 years. It wasn't until after the Civil War (1868) that Atlanta became, once and for all, the state capital; its present capitol building, completed July 4, 1889, was hailed as a testament to the city's recovery. Assuming office in the new building, Governor (and former Confederate general) John Brown Gordon eloquently expressed the sentiments of his consituency: "Built upon the crowning hill of her capital city, whose transformation from desolation and ashes to life . . . and beauty so aptly symbolizes the State's resurrection, this proud structure will stand through the coming centuries as a fit memorial to the indomitable will of this people." And so it does.

Modeled after the nation's Capitol, another neoclassical edifice atop a "crowning hill," its 75-foot dome, covered in 24-karat gold leaf and topped by a statue of Liberty, is a major Atlanta landmark. The building is fronted by a massive 4-story portico with a pediment supported by six Corinthian columns set on large stone piers. Engraved on the pediment is the Great Seal of State, flanked by two figures representing Georgia agriculture and commerce. Inside the magnificent rotunda, with its soaring 237-foot ceiling, are busts of famous Georgians, including signers of the Declaration of Independence and the Constitution.

Tours begin in the entrance hallway of the Main Floor, this level also serving as an information center for city and state attractions. The governor's office is off the main hall. The tours take 45 minutes; allow at least another 30 minutes to browse around on your own after the tour. Highlights of the grounds are detailed in a brochure available at the tour desk. *Note:* Your bag will be searched when you enter.

On the main floor, you'll see display cases of bullet-ridden Georgia Civil War flags and portraits of past governors. Flags suspended from the fourth-floor balustrades can be seen in the Hall of State Flags on this level in the South Wing. Flags that have flown over Georgia (including the British flag and several flags of the Confederacy) are displayed in the Hall of Flags, to the north of the Rotunda. Also in the North Wing are additional governors' portraits, busts of famous Georgians, and a portrait of Martin Luther King, Jr., backed by the Lincoln Memorial.

Grand staircases in both wings rise to the fourth floor, where you'll enter the house of representatives, and, across the hall, the senate chambers. The legislature meets for 40 days, beginning the second Monday in January (it can also be called into special sessions); all of its sessions are open to the public. The fourth floor additionally houses the State Museum of Science & Industry, with exhibits on cotton, peach, and peanut growing; cases of stuffed birds, fish, deer, insects, and other species native to Georgia; weaponry; rocks and minerals; Indian artifacts; and more.

Some events of note: The week before Thanksgiving is Indian Heritage Week at the capitol. A wattle-and-daub Indian dwelling is constructed in the rotunda, and there are Native American lecturers, music, and arts-and-crafts demonstrations. At Christmas, a beautifully decorated 40-foot tree adorns the rotunda. And on January 15, Martin Luther King, Jr's., birthday, there's an annual memorial program; local dignitaries, including the governor, give speeches, and King's family attends.

Admission: Free.

Open: Mon–Fri 8am–5:30pm, Sat 10am–2pm, Sun 1–3pm. Tours are given weekdays only at 10 and 11am and 1 and 2pm. **Closed:** Major holidays, including state holidays. **MARTA:** Georgia State. **Parking:** Lot behind the capitol building on Capitol Avenue is closed to the public during legislative sessions; other lots are on M. L. King Drive at Central Avenue and on Courtland Street between M. L. King Drive and Central Avenue.

UNDERGROUND ATLANTA, bounded by Wall St., Washington St., Martin Luther King, Jr., Dr., and Peachtree St. Tel. 523-2311.

The site of Underground Atlanta is the historic hub of the city, centered on the Zero Milepost that marked the terminus of the Western & Atlantic Railroad in the 1800s. For many years a flourishing locale, the area became so congested in the early 1900s that permanent concrete viaducts were constructed over it, elevating the street system and routing traffic over a maze of railroad tracks. Merchants moved their operations up to the new level, using the lower level for storage space. For most of the 20th century, it remained a deserted catacomb. Then, in 1969, a group of Atlanta businesspeople decided to create an underground entertainment complex of restaurants, shops, and bars in a setting that retained the historic feel of the area. The idea was great, but perhaps the time wasn't right; the complex declined and closed after a little over a decade. More recently, under the auspices of the Rouse Company (operators of New York's South Street Seaport, Baltimore's Harborplace, and Boston's Faneuil Hall), it has become Atlanta's most ballyhooed sightseeing extravaganza.

Occupying 12 acres in the center of downtown, this $142 million entertainment mecca and spirited urban marketplace opened in June 1989. It is heralded by a beacon of oscillating searchlights emanating from a 138-foot light tower, an outdoor staging area used for performances and concerts, and the cascading waters of Peachtree Fountain Plaza. It offers over 100 retail shops with period facades; establishments range from Christmas-year-round to Everything's a Dollar stores, as well as emporia featuring gift items, trendy apparel for men and women, and a wide array of other merchandise. Humbug Square—where street vendors and con artists flourished in the early 1900s—is again a colorful street market with turn-of-the-century pushcarts and wagons displaying offbeat wares. Specialty foods are sold in Packinghouse Row, a site on which meat packers and food wholesalers operated in the 1800s. Clustered around a section called Kenny's Alley, over a dozen restaurants and nightclubs (see Chapter 10, "Atlanta Nights") offer a wide spectrum of food and entertainment. And like Rouse projects everywhere, the Underground has a food court purveying everything from egg rolls to stuffed baked potatoes.

Markers throughout the complex indicate historic sites, and the Atlanta Convention and Visitors Bureau maintains an information center at Underground on the corner of Pryor and Alabama streets: The New Georgia Railroad (tel. 656-0769), a restored vintage train, has its central depot here. You can take an 18-mile Atlanta Loop tour, go to Georgia's Stone Mountain, or enjoy a romantic dinner ride. Details in Chapter 10.

Admission: Free. There is a charge for parking in the garage on Central Avenue off Martin Luther King Drive, but it's reduced if you get your ticket validated at a store or restaurant.

Open: Mon–Sat 10am–9:30pm, Sun noon–6pm. Most restaurants and clubs stay open until midnight (or later) nightly. **MARTA:** Five Points Station has a short pedestrian tunnel that connects directly with Underground Atlanta.

HERITAGE ROW, 55 Upper Alabama St., in Underground Atlanta. Tel. 584-7879.

This informative and highly entertaining attraction tells the story of Atlanta from its humble beginnings as a wilderness village through its eventful 200-year history to its present-day status as an international city. It's divided into six themed sections. Your journey through history begins in "Origins" with the Cherokee and Creek Native Americans who resided near the Chattahoochee River for centuries before Europeans arrived. You'll view the virgin forest that surveyor Stephen Long saw in 1837 when he drove the Zero Mile Post stake marking the terminus of the Western & Atlantic Railroad. An 1845 train depot is re-created. The scenes are enhanced with audio recordings; you'll hear Creek music and train whistles, even the sound of Long driving in the stake.

As you pass through the train station doorway, you'll enter the "Civil War" area. Amidst bombed rubble, with shells bursting in the background, you'll hear readings of the poignant diaries of people who experienced the siege of Atlanta.

In "Atlanta Resurgens—the New South" (through 1895), skyscrapers go up as Atlantans begin recovering from the ravages of war. In a reconstruction of *Atlanta Constitution* editor Henry Grady's office you can hear excerpts from his famous speech advancing the ideals of the "New South." Another audio enhancement is Sousa's "King Cotton March," composed in honor of the 1895 Cotton States and International Exposition in Piedmont Park.

"Forward Atlanta" (through 1945) deals with the surge in the business community and prominent roles played by major companies. It also examines the Jim Crow Laws and the prosperous black-owned stores and businesses and thriving music scene that grew Sweet Auburn, partially because of the segregation laws. You can listen to 12 minutes of Atlanta blues and country-music greats like Fiddlin' John Carson and Bessie Smith. Displays include a walk-through 1920s trolley car, and a video takes you to the movie premiere of *Gone With the Wind*.

"Big League City" (through 1974) documents Atlanta's continued emergence as a business center and as the cradle of the civil rights movement. Stand behind Martin Luther King's pulpit here, while listening to his stirring "I Have A Dream" speech, and view a video of Mayor Hartsfield peacefully integrating the public schools. Also heralded in this section is the arrival of big-time sports in Atlanta.

Transportation and communications are the themes of the final "International City" area, focusing on the role of Turner Broadcasting and Delta Air Lines. You can step inside a 1970 Convair 880 Delta jet cockpit (photos inside contrast the infinitely more complex controls of a present-day jet) and listen to pilots conversing with the tower at Hartsfield International Airport. Baseball buffs will enjoy a video of Hank Aaron's record-breaking home run. The tour ends with a 15-minute high-tech, wide-screen video called *People: The Spirit of Atlanta,* a tapestry of songs, stories, and interviews with community leaders and ordinary citizens. Heritage Row was created by a prestigious committee of historians, and they've done a superb job.

Admission: Adults $3, children 13–18 and seniors $3.50, children 4–12 $2, 3 and under free.

Open: Tues–Sat 10am–5pm, Sun 1–5pm. **Closed:** Mon.

MARTA: Five Points. **Parking:** In garage on Central Avenue off Martin Luther King Dr.

THE WORLD OF COCA-COLA, 55 Martin Luther King Dr. SW, at Central Avenue, adjacent to Underground Atlanta. Tel. 676-5151.

This exposition-like attraction showcases "the world's most popular product." Its vast 3-story pavilion houses a vast collection of Coca-Cola memorabilia, along with numerous interactive displays, high-tech exhibits, and video presentations. A self-guided tour begins on the third level where visitors are greeted by a Rube Goldberg–like kinetic sculpture called a "Bottling Fantasy." Exhibits throughout trace the history of Coca-Cola from its 1886 debut at Jacob's Pharmacy in downtown Atlanta to its current worldwide fame. Highlights include: displays of antique bottling equipment; a re-creation of Barnes Soda Fountain in Baxley, Georgia (ca. 1930), where a soda jerk dispenses Coke lore while making Coke ice-cream floats (a jukebox on the premises plays Coke-themed pop songs of yesteryear like "Sweet Coca-Cola Bush" sung by Shirley Temple); diverse advertising campaigns over the years (did you know that Maxwell House's "good to the last drop" was originally a Coke slogan?); Coke-themed toys, trays, school supplies, games, and the like; a video on the making of the "Hilltop Reunion" Coke commercial (it kicked off the "I'd Like to Teach the World to Sing" campaign); print ads featuring screen stars such as Jean Harlow

Claudette Colbert, Clark Gable, and Cary Grant; and an interactive audio exhibit that lets you listen to Coke commercials sung by pop stars like Al Jarreau, Loretta Lynn, Jerry Lee Lewis, and the Supremes. A high-tech film on the third floor called *Every Day of Your Life* highlights Coca-Cola consumption in over a dozen countries on six continents—from the Imperial Palace of Thailand to the Masai Steppe of Africa. And, in case you've worked up a thirst by this time, you can sample unlimited amounts of 38 Coca-Cola Company beverages at Club Coca-Cola, including 18 international drinks that are not sold in the United States (for example, a pineapple/orange/banana beverage marketed only in Kenya). The tour ends in the first-floor gift shop, which vends a mind-boggling array of Coke-motif items—everything from T-shirts to battery-operated break-dancing Coke cans. There's much, much more; this experience is a total immersion in Coca-Cola.

Admission: Adults $2.50, seniors over 55 $2, children 6–12 $1.50, under 6 free.

Open: Mon–Sat 10am–9:30pm, Sun noon–6pm; last entry one hour before closing time. **Closed:** New Year's Day, Easter, Thanksgiving, Christmas Eve, and Christmas Day.

MARTA: Five Points. **Parking:** Garage on Central Avenue off Martin Luther King Drive.

MICHAEL C. CARLOS MUSEUM OF EMORY UNIVERSITY, 571 S. Kilgo St., near the intersection of Oxford and N. Decatur Rds. on the Main Quadrangle of the Emory Campus. Tel. 727-4282.

Emory University's antiquities collection dates to 1875 and this intriguing museum to 1919, when it was founded to display the art and artifacts collected by Emory faculty in Egypt, Cyprus, Greece, Sicily, the Sea of Galilee, and the sites of ancient Babylon and Palestine. Today the museum also maintains collections of ancient art and archaeology of Rome, Central and South America, the Near East, and Mesoamerica; works of the native cultures of North America; and art and ethnology of Asia, Africa, and Oceania. And a sizable collection of works on paper encompasses illuminated manuscript pages, drawings, and prints from the Middle Ages and the Renaissance to the 20th century. It's all housed in a 1916 beaux-arts building which is on the National Register of Historic Places, its interior redesigned in 1985 by postmodernist architect Michael Graves. At this writing, a major expansion (also by Graves) is underway which will add 35,000 square feet of exhibition space to the facility.

The first-floor galleries feature changing exhibits from the extensive permanent collection—objects that were part of the daily life of people from three continents as early as the third millenium B.C. They include Bronze and Iron Age clay pots, jugs, loom weights, and oil lamps from Palestine; Egyptian mummies, pottery, cosmetic containers, and headrests; Greek and Cypriot pottery, flasks, and statuary; and Mesopotamian pottery, coins, tools, sculpture, and cuneiform tablets inscribed with ancient writing. Also on this level: the Thibadeau Pre-Columbian collection, comprising over 1,300 objects spanning 2,000 years of creativity—gold jewelry, pottery, and statues, including many ceramic, volcanic stone, greenstone, and gold sculptures from ancient Costa Rica.

The upper floor is used for changing exhibits ranging in subject matter from Pueblo Indian pottery to impressionist art. This level also houses a café serving light fare. Throughout the museum, 210 plaster casts of ancient architectural elements—reliefs, friezes, column capitals, and decorative elements from temples and monuments—adorn hallway and lobby walls. There are many interesting workshops, lectures, films, and gallery tours here; call to find out what's on during your stay.

Admission: A donation of $2 is suggested.

Open: Tues–Sat 10am–4:30pm, Sun noon–5pm. **Closed:** New Year's Day, July 4, Thanksgiving, and Christmas.

2. MORE ATTRACTIONS

CHATEAU ELAN VINEYARDS, exit 48 off I-85 in Braselton. Tel. 867-8200 or toll free in Georgia 800/233-WINE.

The town of Braselton, about 30 miles north of downtown Atlanta, is one I'll be watching with interest. Actress Kim Basinger bought the town for $20 million a few years ago, rumor has it to put up a movie studio. Meanwhile, Braselton's premier attraction is Château Elan, a hilltop winery that replicates a 16th-century French estate surrounded by verdant countryside. Its first wines were produced in 1985, and already they have garnered over 140 awards. There's much to do here. Guided tours are given every hour on the hour between 11am and 4pm (you can take self-guided tours from 5pm to closing).

On view are the crushing and pressing machines, oak barrels used to age and flavor wines, the cask room, and the bottling area. Tours conclude with a wine tasting. Vines ripen in July/August, so if you're here during harvesting in August and September, you'll actually see the winemaking procedure. About 300 tons of grapes are harvested and processed each year. The interior of the château, a stage-set version of a Paris street, has a quarry-stone floor, wrought-iron fences, and streetlamps. Walls are adorned with large murals depicting the history of winemaking and two Parisian sites—the train station Gare du Nord and the place des Vosges. The building houses an art gallery offering changing exhibits by regional and national artists, displays of antique European winemaking equipment, and a wine market.

There are also two on-premises restaurants, so plan to dine here. Café Elan, open daily from 10am (closing hours vary; call before you go), features sandwiches, salads, and continental entrées like chicken

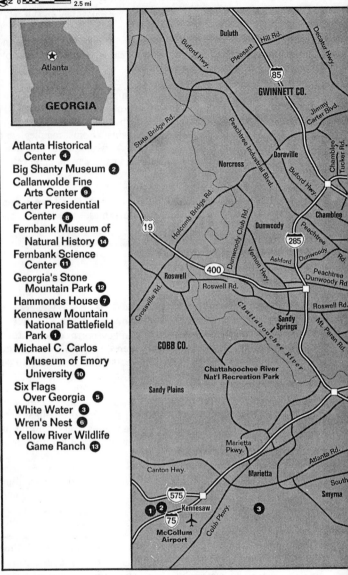

Atlanta Historical Center ④

Big Shanty Museum ②

Callanwolde Fine Arts Center ⑨

Carter Presidential Center ⑧

Fernbank Museum of Natural History ⑭

Fernbank Science Center ⑪

Georgia's Stone Mountain Park ⑫

Hammonds House ⑦

Kennesaw Mountain National Battlefield Park ①

Michael C. Carlos Museum of Emory University ⑩

Six Flags Over Georgia ⑤

White Water ③

Wren's Nest ⑥

Yellow River Wildlife Game Ranch ⑬

sautéed with pecans in red-wine cream sauce for $5 to $7 at lunch, $13.50 to $17.50 at dinner. It's a charming setting, with seating under a green awning. The fancier Le Clos—with pale pink walls, lace-curtained French doors, and tables covered with crisp white linen—is open for dinner only Thursday, Friday, and Saturday evenings, with seatings at 6:30 and 8:30pm. A five-course prix-fixe meal ($40 to $55) features haute-cuisine entrées such as Barbarie duck breast with

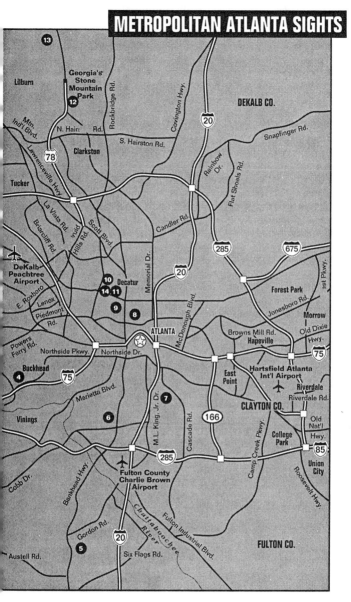

cerise sauce and Dover sole aux champignons meunière; appropriate wines with each course are included. Reservations are imperative. Men are requested to wear a coat and tie. A final dining option: picnic areas on the lovely grounds; custom picnic baskets can be purchased here.

In addition to its interior attractions, Château Elan has nature trails along St. Emilion Creek (forested with tulip poplar, oak, hickory, and beech trees) and by Romanée-Conti pond. Every Saturday evening from Memorial Day to Labor Day there's dancing to live music (fifties and sixties beach songs) in an adjoining outdoor facility called Le Pavillon. An admission cost of $27.50 per person includes dinner (without dinner, $20). Entertainment begins at 7:30pm, but you should arrive at least an hour earlier. In addition, there are numerous events at Château Elan—call to find out what's on during your stay. A gorgeous 18-hole golf course is on the grounds, and a spa and country inn are in the works for the future. If all that's not enough to do, there are designer-outlet malls close by.

Admission: Free.

Open: Daily 10am–10pm. **Closed:** Christmas.

BIG SHANTY MUSEUM, 2829 Cherokee St., Kennesaw. Tel. 427-2117.

On this site began the wild adventure known as "the Great Locomotive Chase." The Civil War had been under way for a year on April 12, 1862, when Union spy James J. Andrews and a group of 21 Northern soldiers disguised as civilians boarded a locomotive called the General in Marietta, buying tickets for diverse destinations to avert suspicion. When the train made a breakfast stop at the Lacy Hotel in Big Shanty, they seized the locomotive and several boxcars and fled northward to Chattanooga. The goal of these daring raiders was to destroy tracks, telegraph wires, and bridges behind them, thus cutting off the Confederate supply route between Virginia and Mississippi.

Conductor William A. Fuller, his breakfast interrupted by the sound of the General chugging out of the station, gave chase on foot, then grabbed a platform car and poled along the tracks. With him were a railroad superintendent and the General's engineer. At the Etowah River, Fuller and crew commandeered a small locomotive called the Yonah and made better progress. Meanwhile, the raiders tore up track behind them, and when the pursuers got close, the raiders slowed them down by throwing ties and firewood onto the tracks. Andrews, a very smooth talker, managed to convince station attendants en route that he was on an emergency mission running ammunition to Confederate general Beauregard in Mississippi. Fuller's chances of catching the General improved when he seized the southbound Texas and began running it backward toward the raiders, picking up reinforcements along the way and eventually managing to get a telegraph message through to General Danville Leadbetter, commander at Chattanooga. The chase went on, with Andrews sending uncoupled boxcars careening back toward Fuller as obstructions. Fuller, however, who was running in reverse, merely attached the rolling boxcars to his engine and kept on. At the wooden-covered Oostanaula bridge, the raiders detached a boxcar and set it on fire in hopes of finally creating an impassable obstacle—a burning bridge behind them. But the Texas was able to push the flaming car off the bridge; it soon burned out, and Fuller tossed it off the track and continued.

By this time the General was running low on fuel and water, the Texas was hot on its heels, and the raiders realized that all was lost. Andrews gave his final command: "Jump off and scatter! Every man for himself!" All were captured and imprisoned within a few days. Some escaped, others were exchanged for Confederate prisoners of war, and the rest were hung in Atlanta, most of them at a site near Oakland Cemetery. Though the mission failed, the raiders, some of them posthumously, received the newly created Congressional Medal of Honor for their valor.

The Big Shanty Museum, occupying a building that was once the Frey cotton gin, houses the General (still in running condition, but don't get any ideas), exhibits of Civil War artifacts, memorabilia and photographs relating to the chase and its participants, and, for good measure, a *Gone With the Wind* exhibit. You can view a 20-minute narrated video about the chase, but if you really want the full story rent the Disney movie, *The Great Locomotive Chase,* starring Fess Parker as the dashing Andrews. To get here, take exit 117 off I-75N and follow the signs. It takes about a half hour. The museum is three miles from Kennesaw Mountain/National Battlefield Park (details below), so consider visiting both of these Civil War–related sights the same day.

Admission: $2.50 for adults, $2 for seniors, $1 for children 7–15; children 6 and under free. Families pay a maximum of $10.

Open: Mar–Nov, Mon–Sat 9:30am–5:30pm; Dec–Feb, Mon–Fri 10am–4pm, Sat 10am–5:30pm, Sun noon–5:30pm.

KENNESAW MOUNTAIN/NATIONAL BATTLEFIELD PARK, Old Highway 41 and Stilesboro Rd., Marietta. Tel. 427-4686.

This 2,882-acre park was established in 1917 on the site of a crucial Civil War battle in the Atlanta campaign of 1863–64. A very popular attraction—perhaps because it commemorates a Confederate victory—it draws some 75,000 visitors annually. The action began in June 1864. A few months earlier, Gen. Ulysses S. Grant had ordered Sherman to attack the Confederate army in Georgia, "break it up, and go into the interior of the enemy's country as far as you can, inflicting all the damage you can upon their war resources." In response to this order, Sherman's army, 100,000 strong, had been pushing back Confederate forces composed of 65,000 men under Gen. Joseph E. Johnston. By June 19, Union troops had driven Johnston's men back to a well-prepared defensive position on Kennesaw Mountain. Southern engineers had built a line of entrenchments in its rocky slopes allowing the Confederates to cover every approach with rifle or cannon. An Ohio officer later commented that if the mountain had been constructed for the sole purpose of repelling an invading army, "it could not have been better made or placed."

On June 27, following a few weeks of skirmishing, Sherman, underestimating the strength and still-feisty morale of the rebels, attempted to break through Confederate lines and annihilate them in a grand no-holds-barred assault from two directions. Confederate Gen. Samuel French described the onset of the attack thusly: "As if by magic, there sprang from the earth a host of men, and in one long, waving line of blue the infantry advanced and the battle of Kennesaw Mountain began."

Sherman's men were repelled by massive bursts of firepower and huge rocks rolling down the mountain at them. Federal casualties far outnumbered Confederate losses. Meanwhile, 8,000 Union infantrymen in five brigades attacked from another angle and were shot down or defeated in brutal hand-to-hand combat, the Union losing 3,000 men, the Confederates 500. Weeks of torrential rain, which had turned these battlegrounds into a muddy mire, added significantly to the misery quotient on both sides. There was no rain the day of the battle, but the day was swelteringly hot and muggy.

Allow at least two hours for exploring. Start your tour at the **Visitor Center,** where you can pick up a map, watch a 10-minute slide show about the battle, and view exhibits of Civil War artifacts and memorabilia. You can drive weekdays (on weekends take a shuttle bus) or hike up the mountain to see the actual Confederate entrenchments and earthworks, some of them equipped with Civil War cannons and artillery. The trail is about one steep mile long, so wear comfortable shoes. Interpretive signs at key spots enhance the experience, and, weekends spring through fall, interpretive programs further elucidate the battle. You'll also want to drive to **Cheatham Hill,** site of some of the fiercest fighting. There are 16 miles of hiking trails for those who want a more extensive tour (trail maps are available at the Visitor Center), and picnicking is permitted in designated areas, some with barbecue grills. The scenery, by the way, is gorgeous, so even if Civil War battles are not your thing (that is, if you're reluctantly accompanying an enthusiastic spouse), it makes for beautiful hiking or driving.

Admission: Free.

Open: The visitor center is open daily 8:30am–5pm, till 6pm weekends June–Aug; front gate closes at 8pm June–Aug, 6pm the rest of the year. **Closed:** Christmas and New Year's Day. **Directions:** I-75 north to the Barrett Parkway exit, then follow the signs.

HIGH MUSEUM OF ART AT GEORGIA-PACIFIC CENTER, 133 Peachtree St. NE, at Houston St. Tel. 577-6940.

This downtown branch of the High Museum of Art is a beautiful facility used to display traveling exhibitions and works from the permanent collection. Opened in 1986, it was designed with the idea of making museum going more accessible to the working public. Its dramatic structure, which has been described as "architecture within architecture," is entered via the imposing lobby of the Georgia-Pacific building, itself the setting for Louise Nevelson's vast indoor environmental sculpture in white wood, *Dawn's Forest.* Spanning three levels, the 12,000-square-foot museum has beautiful walls paneled in an African wood called anegré, and slate-covered pedestrian ramps affording visitors a view of the downtown skyline as they descend to the galleries.

The upper gallery, which is used primarily for traveling and loan exhibitions, has a barrel-vault ceiling with Plexiglas inserts allowing daylight to filter in. The four lower galleries open onto a lobby and sculpture area. Shows here focus on photography and folk art. In addition to exhibits, the museum offers free films, lectures, concerts, and gallery talks at 12:15pm on the second Tuesday of each month and free tours of special exhibits at 12:15pm on the first and third Wednesday of each month. The Georgia-Pacific Building, by the way, occupies the hallowed site of the Loew's Grand Theatre, where *Gone With the Wind* premiered in 1939.

Admission: Free.

Open: Mon–Fri 11am–5pm. **MARTA:** Peachtree Center.

ATLANTA HISTORY CENTER DOWNTOWN, 140 Peachtree St. NE, at Forsyth St., in Margaret Mitchell Sq. Tel. 238-0655.

This downtown branch of the Atlanta History Center (see "The Top Attractions," above, for details) serves as an information station about Atlanta attractions. It occupies the 3-story Hillyer Building, itself a historic site dating from 1911 and listed on the National Register of Historic Places. Upstairs, an 18-minute video presentation called "Greetings from Atlanta" traces the city's history from the days when Cherokee and Creek Indians roamed the pine forests to the present. There are always Atlanta-related exhibits on subjects ranging from city monuments to the history of Underground Atlanta, traditional quilts, and, of course, *Gone With the Wind*. Also of interest is a free noontime lecture series held from the fall through the spring which has featured such noted speakers as Carl Rowan, Calvin Trillin, Arthur Ashe, and Rosalynn Carter.

Admission: Free.

Open: Mon–Sat 10am–6pm. **Closed:** New Year's Day, Memorial Day, Labor Day, Thanksgiving, and Christmas. **MARTA:** Peachtree Center.

ALONZO F. HERNDON HOME, 587 University Place, between Vine and Walnut Sts. Tel. 581-9813.

Alonzo Herndon was born into the last decade of slavery in 1858. After emancipation, from age 13 to 20, he worked as a field hand and sharecropper, supplementing his meager income by selling peanuts, homemade molasses, and axle grease. He arrived in Atlanta in the early 1880s, where he worked as a barber and eventually owned several barbershops of his own. These were outfitted with beautiful fixtures and chandeliers bought on a trip to Europe. He acquired real estate with earnings from these shops. By 1895, with only a year of formal education and less than 40 years out of slavery, Herndon was the richest black man in Atlanta. In 1905, he began buying up insurance companies and reorganizing them. These became the nucleus of the Atlanta Life Insurance Company, today the nation's second-largest black-owned insurance company.

In 1910, Herndon built this elegant 15-room house in the beaux-arts neoclassical style with a stately colonnaded entrance. Today, visitors enter from the back. The tour begins in a receiving room with a 10-minute introductory video called *The Herndon Legacy*. Herndon and his wife, Adrienne McNeil, a Shakespearean actress, were the primary architects of the house, and construction was accomplished almost completely by black artisans. Since the home was occupied until 1977 by their son Norris, much of the original furniture remains, and there are family photographs throughout. Adrienne died about a week after the house was completed. Two years later, Herndon married Jessie Gillespie, who later became the vice president of Atlanta Life.

The tour takes you through the reception hall, where the butler greeted visitors; the music room, with rococo gilt-trim walls and Louis XV–style furnishings; the living room, with a frieze on its walls depicting the accomplishments of Herndon's life; the dining room, furnished in late Renaissance style with family china and Venetian glass displayed in a mahogany cabinet; the butler's pantry; and the sunny corner breakfast room. Upstairs, you'll see Jessie Herndon's bedroom, with its Jacobean suite and Louis XV–style furnishings; Herndon's Empire-furnished bedroom, where a book from a Republican National Convention displayed on a table lets you know his political bent; the collection room (Norris collected ancient Greek and Roman vases and funerary objects); Norris's bedroom; a Victorian sitting room; and a guest bedroom.

Admission: Free.

Open: Tues–Sat 10am–4pm, with tours on the hour. **Closed:** All national and state holidays. **MARTA:** Vine City.

ATLANTA COLLEGE OF ART GALLERY, in the Memorial Arts Building of the Woodruff Arts Center, 1280 Peachtree St. NE. Tel. 898-1157.

The Atlanta College of Art, housed in the Woodruff Arts Center complex, features an ongoing series of gallery shows. Some recent examples: "Songs of My People—African-Americans: A Self-Portrait"; a photojournalism exhibition called "Forced Out: The Agony of the Refugee in our Time"; and "Presswork: Prints by Women." There are also frequent lectures and occasional concerts here. Call for details.

Admission: Free.

Open: Mon–Sat 10am–5pm; fall–spring Sun 2–6pm as well. **MARTA:** Arts Center.

ATLANTA MUSEUM, 537 Peachtree St., between Prescott St. and Linden Ave. Tel. 872-8233.

If, like me, you love to come upon musty collections of curiosities, this will be a thrill. Antiques dealer James Elliott, Sr., started his mini-Smithsonian in 1936; today, his son, James Elliott, Jr., is in charge of its 2,500 or so diverse exhibits. They're displayed in a 1900

Historic Register Victorian home that once belonged to the Rose family, founders of Four Roses liquor (when Georgia went dry in 1907, they moved to Tennessee). Mr. Elliott still runs a cluttery antique shop on the first floor. The museum is upstairs.

Exhibits include: the throne of Haile Selassie, paw signatures of movie dogs, Franklin D. Roosevelt's fishing hat, personal articles (a coat, raincoat, camp mirror, tablecloth, and cigar box) that belonged to Adolf Hitler, a carved stone from King Tut's tomb, a lock of Napoleon's hair and a pair of chairs from his throne room (the latter were given to Admiral Dewey while on a goodwill tour of France), a World War II Japanese field telephone, a vase with an Egyptian curse, the desk on which the Georgia secession was written, General Custer's hairbrush, Davy Crockett's gun, furnishings and books that belonged to Margaret Mitchell, an original model of the cotton gin from Eli Whitney's shop, spoons made by Paul Revere, and a piece of root from the apple tree under which Robert E. Lee stood when he surrendered at Appomattox. Another collector of curiosities, Michael Jackson, once came in and tried to buy a thing or two, but Elliott wouldn't part with his treasures.

Admission: $3 for adults, $2 for children under 12 and seniors.
Open: Mon–Fri 10am–5pm. **MARTA:** North Avenue or Civic Center. **Parking:** On the side and rear of the building.

HAMMONDS HOUSE, 503 Peeples St., between Ralph Abernathy Blvd. and Oak St. Tel. 752-8730.

Occupying the 1857 Eastlake Victorian-style former home of Dr. Otis T. Hammonds, a black anesthesiologist and art patron, Hammonds House is a national center for the exhibition, preservation, research, and documentation of African American art and artists. The house was purchased with these aims in mind by the Fulton County Commission after Hammonds's death in 1985. Hammonds's extensive collection included works by African American and Haitian artists, as well as African masks and carvings. On permanent display are paintings and prints by Romare Bearden and an exhibit of contemporary Haitian art. The facility also presents changing exhibits, including works from the permanent collection and shows of local and national artists.

Admission: $1 for adults, seniors and children under 13 free.
Open: Tues–Fri 10am–6pm, Sat–Sun 1–5pm. **MARTA:** West End (4½ blocks away).

CALLANWOLDE FINE ARTS CENTER, 980 Briarcliff Rd. NE, north of Ponce de Leon Ave. Tel. 872-5338.

A magnificent 16th-century Gothic/Tudor–style mansion, built for Coca-Cola heir Asa Candler in 1920, Callanwolde today serves as a fine-arts center for DeKalb County. Classes are given in pottery, painting, photography, drawing, and more, and there are numerous workshops for adults and children. Though it's a lovely setting for art students, I can't help wishing that some preservation committee had instead restored the house to its former grandeur and re-created its furnishings and appointments. As it is, most of the rooms are bare, and only Callanwolde's exquisite walnut paneling, beautifully carved ceilings and moldings, grand staircase, magnificent marble and stone fireplaces, and leaded-glass windows evoke its luxurious past.

The estate occupies 12 acres (originally 27) in the Druid Hills section of Atlanta, an area planned by Frederick Law Olmsted, designer of New York's Central Park. Its name derives from the Candler family's ancestral home, Callan Castle, in Ireland. *Callan* is the Irish name for Candler, and *wold* is an old English word for wood or forest. Visitors are welcome to peruse shows of local artists in the Petite Hall gallery upstairs; enjoy the lawns, formal gardens, and nature trails, which are maintained by the county; and participate in the many events here—concerts, storytelling festivals, dance performances (see the "Calendar of Events" in Chapter 2). Attending a function here is the best way to experience the estate.

Admission: Free. Guided tours, by special appointment only, cost $1.50 for adults, 50¢ for children under 12. If you're interested in a tour, call to arrange it as far in advance as possible.

Open: Mon–Sat 10am–3pm.

RHODES MEMORIAL HALL, 1516 Peachtree St. NW, at Peachtree Circle. Tel. 881-9980.

Rhodes Hall is one of only two remaining pre–World War II Peachtree Street mansions. It was designed by Willis Franklin Denny (at the time Atlanta's leading residential architect) in 1903 as a residence for affluent Atlanta businessman Amos Giles Rhodes and his family. Its medieval baronial-cum-high Victorian Romanesque style was inspired by Rhineland castles. The granite exterior is replete with arched Romanesque windows, battlements and buttresses, parapets, towers, and turrets. A large Syrian-arched veranda wraps the east and north facades. And the interior is grandiose, with maple-bordered oak floors laid in herringbone pattern, mosaics surrounding the fireplaces, and a gracefully winding hand-carved Honduran mahogany staircase with nine stained-glass stairwell panels depicting "The Rise and Fall of the Confederacy." The house and stables originally occupied 150 acres of land and included servants' quarters, a carriage house, and other outbuildings. At the turn of the century, this site was in suburbia, an afternoon's drive from downtown (via mule-drawn streetcar) to Rhodes Hall.

Upon Rhodes's death in 1928, his residence was deeded to the state of Georgia in keeping with his desire to preserve it. The house was entered on the National Register of Historic Places in 1974. Today it is headquarters for the Georgia Trust for Historic Preservation and is in an ongoing process of restoration. To date, the original dining-room suite and some other furnishings are in place, and Scalamandre has replicated the parlor's silk wall coverings. Original landscaping—with white and red cedars, dogwoods, banana trees, and a circular flower bed—is being re-created in the front yard. Tour guide Elva Spangenberg, who celebrated her 104th birthday October 30, 1991, greets visitors.

Admission: $2 for adults, 50¢ for children under 12.

Open: Mon–Fri 11am–4pm. Tours are given on a continuous basis throughout the day. **MARTA:** Arts Center.

THE MARGARET MITCHELL HOUSE, 999 Peachtree St. NE, at 10th St. Tel. 870-2360.

In Atlanta, *Gone With the Wind* comes up daily, and Margaret Mitchell is an almost-hallowed name. So it's rather surprising that only at this late date has the city begun restoring the dilapidated turn-of-the-century Tudor-revival apartment house at 999 Peachtree where Mitchell lived with her husband, John Marsh, from 1925 to 1932 (they called it "The Dump"), and wrote most of her epic novel. They even held their wedding reception there. Preservationists are currently raising money for the restoration, scheduled for completion in time for the 1996 Olympics. Since everyone comes to Atlanta seeking *GWTW*-related attractions, and few exist (the white-colonnaded mansion at 1401 Peachtree Street, where Mitchell grew up, was razed in 1952), it is estimated that the restored home will draw millions of visitors annually. Plans call for a re-creation of Mitchell's apartment and utilization of the rest of the building for a museum of *GWTW* memorabilia. At this writing, this project is in the earliest stages and not open to the public, but I include it for those who'd like to pass by and view the shrine.

PARKS

PIEDMONT PARK, Piedmont Ave. at 14th St. (main entrance).

Piedmont Park, the city's most popular and centrally located recreation area, was created at the turn of the century for the Cotton States Exposition. Its designer was Frederick Law Olmsted, America's most noted landscapist. "The beauty of a park," said Olmsted, "should be the beauty of fields, the meadow, the prairie, of green pastures, and still waters. What we want to gain is tranquility and rest of the mind." To this end, he transformed a woodsy meadow into a 180-acre parkland with a varied terrain of rolling hillsides, verdant lawns, and lush forest around beautiful Lake Clara Meer.

The park is the setting for many popular regional events: jazz and symphony concerts, art and music festivals, marathons, and more. It contains a large baseball field, tennis courts, a large public swimming pool, and paths for jogging, skating, and cycling. And the magnificent Atlanta Botanical Garden (see "Top Attractions," above) is adjacent.

Admission: Free.

Open: Daily 6am–1am. **MARTA:** Midtown or Arts Center.

GRANT PARK, bordered by Sydney St. and Atlanta Ave., Boulevard and Cherokee Ave.

Named for Confederate captain Lemuel P. Grant, who helped build Atlanta's defense line, Grant Park still contains vestiges of his fortifications. Grant also donated its 100 acres to the city for a park on this site. Near the intersection of Boulevard and Atlanta Avenue, you can see the remaining earthwork slopes of Fort Walker, a commanding artillery bastion with its original gun emplacements. Its cannons and caissons can be seen in the museum area of Cyclorama (see "Top Attractions," above), one of Grant Park's two major attractions. The other is Zoo Atlanta (see "Cool for Kids," below).

Admission: Free.

Open: Daily 6am–1am.

3. COOL FOR KIDS

Though the following attractions are great choices if you're traveling with kids, don't pass them up if you're not. I especially love Wren's Nest, the Center for Puppetry Arts, the Yellow River Wildlife Game Ranch (visit in conjunction with Stone Mountain), and Zoo Atlanta (visit in conjunction with Cyclorama and Oakland Cemetery).

ZOO ATLANTA, 800 Cherokee Ave., in Grant Park. Tel. 625-5600.

This absolutely delightful 40-acre zoo dates from 1889, when George W. Hall (aka "Popcorn George") brought his traveling circus to town. Employee claims against Hall for back wages forced him to relinquish his menagerie, and the animal entourage was purchased by a prominent Atlanta businessman who donated the collection to the city as the basis for a zoological garden in Grant Park. It's grown considerably since then, but the real turnaround came in 1985, when the zoo began a still-ongoing multimillion-dollar renovation.

Today, Zoo Atlanta is a very exciting and creatively run facility, with animals housed in large open enclosures which simulate their natural geographical habitats. The zoo is engaged in a breeding program, much of it centering on endangered species. Signs, some translated into Swahili, use a cartoon format to inform visitors about environmental and conservational issues pertinent to wildlife. All areas are beautifully landscaped and adorned with animal sculptures. There are video displays in the Elephant Barn and Gorilla museum, and safari carts throughout the zoo serve as additional informational stations. Do plan to catch entertaining and educational animal shows in the Kroger Wildlife Theater, presented daily at 11:30am and 12:30, 2:30, and 3:30pm April through October. Ditto the African Elephant Demonstration given daily year round at 11am, 1, and 3pm. Admission is free.

Flamingo Plaza is the first habitat you'll see upon entering the zoo. Farther on, **Masai Mara** houses elephants, rhinos, lions, zebras, giraffes, gazelles, and other African animals and birds. Its landscape resembles the plains of East Africa, with honey locust trees and yuccas; and the lion enclosure replicates an East African kopje (rocky outcropping). A café called the **Swahili Market** overlooks the zebras. Frequent animal demonstrations, African storytelling, and educational programs take place under the Elder's Tree in Masai Mara.

The lushly landscaped **Ford African Rain Forest** centers on four vast gorilla habitats separated by moats. Studies on gorilla behavior take place here, and there are always quite a few adorable babies. A gorilla named Willie B. is the zoo's mascot. Also in the section: a walk-through aviary of West African birds; small African primates; and the Gorillas of Cameroon museum. Landscaping includes burned-out areas of forest and deadfall trees—gorillas do not live in manicured gardens.

Sumatran tigers (a very endangered species) and orangutans live in the **Ketambe** section, an Indonesian tropical rain forest with clusters of bamboo and a waterfall. Ketambe also includes a Reptile House and a special exhibit area, often used to house visiting animals.

A zoo train travels through the **Children's Zoo** area, a peaceful enclave where kids can pet baby llamas, sheep, pigs, and goats. There are aviaries here, too, and a duck and swan pond. In the works are **Okefenokee Swamp** and **Coastal Georgia** exhibits. There are shops and snack bars throughout the zoo and tree-shaded picnic areas in Grant Park.

Admission: $7 for adults, $4.50 for children 3–11, children 2 and under free. Strollers can be rented.

Open: Daily 10am–5pm, till 6pm during Daylight Savings Time. **Closed:** New Year's Day, Martin Luther King Day, Thanksgiving, Christmas. **Directions:** By car, take I-75 south to I-20 east. Get off at the Boulevard exit and follow the signs to Grant Park.

WREN'S NEST, 1050 Ralph Abernathy Blvd., two blocks from Ashby St. Tel. 753-7735.

Named for a family of wrens that once nested in the mailbox, Wren's Nest is the former home of Joel Chandler Harris, who chronicled the wily deeds of Br'er Rabbit and Br'er Fox. It's been open to the public since 1913, when his widow sold it to the Uncle Remus Memorial Association. Harris's literary career began at the age of 13, when he apprenticed on *The Countryman,* a quarterly plantation newspaper. In four years spent learning journalism there, young Harris spent many an evening hanging about the slave quarters, drinking in African folk tales and fables spun by George Terrell, a plantation patriarch who became the prototype for Uncle Remus. Sherman's army put *The Countryman* out of business, and Harris went on to other newspapers, working his way up to editorial writer at the *Atlanta Constitution* by age 28. There, plagued by writer's block one gloomy winter afternoon, he remembered the plantation stories of his youth and evoked Uncle Remus to fill his column. Enthralled readers clamored for more, and the rest is history.

The house itself is an 1870s farmhouse with a Queen Anne Victorian facade added in 1884. Harris lived here from 1881 until his death in 1908, doing most of his writing in a rocking chair on the wraparound front porch. On a 30-minute tour, including a slide presentation about Harris's life, you'll see much Uncle Remus memorabilia, including a humidor sculpture of Br'er Fox arresting Br'er Rabbit for stealing beets, a gift from the town of Carlsbad, Austria. The stuffed great horned owl over the study door was a gift from Theodore Roosevelt, whose White House Harris visited. The original wren's nest mailbox reposes on the study mantel, and all of Harris's books, along with signed first editions of major authors of his day (Mark Twain and others) are displayed in a bookcase.

The house is restored to its 1900 appearance, and an interpretation center is in the works. Call ahead to find out when storyteller-in-residence Akbar Imhotep will be telling stories culled from African and African-American folklore; it's a real treat. Mid-June through mid-August, Akbar and storytellers perform daily at 11:30am and 12:30 and 1:30pm.

Joel Chandler Harris died at the age of 62 on July 3, 1908. He penned his own epitaph, which appears on his gravestone:

I seem to see before me the smiling faces of thousands of children—some young and fresh—and some wearing the friendly marks of age, but all children at heart, and not an unfriendly face among them. And while I am trying hard to speak the right word, I seem to hear a voice lifted above the rest saying, "You have made some of us happy." And so I feel my heart fluttering and my lips trembling and I have to bow silently and turn away and hurry into the obscurity that fits me best.

Admission: $3 for adults, $2 for seniors and students 13–19, $1 for children 4–12, under 4 free; storytelling $1 per person additional.
Open: Tues–Sat 10am–4pm, Sun 1–4pm, with tours departing every 30 minutes on the hour and half hour. **Closed:** Mon, Jan 1, Thanksgiving, Dec 24 and 25. **Directions:** MARTA: West End (3 long blocks away); by car, Take I-20 to Ashby St., turn left on Ashby, right on Ralph Abernathy Blvd.; Wren's Nest is 2 blocks down on the left.

CENTER FOR PUPPETRY ARTS, 1404 Spring St. NW, at 18th St. Tel. 873-3089, box office 873-3391.

If you're traveling with the kids, this is in the not-to-be-missed category. In fact, I wouldn't miss it even without kids in tow. The center is dedicated to expanding public awareness of puppetry as a fine art and to presenting all its international and historical forms. Opened in 1978, with Kermit the Frog cutting the official ribbon (he had a little help from the late Jim Henson), it contains a 300-seat theater, a 90-seat black-box theater, two smaller theaters, gallery space, and a permanent museum. The puppet shows are marvelous—sophisticated, riveting, full-stage productions with elaborate scenery. Some are family oriented (*Pinocchio, Cinderella*); others, with nighttime showings, are geared to adults. There are always performances Monday to Friday at 10 and 11:30am (an extra matinee show takes place Wednesday at 1pm) and Saturday at 10:30am and 12:30pm. Reservations are essential. Call a week or so in advance to enroll yourself or your kids in a puppet-making workshop here.

The museum area displays puppets ranging from Shakespearean characters to Punch and Judy figures. It's an excellent collection, one of the largest in North America, including turn-of-the-century Thai shadow puppets, Indonesian wayang golek puppets used to tell classic stories (a centuries-old tradition), Chinese hand puppets, rod-operated marionettes from all over Europe, original Muppets, a German puppet made of scarves, pre-Columbian clay puppets that were used in religious ceremonies circa A.D. 1200, Turkish shadow figures made of dried animal skins, and a Nigerian Yoruba puppet, among many, many others. The permanent collection is augmented by short-term exhibits such as a recent Bill Baird retrospective (he created the puppets used in *The Sound of Music*).

Admission: $3 for adults, $2 for children; free if you see the show or take a workshop. Show prices vary; call ahead for details.

Open: Mon–Sat 9am–4pm. **Closed:** New Year's Day, Memorial Day, July 4, Labor Day, Thanksgiving, and Christmas. **MARTA:** Arts Center.

YELLOW RIVER WILDLIFE GAME RANCH, 4525 Hwy. 78, Lilburn. Tel. 972-6643.

This 24-acre animal preserve bordering the Yellow River is one of the most special places I've ever visited. Owner Art Rilling has created an environment that offers close encounters of the four-legged kind—a chance to view, pet, feed, and generally mingle with some 600 animals (always including quite a few babies) living in open enclosures, or right out in the open, along a one-mile oak- and hickory-shaded forest trail. Art knows every animal on the ranch by name and can give you chapter and verse on the personality, preferences, and in some cases, even romantic history of them. You'll feel like you're in a Disney movie when the deer sidle up and nuzzle you. The animals know they're among friends here and are highly socialized, so you have a unique chance to study them up close. Inhabitants include donkeys named Rhett and Scarlett, the goats at Billy Goat Gruff Memorial Bridge (they climb it to get food at the top), dozens of rabbits in Bunny Burrow (kids can walk right into this enclosure and pet the bunnies), a wide assortment of interesting-looking chickens, a herd of buffalo, a talking crow, a skunk named General Sherman (we are in Atlanta, after all), and a groundhog named General Lee. You can get animal food in the gift shop at the entrance or buy it along the trail.

Some animal exhibits are enhanced by interesting audio programs (did you know, for instance, that a buffalo can outrun a horse?). Bring your camera (or sketchbook), wear comfortable shoes, and do consider bringing a picnic lunch; there are tables throughout the property, and one especially nice picnic area overlooks the river. An exciting time to visit is Sheep Shearing Saturday in early spring.

Admission: $3.50 for adults, $2.50 for children 3–11, children under 3 free.

Open: Memorial Day–Labor Day daily 9:30am–dusk; till 5:30pm the rest of the year.

SCITREK (Science and Technology Museum of Atlanta), 395 Piedmont Ave., between Ralph McGill Blvd. and Pine St. Tel. 522-5500.

Opened in 1988, this museum offers hands-on adventures for adults and kids in science and technology. There are over 100 interactive exhibits, divided into categories.

In Electricity and Magnetism you can create a magnetic field to hurl a disc upward, change light into electricity, produce electric current using your own hand as a "battery," see how much electricity you can generate pedaling a bicycle (how many bulbs can you light up?), and test various metals for electrical conductivity.

In Light and Perception, a kinetic light sculpture lets you vary frequency, intensity, and revolutions to create an infinite variety of designs. You can also examine the range of your peripheral vision here, step inside a kaleidoscope, watch yourself on video while walking through a distorted room (demonstrating how the brain visually perceives things based on past experience), mix over 16 million colors (time permitting) on a computer, bend light beams, and look into infinity. This section houses my favorite exhibit, the frozen shadow room, in which you can "freeze" your shadow on a wall of light-sensitive phosphorous vinyl film; a bright flash causes the panel to glow except in the area your body shields from the light. It's lots of fun dancing and jumping to create shadow art on the wall.

Kidspace has simple exhibits geared to the 2- to 7-year-old set. Here the kids can paint their faces in a mirror, explore a crystal cave, blow enormous bubbles, squirt water to float toys downstream, play electronic instruments, make images on heat-sensitive liquid crystal with their hands, and use furnished play environments including an office, puppet theater, and a TV news/weather station. There are also very easy computer games.

Pulleys, levers, wheels, axles, and suchlike are explored in Mechanics. You can lift billiard balls with a screw auger, become a human gyroscope, and suspend a ball in the air using a Bernouilli blower (don't ask me to explain what that is; I'm low tech).

The most recently added exhibition area is Mathematica, where a history wall portrays the achievements of major mathematicians from the 12th century to the present. Other hands-on displays here demonstrate various aspects of mathematics from the laws of planetary motion to probability theory.

Exhibits are supplemented by an ongoing series of lectures, demonstrations, workshops, temporary shows, and exhibits such as Dinamations "Sea Creatures Past and Present" and "Mission to Mars." Phase II of SciTrek, now in the works, will highlight technology with many new permanent exhibits.

Admission: $6 for adults, $4 for seniors and children 3–17, free for children under 3; $15 for families. There's parking at $3 per car.

Open: Tues–Sat 10am–5pm, Sun noon–5pm, with later hours on occasional selected evenings. **Closed:** Monday, Thanksgiving, Christmas, Easter, New Year's Day. **MARTA:** Civic Center.

FERNBANK SCIENCE CENTER, 156 Heaton Park Dr. NE, at Artwood Rd. (off Ponce de Leon Ave.). Tel. 378-4311.

Owned and funded by the DeKalb County School System, this museum/planetarium/observatory, located on 65 verdant acres of Fernbank Forest, recently became part of the Fernbank Museum of Natural History (details above in "Top Attractions"). Plan to visit the entire complex the same day. There's a 2½-mile forest trail here, with trees (oaks, pines, magnolias, dogwoods, sweet gums, red maples, tulip poplars), shrubs, ferns, wildflowers, mosses, and other plants (rhododendrons, honeysuckle, greenbrier, wild onion, Oconee bells) marked for identification. This unspoiled natural environment is home to many animals and birds, and a small pond teems with aquatic life.

The indoor facility houses museum exhibits such as: a video display on geological phenomena (volcanoes, earthquakes, mountain formation); a gem collection; development of life in Georgia from 500 million years ago to a million years ago; a complete weather station with a meteorologist on duty; fossil trees; the original *Apollo 6* space capsule and space suit (on loan from the Smithsonian); computer games; a replica of the Okefenokee Swamp, complete with sound effects; and replicas of dinosaurs that roamed Atlanta in prehistoric times. There are planetarium shows, and, at the Observatory, which contains the largest telescope in the world dedicated to public education, an astronomer gives a talk and lets visitors use the telescope.

If you're here on a Sunday, allow time to visit the nearby Greenhouse, about 2½ miles from the center. A horticulturist gives a talk to visitors, and children can pot a plant and take it home. There are many workshops, lectures, tours, and films for adults and children on subjects ranging from nature photography to weather forecasting.

Admission: $2 for adults, $1 for students, free for senior citizens. *Note:* Children under 5 are not admitted to the planetarium.

Open: Mon 8:30am–5pm, Tues–Fri 8:30am–10pm, Sat 10am–5pm, Sun 1–5pm. Planetarium shows at 8pm Tues–Fri and 3pm Wed and Fri–Sun. The Observatory is open Thurs–Fri 8:30–10pm, weather permitting. Forest trails are open Mon–Fri 2–5pm, Sat 10am–5pm, Sun 1–5pm. The Greenhouse is open Sun only 1–5pm.

SIX FLAGS OVER GEORGIA, 7561 Six Flags Rd. SW, at I-20 W. Tel. 948-9290.

One of the state's major family attractions, this vast theme park offers over 100 rides, shows, and attractions. It's a great day's entertainment. Arrive early (at least 15 minutes before opening), note where you've parked in the vast lot, and take 10 minutes or so to plan the day's schedule. The park is southern-themed, with Cotton States, Confederate, and Georgia sections. There's a Bugs Bunny Land geared to young children, and costumed Looney Tune characters such as Sylvester, Bugs, and Daffy Duck roam the park greeting young visitors. Holiday times are especially event-filled.

Thrill rides include: Ninja, the "black belt" of roller coasters, turns riders upside down five times and offers thrilling loops, dives, and corkscrew turns; the Georgia Cyclone, a classic wooden roller coaster with 11 dramatic drops, patterned after the famed Coney Island coaster; the Great Gasp, a 20-story parachute jump; Thunder River, a simulated white-water rafting adventure; the Mind Bender, a triple-loop roller coaster; and Free Fall (ever wondered what it would be like to fall off a 10-story building?). A less dizzying highlight is Monster Plantation, a Disneyesque boat ride through an antebellum mansion haunted by over 100 animated monsters. There's much, much more.

Shows vary from year to year, but they usually include a major musical revue, a high-dive show, a golden-oldies show, thrill cinema adventures on a 180-degree screen, a magic show, a Don Rickles–style comic (much modified, of course) in the form of a sharp-tongued bird named Buford Buzzard, and an animated character show. In addition, headline performers such as Willie Nelson, the Smithereens, Eddie Money, and Tanya Tucker play the 8,072-seat (with lawn seating for 4,000) Southern Star Amphitheatre.

There are restaurants and snack bars throughout the park, though you might consider bringing a picnic. Gift shops also abound.

Admission: $22 for adults, $15.70 for children ages 3–9, $10.48 for seniors (55 and over), under 3 free. 2-day tickets available. Amphitheatre concerts are free with park admission.

Open: Daily Memorial Day–late Aug, weekends only (those weekends sometimes including a Fri or Mon) early Mar–Memorial Day and Sept–Oct 31, also many evenings late Nov–Dec for special "Holiday in the Park" celebrations. Gates open 10am daily; closing hours vary. **Parking:** $5.

WHITE WATER, Exit 113 off I-75 on North Cobb Pkwy., Marietta. Tel. 424-WAVE.

Forty acres of wet, splashy fun await you at White Water, the largest water-theme park in the Southeast. Its attractions include: the $500,000 Black River Falls, with two enclosed 400-foot flumes creating a twisting "river of darkness" enhanced by strobe lights; the "Atlanta Ocean," a 710,000-gallon pool generating continuous 4-foot waves; Tidal Wave, two 250-foot water slides that you can descend with or without a tube and splash into a pool that merges with the Little Hooch River; Bahama Bob-Slide, a group tube ride down a chute the length of two football fields; Caribbean Plunge, a 100-foot free-fall water flume drop; and Dragon's Tail Falls, which sends riders plummeting down a 250-foot triple drop at speeds up to 30 miles per hour. There's much more, including a special section for children 48 inches and under called Little Squirt's Island, offering 25 tot-size water attractions. Captain Kid's Cove, adjacent to it, has dozens of additional activities for kids 12 and under. Restaurants and snack bars are on the premises, as are rental lockers and shower facilities. Swimsuits are essential. Over 300 lifeguards and ride attendants are on staff.

Adjacent to White Water is **American Adventures** (tel. 424-9283), an $8.5 million, indoor/outdoor old-fashioned amusement park featuring miniature golf; eight children's rides in Fun Forest (bumper cars, a small roller coaster, a tilt-a-whirl); a classic carousel; a penny arcade with over 130 games; and Professor Plinker's Laboratory—a large children's play area with ball crawls, nets to climb, a shadow room, and more. It's all geared to children 12 and under. A highlight: you can experience car-racing thrills on the Great Race, a 1,200-foot track. A 180-seat family-style restaurant is on the grounds. Admission to American Adventures is free (you pay per ride; a pass for unlimited rides is $9.99 for children, $1.99 for adults; adults ride free with toddlers). The park is open 365 days a year (hours vary seasonally).

Admission: $15.50 for adults, $9.50 for children over age 4 up to 48 inches tall; children under 4 and senior citizens free.

Open: Weekends only in May and Sept, daily Memorial Day–Labor Day from 10am; closing hours vary. **Closed:** Oct–Apr.

4. ORGANIZED TOURS

SIGHTSEEING BUSES

GRAY LINE OF ATLANTA, 37–45 Industrial Blvd. Tel. 767-0594.

This company offers several comprehensive tours aboard comfortable sightseeing buses. Departures are from the Hyatt Regency Downtown. Since departure times and prices are subject to change, call before you go.

All Around Atlanta is a 3½-hour excursion that takes in Peachtree Street, Peachtree Center (you'll see the city's notable downtown architecture), the capitol, Georgia Tech, Coca-Cola headquarters, the Governor's Mansion, the Martin Luther King, Jr., Historic District (his birthplace, tomb, church, and the King Center), the Woodruff Arts Center, Swan House, and Cyclorama. It's a great introduction to the city. Adults pay $15, children 6 to 11 pay $10, under 6 free. Departures are daily at 8:30am and 1pm.

The Atlanta Grand Circle, a 7½-hour tour, includes all of the above plus the city's grand homes, history-rich Five Points, the CNN complex, Underground Atlanta, and Georgia's Stone Mountain. Adults pay $25, children $18. Departures are daily at 8:30am.

The Black Heritage Tour, a 3½-hour trip, concentrates on the Sweet Auburn district, where Dr. Martin Luther King, Jr., spent his boyhood years. In addition, you'll visit the Herndon mansion and the world's largest predominantly black center for higher education—the Atlanta University complex. Adults pay $15, children $10. Departures are on Saturdays only at 1pm.

GUIDED WALKING TOURS

THE ATLANTA PRESERVATION CENTER, 156 7th St. NE, Suite 3. Tel. 522-4345.

This private, nonprofit organization is dedicated to "the preservation of Atlanta's architecturally, historically, and culturally significant buildings and neighborhoods," and offers eight 1½- to 2-hour guided walking tours in the city. Cost of each tour is $6 for adults, $3 for students and senior citizens, free for children under five. Tours of the Fox Theatre District are given year round; the remaining tours are offered April through November only. Call for days and hours.

The **Fox Theatre District Tour** is a must. You'll explore in depth this restored 1920s Moorish movie palace, a theater whose auditorium resembles the courtyard of a Cairo mosque and whose architecture and interior were influenced by the discoveries at King Tut's tomb. The tour also includes turn-of-the-century buildings in the area.

Also in the not-to-be-missed category: the **Oakland Cemetery Tour.** Oakland Cemetery, dating from 1850, has a wonderful collection of Victorian monuments on 88 beautiful wooded acres. Many noted Atlantans are buried here. It's a fascinating excursion.

The **Historic Downtown Tour** is an architectural survey of Atlanta's downtown edifices from Victorian mansions to modern high rises. You'll learn about the architects, the businessmen, and the prominent families who created the city's early commercial center.

The **Inman Park Tour** visits Atlanta's first garden suburb, where you'll see preserved and restored Victorian mansions. Highlights include the homes of Coca-Cola magnates Asa Candler and Ernest Woodruff and the interior of the Inman Park Methodist Church.

The **Underground and Capitol Area Tour** explores the State Capitol, visits three churches established before the Civil War, and provides a unique opportunity to learn about the history of Underground Atlanta.

The **Sweet Auburn Tour** focuses on the area black 20th-century entrepreneurs developed into a prosperous commercial hub. You'll also visit Martin Luther King's boyhood home and the church where he preached.

Walking Miss Daisy's Druid Hills explores the neighborhood that was the setting for the play and film *Driving Miss Daisy*. The gracious parklike area was laid out by Frederick Law Olmsted and contains many architecturally notable homes.

Finally, the **West End and Wren's Nest Tour** focuses on the home of Joel Chandler Harris (author of the Uncle Remus stories), while also noting Victorian homes and churches in the West End area.

5. SPORTS & RECREATION

Spectator sports are a favorite pastime in Atlanta. This is, after all, the town where Hank Aaron (Atlanta Braves) made his record-breaking 715th home run, breaking Babe Ruth's record. Take a break from museum going and catch a Falcons, Braves, or Georgia Tech game. Or get out on a playing field, tennis court, or golf course yourself.

SPECTATOR SPORTS

In addition to the suggestions listed below, check the papers to see what's on during your stay or call **Real Talk** (see box on p. 213)

GEORGIA DOME, 285 International Blvd. NW. Tel. 656-0920.

Atlanta's new $214 million, 70,500-seat domed megastadium, built to accommodate Super Bowl XXVIII in 1994 and Olympic events in 1996, is also the new home of the Atlanta Falcons (NFL), who play 10 to 12 games here each year. A Falcons exhibition game in August 1992 was the dome's very first event. The facility combines with the adjacent 2-million-square-foot Georgia World Congress Center to form the world's largest entertainment complex. Its oval shape provides a close view of stadium action from every seat. It is also the site for the annual Peach Bowl, while other targeted events include the NCAA Final Four, the NBA All-Star Game, and the ACC Basketball Championship. The dome additionally hosts tennis matches, tractor pulls, college basketball, and Supercross events. Check the papers or call the above number to find out what's on during your stay.

Prices: Vary with events. Tickets to Falcon games are $27, Peach Bowl tickets are in the $35 range, Super Bowl tickets about $150.

Open: Year round. **MARTA:** Omni or Vine City.

OMNI COLISEUM, 100 Techwood Dr. NW. Tel. 681-2100.

SUPER BOWL TICKETS

Tickets to Super Bowl XXVIII in 1994 will be available to all NFL season-ticket holders through the respective teams. If you're not a season-ticket holder, the NFL will conduct random drawings of all requests sent by certified mail between February 1, 1993, and June 1, 1993, with a limit of two tickets per request and no multiple requests from individuals or organizations. Send requests to: Super Bowl Tickets, National Football League, 410 Park Ave., New York, N.Y. 10022.

The 16,000-seat oval-shaped Omni Coliseum is home to the Atlanta Hawks (NBA), who play 41 games here during their fall-to-spring season, plus preseason and, with luck, playoff games. Call 827-3800 for information. In mid-March there are opening-round NCAA Basketball Tournament games. Also fall through spring, the Atlanta Knights hockey team (IHL) plays about 40 games here. In September, the Omni hosts NHL exhibition games. WCW professional wrestling takes place year round here. And there are tractor pulls in October and January. At other times, the Omni is used for varied sporting and entertainment events. Call or check the papers to find out what's on during your stay.

Prices: Vary with events. Tickets to Hawks games are mostly in the $10–$25 range. For all events here, tickets are usually available through Ticketmaster (tel. 249-6400).

Open: Year round. **MARTA:** Omni.

ATLANTA-FULTON COUNTY STADIUM, 521 Capitol Ave. SW, between Fulton St. and Georgia Ave. Tel. 522-1967.

The circular open-air Atlanta-Fulton County Stadium, built in 1965, has 52,000 seats for baseball and 60,000 for football. The Atlanta Braves (NL) play 81 games here during baseball season. Call 522-7630 for information about games. Charge tickets via Ticketmaster (tel. 249-6400). The stadium is also used for college football games and Motocross events.

Prices: Tickets to football games are $17–$25, baseball tickets are $6–$10, Motocross tickets are $11–$20. Parking is $5–$7, depending on the event.

Open: Year round. Baseball season is Apr–Sept. **MARTA:** Shuttle-bus service (fare is 85¢) operates between the stadium and downtown Atlanta, starting 2½ hours before game time; call 848-4711 for shuttle-bus information.

BOBBY DODD STADIUM/GRANT FIELD, Georgia Institute of Technology, North Ave. and Techwood Dr. Tel. 894-5447.

Since 1913, this 46,000-seat stadium has been the home of those "Ramblin' Wrecks from Georgia Tech"–the Yellow Jackets college football team. For ticket information call the above number. Charge tickets via Ticketmaster (tel. 249-6400).

Prices: Tickets are $17–$21.

Open: Sept–Nov for football season. **MARTA:** North Avenue.

MOTOR SPORTS

ROAD ATLANTA, Georgia Hwy. 53 between I-85 and Georgia 365. Tel. 967-6143.

Situated on 1,000 scenic wooded acres about 50 miles north of downtown Atlanta, this is the Southeast's premier motor-sports facility. Its 2.5-mile Grand Prix racecourse offers a challenging combination of turns, elevation changes, and high-speed straights.

Events include sports car, motorcycle, vintage/historic, and go-kart racing, including the annual International Motor Sports Association (IMSA) Camel GT for prototype sports cars, AMA Camel Pro motorcycle road races, and Sports Car Club of America (SCCA) National Championship Valvoline Runoffs. The property includes a 5-acre lake with a sandy beach. Tickets are available through the above number or Ticketmaster (tel. 249-6400). You can camp free on the property if you're attending an event.

Prices: Tickets are $20–$45.

Open: Year-round season of events. **Directions:** Route 85N to Exit 49 and follow the signs.

RECREATION

Atlanta's fine climate is very conducive to participation in outdoor sports, and facilities abound.

FISHING

THE FISH HAWK, 283 Buckhead Ave. NE, between Peachtree and Piedmont Rds. Tel. 237-3473.

The Fish Hawk is the largest supplier in Atlanta for quality tackle. It carries all manner of fishing gear and outdoor clothing and can also supply the requisite license ($7 for seven days, $13 for a trout-fishing license valid for one year). There's good trout fishing on the Chattahoochee River, just 10 minutes from the store, or in the North Georgia Mountains, about 1½ hours from here. Many lakes in the area are good for bass and striper, including Lake Lanier, a 38,000-acre reservoir about 45 minutes away. For saltwater fishing, you'll have to drive about five hours from Atlanta to the East Coast. Owner Gary Merriman is extremely knowledgeable and can tell you where to find the fish you seek. He can also tell you all applicable state regulations.

For additional information, serious fisherfolk can write or call the Georgia Department of Natural Resources, Game and Fish Division, Suite 1358, Floyd Towers East, 205 Butler St. SE, Atlanta, GA 30334 (tel. 404/656-4817).

Open: Mon–Fri 9am–6pm, Sat 9am–5pm.

GOLF

GEORGIA'S STONE MOUNTAIN PARK GOLF COURSE, Stone Mountain Park. Tel. 498-5717.

Stone Mountain's 36-hole Robert Trent Jones nationally ranked layout is a beautiful facility, with nine holes adjacent to the park's lake. To quote *Gene's Guide to Atlanta's Public Courses,* "Its narrow rolling fairways lead to well trapped, tiered bent grass greens. When the tees are back this course demands both strength and accuracy." I don't know what that means, but if you're a golfer I guess it communicates something. A pro shop is on the premises, and lessons are available. For weekends and holidays reserve the Tuesday prior to the day you want to play; other times it's first come, first served.

Admission: $36 green fees, including the cart. There is a fee of $5 per vehicle to enter the park.

Open: Mon–Fri 8am–dark, from 7am until dark weekends and holidays.

HOT-AIR BALLOONING

SUNDANCE BALLOON, 395 8th St. NE. Tel. 972-3618.

Aeronaut/owner Chuck Deafenbaugh, a fully licensed and insured hot-air balloonist, has been flying balloons professionally since 1972. He offers sunrise and sunset flights in a wicker airship over verdant farmland, horse country, woods, and lakes. On landing, you're greeted with champagne, fruit, and cheese. Call for reservations.

Prices: $150 for one or two people, $325 for three.

Open: Daily.

A similar operation is **Southeastern Balloon Services** (tel. 985-8079).

RIVER RAFTING

SOUTHEASTERN EXPEDITIONS, 2936-H N. Druid Hills Rd. Tel. 329-0433 or toll free 800/868-RAFT.

Southeastern offers white-water adventures on the scenic Chattooga River in North Georgia (it's the one you saw in the movie *Deliverance*) and the Ocoee in Tennessee. Put-in points for both rivers are about a 2-hour drive from Atlanta. Trips vary in length (from a few hours to a few days) and difficulty. A favorite of mine is a sunrise trip on the Chattooga; you'll find the exquisite morning peacefulness of river and forest soon contrasted by the thrill of running some of the toughest rapids around. After lunch you can hike to the magnificent Opossum Creek Falls. Days like that are magical. The Chattooga offers Class II and III rapids in Section III and Class III, IV, and V rapids in Section IV. The roller-coasterlike Ocoee has Class III and IV rapids only. Kids must be at least 10 for easy trips, 12 or 13 for more difficult rapids. The company also offers canoeing and kayaking. All of these expeditions are immensely popular, so make your reservations as far in advance as possible.

Prices: Vary depending on length and difficulty, and weekends are more expensive than weekdays. Half-day trips begin at about $28, full-day trips at $47, both rates including lunch, equipment, a guide, and transportation from the outpost to the river.

Open: Rafting season is Apr 1–Oct 31, with occasional trips in Mar and Nov.

ROLLER SKATING AND BICYCLING

SKATE ESCAPE, 1086 Piedmont Ave. NE, at 12th St. Tel. 892-1292.

Conveniently located close to Piedmont Park, Skate Escape offers all kinds of bicycles and skates for rent or sale, as well as helmets, bicycle locks, and accessories. You can also buy skateboards here.

Prices: Rental per hour $5 for single-speed children's bike or tandem. Conventional or in-line skates are $4 per hour, $12 per day. A driver's license or major credit card is required for ID, or you can leave a deposit of $100 for skates, $200 for bicycles.

Open: Mon–Sat 10am–7pm, Sun 11am–7pm. **MARTA:** Midtown.

SWIMMING

Almost every Atlanta hotel features a swimming pool. In addition, there's a large public swimming pool in Piedmont Park.

TENNIS

TENNIS TECH, Lenox Park Tennis Center, 3375 Standard Dr., off Peachtree Rd. 1 mile north of Lenox Sq. Tel. 237-7339.

Tennis Tech, a tennis management group, operates 11 public courts (3 indoor clay, 7 outdoor clay, and 1 outdoor hard court) at Lenox Park. Four of the outdoor courts are lit for night play. You can reserve 24 hours in advance or just show up. Tennis lessons are available for adults and children. There are showers, lockers, and a pro shop on the premises.

Open: Daily year round from 9am–9 or 10pm.

Prices: $3 per person per hour for outdoor courts; $15 per hour/per court for indoor facilities weekday and nonholiday afternoons, $24 at all other times.

PIEDMONT PARK, Piedmont Avenue and 14th St. Tel. 872-1507.

The City of Atlanta Parks and Recreation Department operates 12 outdoor hard courts at Piedmont Park, all of them lit for night play. Although it's not required, it's best to reserve 24 hours in advance. There are showers, lockers, and a pro shop on the premises.

Open: Weekdays 10am–9pm, Sat–Sun 9am–6pm.

Prices: $1.50 per person per hour during the day, $1.75 per person per hour when courts are lit for night play.

BITSY GRANT TENNIS CENTER, 2125 Northside Dr., between I-75N and Peachtree Battle Ave. Tel. 351-2774.

Also operated by the Atlanta Parks and Recreation Department are these 13 outdoor clay courts (6 of them lit for night play) and 10 outdoor hard courts (4 lit). Courts are available on a first-come, first-served basis. No reservations. There are showers, lockers, and a pro shop on the premises.

Open: Mon–Fri 9am–9pm, Sat–Sun 8am–8pm.

Prices: $2.50 per person per hour for clay courts, $1.50 per person per hour for hard courts.

CHAPTER 8

STROLLING AROUND ATLANTA

1. DOWNTOWN
2. SWEET AUBURN

I t's my feeling that you never really understand a city unless you walk around it a bit. Atlanta's lovely climate makes walking tours a marvelous option just about year round. In addition to the suggestions below, consider the excellent guided walking tours listed in Chapter 7, "What to See and Do in Atlanta." Also, note that the following attractions detailed in that chapter comprise walking tours in and of themselves: Stone Mountain; Oakland Cemetery; and the Atlanta Historical Society in Buckhead.

WALKING TOUR 1 — Downtown

Start: Peachtree Center at the corner of Harris Street and Peachtree Center Avenue.
Finish: Hurt Plaza.
Time: Allow approximately two hours, not including museum perusal and browsing in shops; allow one hour if you only walk the Peachtree Center portion.

Atlanta's downtown section, around which the city grew, is one of the nation's most attractive commercial centers. It makes for a varied and fascinating architectural tour.

FROM HARRIS ST. TO ELLIS ST. We'll first explore Peachtree Center, an extremely impressive project realized by visionary 20th-century architect/developer John Portman. I don't think any other American city has a downtown that is so largely one person's conception. The complex occupies 14 city blocks and is still growing. Numbers 1 through 14 on your map are all Portman's Peachtree Center buildings, connected by walkways and bridges and beautified by fountains, gardens, and plazas. Portman's "urban village" is based on the premise that "people enjoy living, working, and shopping in a space that is as large as possible without the need of transportation." Start at:

1. **The Marriott Marquis,** Peachtree Center Avenue between Baker and Harris streets, one of Portman's most dramatically

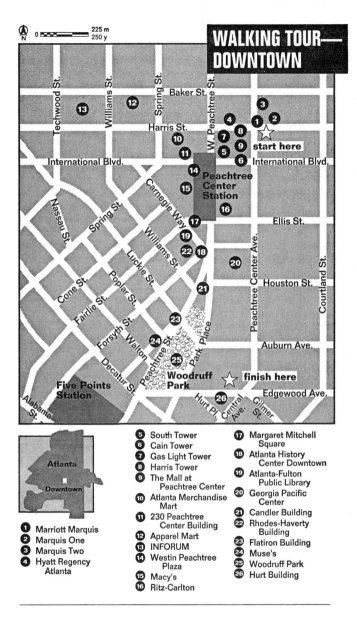

WALKING TOUR— DOWNTOWN

- **1** Marriott Marquis
- **2** Marquis One
- **3** Marquis Two
- **4** Hyatt Regency Atlanta
- **5** South Tower
- **6** Cain Tower
- **7** Gas Light Tower
- **8** Harris Tower
- **9** The Mall at Peachtree Center
- **10** Atlanta Merchandise Mart
- **11** 230 Peachtree Center Building
- **12** Apparel Mart
- **13** INFORUM
- **14** Westin Peachtree Plaza
- **15** Macy's
- **16** Ritz-Carlton
- **17** Margaret Mitchell Square
- **18** Atlanta History Center Downtown
- **19** Atlanta-Fulton Public Library
- **20** Georgia Pacific Center
- **21** Candler Building
- **22** Rhodes-Haverty Building
- **23** Flatiron Building
- **24** Muse's
- **25** Woodruff Park
- **26** Hurt Building

futuristic hotel designs, with a soaring 48-story atrium and vines suspended from balcony railings creating a hanging-garden effect. Step into the lobby, gawk, and, just for the fun of it, ride to the top floor in one of the bubble-glass elevators.

Two 30-story office towers adjoin the hotel:

2. Marquis One and

3. Marquis Two.

4. **The Hyatt Regency Atlanta,** at the corner of Peachtree and Harris streets, is not only Portman's prototype for later downtown hotels but the model for hundreds of properties built across the nation. Like the Marriott, it features a lofty open-air atrium, indoor-garden design. The blue dome atop Polaris, the Hyatt's revolving rooftop restaurant, is a city landmark.

On the square block bounded on the east by Peachtree Center Avenue, on the west by Peachtree Street, on the south by International Boulevard, and on the north by Harris Street, are some Peachtree Center office buildings, built in the 1970s:

5. **South Tower,** 25 stories;
6. **Cain Tower,** 30 stories;
7. **Gas Light Tower,** 25 stories; and
8. **Harris Tower,** 30 stories.

Do stop in at:

9. **The Mall at Peachtree Center,** also in this square block. It's a 3-level complex of shops and restaurants.

The square block immediately west contains:

10. **Atlanta Merchandise Mart,** a wholesale showroom space for gifts, furniture, and floor covering. Opened in 1961, it was the first Peachtree Center building.

Also in this block is:

11. **230 Peachtree Center Building.**

One and two blocks east, respectively, between Harris and Baker streets, are:

12. **The Apparel Mart,** another major wholesale showroom; and
13. **INFORUM,** a showroom for the technology/information industry.

At the corner of Peachtree Street and International Boulevard you'll note the gleaming steel and glass tower of:

14. **The Westin Peachtree Plaza,** the world's tallest hotel. Its mirrored exterior is meant to reflect the surrounding environment.

Just below the Westin is the downtown branch of:

15. **Macy's,** a department store in the grand tradition dating from 1927. Its architectural style is "modified Renaissance." You might want to stop in and do some shopping or have a snack in the Cellar.

Or, plan your walking tour to arrive at:

16. **The Ritz-Carlton,** just across the street, in time for a lavish afternoon tea (see Chapter 6, "Atlanta Dining").

That could very nicely complete a minitour of Peachtree Center. If you have energy, continue on.

FROM PEACHTREE AND ELLIS STS. TO HURT PLAZA

Proceed south from the Ritz-Carlton on Peachtree to Forsyth Street, site of:

17. **Margaret Mitchell Square.** Here you'll find the downtown branch of:

18. **The Atlanta History Center Downtown,** which always features interesting city-related exhibits. There are fascinating free noontime lectures here from the fall through the spring; you might call 238-0655 to find out who's on during your stay and make a lecture part of the tour.

    At the same junction is:

19. **The Atlanta-Fulton Public Library.** You might want to stop in and see the permanent exhibit on Margaret Mitchell on the first floor.

REFUELING STOP   Delectables, down a flight of steps from the library (tel. 681-2909), is a lovely place for low-priced lunch fare. It's open weekdays only. Weekends, you can eat in any of the hotels mentioned on this tour (see Chapter 5 for details on all your options). Also check out downtown restaurants in Chapter 6.

---

20. **The Georgia Pacific Center,** at Peachtree and Houston streets, constructed on red granite from Texas, houses the downtown branch of the High Museum and a vast Louise Nevelson indoor environmental sculpture in white wood called *Dawn's Forest.* Admission is free. Definitely plan to spend some time here.

    Just below Houston Street is:

21. **The Candler Building.** Built at the turn of the century, it's made of white Georgia marble and adorned with ornamental friezes and busts of famous artists, writers, statesmen, and scientists (these portraits range from Michelangelo to Buffalo Bill Cody). It's marvelously opulent (do walk inside), with ornate marble carvings, Tiffany glass, and crystal chandeliers. Asa G. Candler bought the rights to Coca-Cola in 1891 for $2,300—the best buy since the Dutch purchased Manhattan.

    Across the street is:

22. **The Rhodes-Haverty Building,** completed in 1929, a foray into the world of modern architecture.

    Atlanta has a triangular building:

23. **The Flatiron Building,** Peachtree and Luckie streets, designed by Brad Gilbert in 1897.

    Farther down the street is:

24. **Muse's,** a 1921 building occupying a clothing store that was established by George Muse in 1879.

    Across the street is:

25. **Woodruff Park,** named for Coca-Cola magnate Robert W. Woodruff. Though city workers congregate here at lunchtime (it's de rigueur to purchase a char-broiled hot dog from Barker's cart), the park is in a rather seedy phase at this writing.

    Cross the park to Park Place and proceed to Hurt Plaza at Edgewood Avenue.

    Here is:

26. The Hurt Building, built in 1912, one of Atlanta's most magnificent, its entrance flanked by Corinthian columns heralding a marble-walled rotunda. Inside is one of the city's top restaurants, the City Grill (see Chapter 6, "Atlanta Dining"); if you can afford lunch here, there is no better way to wind up your downtown tour.

WALKING TOUR 2 — Sweet Auburn

Start: MLK, Jr., Center for Non-Violent Social Change, 449 Auburn Ave.
Finish: Auburn Avenue and Courtland Street.
Time: Allow at least half a day to explore this area thoroughly.

Sweet Auburn includes the Martin Luther King, Jr., National Historic District, which comprises about 12 blocks along Auburn Avenue. A neighborhood that nurtured scores of 20th-century black businesspeople and professionals, it contains the birthplace, church, and gravesite of Martin Luther King, Jr. Under the auspices of the National Parks Service, portions of Auburn Avenue are in an ongoing process of restoration as an important historic district. Eventually, many of the homes and businesses on the "Birth Home" block will resume their 1920s appearance. This tour provides insight into black history, the civil rights movement, and black urban culture in the South. If you're traveling with children, it's a wonderful opportunity to teach them about a great American. The major attractions are covered in detail in Chapter 7.

Begin your stroll at:

1. **The Martin Luther King, Jr., Center for Non-Violent Social Change,** 449 Auburn Ave., is an organization that continues the work to which King was dedicated—reducing violence within the community and among nations. Freedom Plaza, on the premises, is his final resting place. The center functions as an information station for area attractions. This is where you obtain tickets to view the Birth Home of Martin Luther King, Jr. (on weekends, especially, arrive early, since demand for tickets often exceeds supply). Here, too, you can take a self-guided tour of exhibits on King's life and the civil rights movement and see videos which include some of his most stirring speeches. Including the videos (which shouldn't be missed), plan to spend at least two hours at the center.

   Now, for further orientation, proceed, a few blocks east to:
2. **The Visitor Center,** 522 Auburn Ave., between Howell and Hogue streets (tel. 331-3920), where you can pick up a comprehensive area map/brochure provided by the National Park

Service and view a 15-minute slide show about the history of the community. Often, other relevant videos/slide shows are offered, as are occasional exhibits. This orientation center itself is the elegant restored turn-of-the-century home of two prominent black citizens, the Reverend Peter James Bryant, and, later, of developer Antoine Graves. The center is open Monday to Friday 9am to 5pm.

Cross the street and walk west a bit to:

3. The Birth Home of Martin Luther King, Jr., 501 Auburn Ave., where free half-hour guided tours are given on a continual basis September through May 10am to 5pm, the rest of the year 10am to 7pm. Get tickets at the MLK, Jr., Center listed above.

After you leave, note some turn-of-the-century homes in the area such as:

4. The Double "Shotgun" Row Houses, 472–488 Auburn Ave., two-family dwellings with separate hip roofs which were built in 1905 to house workers for the Empire Textile Company. They were so named because rooms were lined up in a row; if you so desired, you could fire a shotgun right through them.

At the corner of Auburn and Boulevard is:

5. Fire Station No. 6, one of Atlanta's eight original firehouses, completed in 1894. The 2-story Romanesque-revival building was situated to protect the eastern section of the city. Note the Italianate arched windows on the second story. A museum is in the works here for the future.

REFUELING STOP The Martin Luther King, Jr., Center for Non-Violent Social Change, 449 Auburn Ave., (tel. 526-8920), houses the **South Fork Restaurant,** a very nice cafeteria serving home-cooked southern fare. For about $5, you can dine here on baked chicken with biscuits, candied yams, and fresh veggies. There's fresh-baked peach cobbler for dessert. Open daily 7:30am to 6pm. No credit cards.

Continuing west, a notable stop on your tour is:

6. Ebenezer Baptist Church, 407 Auburn Ave., founded in 1886, where Martin Luther King, Jr., served as co-pastor from 1960–68. You can view a video here on the history of the church.

REFUELING STOP At the corner of Auburn Avenue and Jackson Street is another very good, and very inexpensive, southern/soul food cafeteria, the **Beautiful Restaurant** (tel. 233-0800). It's open daily from 7:30am to 8pm. No credit cards. See Chapter 6 for details.

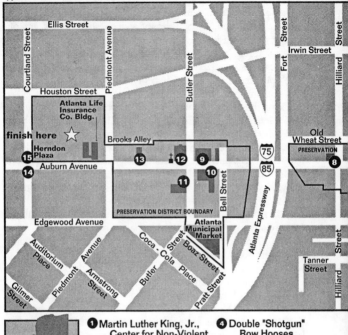

One block west is the:

7. Wheat Street Baptist Church, 365 Auburn Ave., built in the 1920s, but serving a congregation since the late 1800s. Auburn Avenue was originally called Wheat Street in honor of Augustus W. Wheat, one of Atlanta's early merchants. The name was changed in 1893.

Further west, on Auburn between Hilliard and Fort streets, is:

8. The Prince Hall Masonic Building, an influential black lodge led for several decades by John Wesley Dobbs. Today it houses the national headquarters of the Southern Christian Leadership Conference.

REFUELING STOP The corner of Auburn Avenue and Fort Street is the site of the famous **Auburn Avenue Rib Shack** (tel. 523-8315). There are only three booths and a counter, plus, in good weather, a few umbrella tables outside. Arrive early or late to avoid a wait for seating. Everything is homemade— fabulous barbecued chicken, pork, or beef, ribs, potato salad,

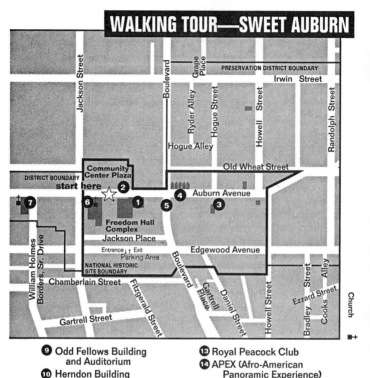

PRESERVATION DISTRICT BOUNDARY

Jackson Street

Boulevard

Grape Place

Irwin Street

Ryder Alley

Hogue Street

Howell Street

Randolph Street

Hogue Alley

Old Wheat Street

DISTRICT BOUNDARY

Community Center Plaza

start here

❷

❻ ❶ ❺ ❹ Auburn Avenue ❸

❼

Freedom Hall Complex

Jackson Place

Entrance ↓↑ Exit

Parking Area

Edgewood Avenue

NATIONAL HISTORIC SITE BOUNDARY

William Holmes Borders, Sr. Drive

Chamberlain Street

Fitzgerald Street

Boulevard

Gartrell Place

Daniel Street

Howell Street

Bradley Street

Ezzard Street

Cooks Alley

Church

Gartrell Street

❾ Odd Fellows Building and Auditorium

❿ Herndon Building

⓫ Butler Street YMCA

⓬ Big Bethel African Methodist Episcopal Church

⓭ Royal Peacock Club

⓮ APEX (Afro-American Panoramic Experience) Museum

⓯ Herndon Plaza

collard greens, candied yams, and more. Prices are low. Open Tuesday 11:30am to 4pm, Thursday 11:30am to 7pm, Friday 11:30am to 9:30pm, and Saturday noon to 9:30pm. No credit cards.

On the other side of the expressway, note:

9. The Odd Fellows Building and Auditorium, 228–50 Auburn Ave., another black fraternal lodge, which originated in Atlanta in 1870. Completed in 1914, the building later became headquarters for an insurance company.

Across the street is:

10. The Herndon Building, 231–45 Auburn Ave., named for Alonzo Herndon, an ex-slave who went on to found the Atlanta Life Insurance Company. It was erected in 1924. By 1930, the Auburn business district supported 121 black-owned businesses and 39 black professionals.

Make a left and you'll see:

11. The Butler Street YMCA, built in the early 1900s.

Go back to Auburn Avenue, and across the street is:

12. The Big Bethel African Methodist Episcopal Church, at no. 220, originally built in the 1890s and then rebuilt in 1924 after a fire. In the 1920s, John Wesley Dobbs called the Bethel "a towering edifice to black freedom."

Farther along is:

13. The Royal Peacock Club, 184–186 Auburn Ave. Its walls painted floor to ceiling with peacocks, it presented top black entertainers such as Ray Charles, Aretha Franklin, and Dizzy Gillespie in its heyday. There is talk of restoring the club to its former glamour.

At Auburn Avenue and Courtland Street is:

14. The APEX (African-American Panoramic Experience) Museum (tel. 521-APEX), featuring exhibits on the history of Sweet Auburn and changing exhibits relating to the African-American experience.

Cross the street to see the final sight on this tour:

15. Herndon Plaza, where exhibits on the Herndon family can be seen.

CHAPTER 9

ATLANTA SHOPPING

1. SHOPPING AREAS
2. DEPARTMENT STORES & MALLS
3. SHOPPING AROUND TOWN

Atlanta is the shopping mecca of the Southeast. Its vast—and very chic—malls serve not only locals but a large number of consumers who come from neighboring states just to shop. Buckhead boutiques such as Sasha Frisson can hold their own with the most fashionable emporiums of New York and Los Angeles. There are also browsable areas of quaint shops in Little Five Points and Virginia-Highland. This is a great town for antiquing, and I love the big old-fashioned downtown Macy's.

1. SHOPPING AREAS

CHAMBLEE'S ANTIQUE ROW

Antique Row, on Peachtree Road between Chamblee-Dunwoody and North Peachtree roads (tel. 458-1614), is a quaint complex of over 30 shops located in historic homes, churches, and other buildings. Some of them date as far back as the 1800s. There are dealers of antique American and European furniture, glassware, pottery, Victoriana, Orientalia, wicker, collector toys, quilts, jewelry, architectural antiques, and crafts items. Country antiques are especially well represented. It's a great afternoon ramble. See also Virginia-Highland, Little Five Points, and Stone Mountain Village, below, for more stores selling antiques. Hours vary with each store. Almost all are open Monday through Saturday from 10:30am to 5pm; most are open Sunday from 1 to 5pm as well. You can take a MARTA train to Chamblee Station; it's about three-fourths of a mile from the shops. On weekdays you can get the Tilly Mill bus from there; on weekends walk or take a taxi.

VIRGINIA-HIGHLAND

This charming area of town, centered on Highland Avenue between Virginia and Ponce de Leon Avenue, teems with antique shops, junk stores, trendy boutiques, and art galleries. Since you'll want to browse through all its shops in one excursion, they're grouped together here in the order in which you will find them while walking north through the neighborhood. Take a lunch break at Murphy's (see Chapter 6, "Atlanta Dining").

ANTIQUES AND GIFTS

ANTIQUES, ETC., 1003 Virginia Ave. NE, at N. Highland Ave. Tel. 874-7042.

Not a highbrow antiques shop, but rather a campy nostalgia trip, Antiques, Etc. is aclutter with fifties blond-wood furniture, Elvis trading cards, back issues of *Life* magazine, art deco and art nouveau lamps and furniture, antique radios and telephones, whimsical clocks, Marilyn Monroe drinking cups, gum-ball machines, miniature Wurlitzers, and much more. Open Sun–Wed 11am–6pm, Thurs–Sat 11am–9pm.

20TH CENTURY, 1044 N. Highland Ave., between Los Angeles and Virginia Aves. Tel. 892-2065.

As its name implies, this shop specializes in international antiques and reproductions made during this century. The inventory is wide-ranging, including some terrific jewelry, Limoges porcelain boxes, suits of armor, whimsical clocks, art nouveau lamps, art deco items, tapestry-covered hatboxes, patchwork quilts, and much more. Great browsing. Open Mon–Wed 11am–7pm, Thurs–Sat 11am–9pm, Sun noon–6pm.

AFFAIRS, 1401 N. Highland Ave., just below University Dr. Tel. 876-3342.

This charming shop, its ambience enhanced by well-chosen classical and jazz tapes, offers many exquisite giftware items. Some examples: a mother-of-pearl toothbrush, a rabbit- or cow-shaped clock, one-of-a-kind picture frames, stuffed dolls and animals, beautiful dinnerware, and floral chintz-lined baskets. Affairs also carries French and Italian kitchenware and a full line of Crabtree & Evelyn products. Delightful browsing. Open Mon–Sat 10am–9:30pm, Sun noon–6pm.

BODY AND BATH

NATURAL BODY, 1403 N. Highland Ave., just below University Dr. Tel. 876-9642.

This very appealing shop invites you to pamper yourself with all manner of skin treatments, bubble baths, massage and body oils, potpourris, soaps, lotions, and cosmetics. All of their products are 100% natural, chemical free, and biodegradable, and none are tested on animals. They carry, among other lines, Kiehl (from New York), Aveda, Ahava (made in Israel with minerals from the Dead Sea), and Bindi (products made in India from ayurvedic herbs, roots, and flowers). Natural Body also runs a spa around the corner (tel. 872-1039), offering massages, facials, aroma therapy, manicures, pedicures, and other beauty spa treatments. Open Mon 10:30am–6pm, Tues–Sat 10:30am–9pm, Sun 1–6pm.

CLOTHING BOUTIQUES

MITZI & ROMANO, 1038 N. Highland Ave., between Virginia and Los Angeles Aves. Tel. 876-7228.

Mitzi Ugolini buys designer clothes in New York, California, and Europe. The women's clothing is fashion-forward—the kind that makes a statement instead of blending in with the crowd. Great jewelry and accessories, too. Prices are affordable. Open Mon 11am–7pm, Tues–Thurs 11am–8pm, Fri–Sat 11am–10pm, Sun noon–6pm.

PORTER'S, 994 Virginia Ave., just off N. Highland Ave. Tel. 874-7834.

Stop by for carefully chosen men's clothing and men's and women's accessories, unique imported and designer ties for men, beautiful T-shirts, jewelry, Beatrix Potter drawer-lining paper, and other lovely items. Open Tues–Thurs 11am–9pm, Fri–Sat 11am–10pm, Sun 12:30–6pm.

MOONCAKE, 1019 Virginia Ave. NE, just off N. Highland Ave. Tel. 892-8043.

Whimsical wearables for women here include traditional styles in lacy wedding gowns, colorful woolen mittens from Turkey, California-look floral tier skirts, sexy and elegant lingerie, mukluks from Pakistan, and oddments that range from ethnic and handcrafted jewelry to rosette-embellished ballet slippers. The retro-style clothing looks vintage, but it's all new. Open spring through fall Mon–Sat 11am–9:30pm, Sun noon–6pm; winter Mon–Sat 11am–7pm, Sun noon–6pm.

AN ART GALLERY

ALIYA GALLERY, 1402 N. Highland Ave. NE, in the Highland Walk Center between University and Morningside Drs. Tel. 892-2835.

Steve Fleenor and Gary Alembik (Gary lived a year in Jerusalem, hence the name Aliya), are the owners of this very lovely gallery. Light jazz or classical music sets the tone for viewing their extremely well-chosen art displays. They represent 30 artists whose works range from contemporary paintings (abstracts, landscapes, and figurative), to pottery, sculpture, and jewelry. Open Sun–Thurs 11:30am–10pm, Fri–Sat 11:30am–11pm.

NEW AGE

ATLANTIS CONNECTION, 1402 N. Highland Ave., between University and Morningside Drs. Tel. 881-6511.

Atlantis is essentially a New Age bookstore offering tomes on color healing, meditation, the *I Ching,* Indian philosophy, astrology, and juice fasting, among other esoterica. It also carries related items—crystals, New Age and Indian jewelry, Tibetan prayer bowls, Zuni fetishes, and incense. Open Mon–Thurs 11am–9pm, Fri–Sat 11am–10pm, Sun 1–6pm.

LITTLE FIVE POINTS

An area similar to Virginia-Highland (see above)—though a little funkier—Little Five Points reminds me of Berkeley in the 1960s. There are still authentic hippies here. It is also close to Virginia-Highland, so if you crave additional boutique browsing, both areas are easily covered in a few hours. While you're shopping here, plan a leisurely lunch at the delightful Bridgetown Grill (details in Chapter 6). Begin your shopping stroll at Euclid and Moreland avenues and proceed southwest along Euclid. Because shopping here is more of a browsing experience than a search for specific merchandise, stores in this area are listed in geographic order rather than by type of store.

CRYSTAL BLUE, 1168 Euclid Ave., between Moreland and Colquitt Aves. Tel. 522-4605.

Wayne and Debbie Vaillancourt's esoteric emporium specializes in crystals and minerals touted for healing and other purposes. For example: black tourmaline promotes balance to the endocrine system, rose quartz perks up the kidneys and circulatory system, and meteorite helps reveal past lives from other planets and galaxies. Other items here include New Age books and cassettes, incense, chimes, chakra oils, and Acusphere exercise balls to stimulate acupuncture points. Open Mon–Sat 11am–7pm, Sun noon–6pm.

STEFAN'S, 1160 Euclid Ave., between Moreland and Colquitt Aves. Tel. 688-4929.

Most of Stefan's merchandise is vintage clothing for men and women from the 1890s through the mid-1960s, the rest accessories like belts, suspenders, cummerbunds, and glitzy period costume jewelry. There are 1950s net-skirt prom dresses, Mamie Eisenhower gowns, tuxedos, wedding gowns, Hawaiian shirts, and many, many hats. Prices are low. Open Mon–Sat 11am–7pm, Sun noon–6pm.

BOOMERANG, 1145 Euclid Ave., between Moreland and Colquitt Aves. Tel. 577-8158.

This eclectic shop carries funky furniture (it ranges from a 1950s vanity table to a leopardskin velvet-upholstered loveseat), and a wide array of gift items—pink French poodle salt and pepper shakers, Mona Lisa magnets, Indian cut-tin wall ornaments, Mexican candlesticks, Chilean wood animals, and more. Open Wed–Sat noon–6pm, Sun 1–5pm.

RENE RENE, 1142 Euclid Ave., between Moreland and Colquitt Aves. Tel. 522-RENE.

Atlanta magazine, in it's "best and worst" awards issue, named Rene Rene the city's "best women's clothing" shop in the "funky club scene" category. It's true, but some of owner Rene Sanning's designs are more sophisticated—even possibly wearable for business. She recently added high-fashion menswear to her line ("not for the IBM man," says Rene). Interesting accessories here, too, such as black gloves adorned with silk roses. Open Mon–Fri 11:30am–6:30pm, Sat 11am–7pm, Sun 1–5pm.

PRINCESS PAMELA'S TCHOTCHKA PALACE, 1141 Euclid Ave., between Moreland and Colquitt Aves. Tel. 222-9514.

This store specializes in small, inexpensive gift items—posters, cards, wind-up toys, hand buzzers, Elvis key chains, puppets from Sri Lanka, sushi-shaped pencil sharpeners, antique and imported toys, and oddities such as a Chippendale's male-stripper movie viewer. Also offered here: a large selection of international masks and folk art, sequin-covered Haitian voodoo flags and bottles, and new and used tapes and CDs. Open Mon–Sat 11am–7pm, Sun noon–6pm.

THROB, 1140 Euclid Ave., between Moreland and Colquitt Aves. Tel. 522-0355.

Throb specializes in unconventional (to put it mildly) club wear for men and women. You can shop here for see-through vinyl minis, hot pants, bondage-look clothing, black fishnet and silver vinyl dresses, intergalactic plastic jewelry, leather lingerie, lingerie meant to be worn as outerwear, chartreuse wigs, and, to complete the look, wild hair dye and make-up colors. Open Mon–Sat 11am–7pm, Sun noon–6pm.

THE JUNKMAN'S DAUGHTER, 1130 Euclid Ave., between Moreland and Colquitt Aves. Tel. 577-3188.

This funky store looks like a transplant from New York's East Village. Owner Pamela Mills, whose parents and grandparents were in the salvage/junk-store business, inherited a bizarre assortment of family treasures, including cartons of Mickey Mouse toys, the remains of a perfume factory, and cases of stockings from 1932. This legacy formed the nucleus of her collection, which today includes Elvis earrings, a large selection of costumes (everything from a California Raisin to a giant crayfish), Japanese military capes, new and used clothing, 1950s saddle shoes and crinolines, feather boas, leather jackets, antique furs, beaded and sequined gowns, Doc Martin's boots and shoes from London, papier-mâché pig's head masks, and much, much more. Open Mon–Sat 11am–7pm, Sun noon–6pm.

A CAPPELLA BOOKS, 1133 Euclid Ave., at Colquitt Ave. Tel. 681-5128.

This is the kind of offbeat bookstore that makes great browsing. They carry new, used, and out-of-print books, many of them relating to counterculture, literature, history, and the arts. Signed editions here, too. Open Mon–Sat 11am–7pm, Sun noon–6pm, with extended hours spring and summer.

BERMAN GALLERY, 1131 Euclid Ave., at Colquitt Ave. Tel. 525-2529.

Specializing in contemporary folk art and ceramics created by untrained artists—most of them black or from rural Appalachia— the Berman Gallery also features Amish and Early American quilts. The owners are potters who sometimes work on a wheel in the shop. Open Tues–Sat 10am–5:30pm.

AFRICAN CONNECTIONS, 1107 Euclid Ave., between Colquitt and Washita Aves. Tel. 589-1834.

This fascinating shop carries: soapstone carvings from Kenya; textiles, such as asooke cloth from Nigeria and kente cloth from Ghana; handcrafted jewelry from Africa, India, and Indonesia, as well as pieces made by African American jewelers using African materials; traditional and contemporary clothing from the Ivory Coast, Ghana, and Nigeria; traditional West African masks; Nigerian Fulani wedding bead necklaces; Indonesian and African baskets; and African ceremonial combs and medicine bowls. There's much more. Open Tues–Sat 11am–6pm, Sun 1–6pm.

STONE MOUNTAIN

Stone Mountain Village, just outside the West Gate of Georgia's Stone Mountain Park (bounded by Second and Main streets north and south, Poole and East Mountain streets east and west; tel. 296-8058), is well worth a visit. It's been developing since the 1800s, and many of the 70-plus shops are housed in historic buildings (for example, an antique shop in a 150-year-old log cabin). Merchants here keep to a very high standard, and their wares are tasteful and of good quality. A lot of the stores specialize in antiques, crafts, and collectibles. Some examples: country furniture, canning jars, dried-flower wreaths, imported toys, handmade candles, dolls, baskets, homemade jams, potpourri, patchwork quilts and quilting fabrics, handcrafted dulcimers, Civil War memorabilia, and out-of-print books.

It's great fun to wander about this quaint village, and there's usually some festive event going on—perhaps an arts-and-crafts fair or live entertainment. During Christmas season, the streets are candlelit and the village becomes a magical place populated by St. Nick, elves, carolers, and harpists. Hours for most shops are Monday through Saturday from 10am to 5pm; some also open Sunday from 1 to 5pm.

Stop for breakfast or lunch at the nearby **Basket Bakery and Garden Café**, 6655 Memorial Drive, at Main Street (tel. 498-0329). For breakfast there are croissants or ham-and-egg platters with homemade biscuits. Later, you can opt for sandwiches on fresh-baked breads, homemade salads, quiche, soups, and home-baked desserts. The café is closed on Monday.

2. DEPARTMENT STORES & MALLS

So many malls, so little time. I've covered the most central shopping clusters only; there are many more in suburbia.

MACY'S PEACHTREE, 180 Peachtree St., between International Blvd. and Ellis St. Tel. 221-7221.

Opened in 1927, this downtown branch of Macy's is a department store in the grand tradition, its main floor featuring 30 lofty fleur-de-lis-topped columns, marble floors, and glittering crystal chandeliers. However, it's perfectly up to date when it comes to merchandise. Like most branches of Macy's nowadays, it has a Cellar—a street market with tiled brick floors and shops specializing in gourmet food and housewares. It's the scene of frequent food tastings. There's also a conveniently located visitor's center on the Cellar level; stop in for information on Atlanta attractions and a complimentary cup of coffee. Six floors of merchandise comprise everything you'd expect—clothing and shoes for the whole family, china, silver, bedding, the works. And dining options range from grilled seafood to a buttery hot cinnamon bun. Open Mon–Sat 10am–6pm, Sun noon–6pm. **MARTA:** Peachtree Center.

UNDERGROUND ATLANTA, Alabama St., between Peachtree St. and Central Ave. Tel. 523-2311.

This 12-acre mix of colorful shops, nightclubs, and restaurants makes for a fun-filled day or evening. There are dozens of shops here, plus vendors in Humbug Square selling merchandise off antique pushcarts. Shopping options include numerous clothing shops for men, women, and children, running the gamut from upscale T-shirts at Dallas Alice, to leather clothing at Tannery West, to Victoria's Secret's very sexy lingerie. An especially interesting shop is Antiquities Historical Galleries (for limited-edition, signed and numbered historical documents). Gift shops run the gamut from Georgia Grande General (Georgia-related gifts and crafts) to Papier D'Couleur (papier-mâché birds, fruits, and animals). And there are also novelty stores such as Santa's Alley (Christmas year round) and the bargain mecca, Everything's A $1. Other merchants here sell books, jewelry, shoes, music tapes and videos, and items related to the 1996 Olympics. And of course, eateries—from pizza and taco stands to elegant restaurants—abound. If you're driving, there's parking in a garage on Central Avenue off Martin Luther King Drive. Be sure to get your ticket validated inside for discounted parking. Open Mon–Sat 10am–9:30pm, Sun noon–6pm. **MARTA:** Five Points.

LENOX SQUARE MALL, 3393 Peachtree Rd. NE, at Lenox Rd. Tel. 233-6767 or 800/344-5222.

The largest shopping mall in the Southeast, the upscale Lenox Square was built in 1959 and has since undergone three major expansions. Anchors include Neiman-Marcus, Macy's, and Rich's department stores, and the J. W. Marriott hotel. There are six movie theaters in the complex, 25 restaurants (two of which, Mick's and the Fish Market, are detailed in Chapter 6, "Atlanta Dining"), and over 200 specialty shops. Among the best-known emporia are Ann Taylor, Victoria's Secret, Britches, Forgotten Woman, Benetton, Muse's, Cartier, Disney Store, The Sharper Image, Laura Ashley, The Limited, The Nature Company, Alfred Dunhill of London, Brooks Brothers, Banana Republic, the Gap, Polo/Ralph Lauren, B. Dalton, Waldenbooks, Radio Shack, Williams-Sonoma, Charles Jourdan, Florsheim Shoes, Bally of Switzerland, Buster Brown, Hoffritz for Cutlery, F.A.O. Schwarz, and Louis Vuitton. Basically, you can purchase just about anything here, from a Siamese kitten to a diamond bracelet (there are nine jewelry stores). A full complement of service shops are here as well—shoe repair, optician, locksmith, post office, airline offices, you name it. Open Mon–Sat 10am–9:30pm, Sun 12:30–5:30pm, with extended hours during the Christmas season. **MARTA:** Lenox.

PHIPP'S PLAZA, 3500 Peachtree Rd. NE, at the Buckhead Loop. Tel. 262-0992.

Atlanta's most exclusive shopping venue (it's almost too swank to be called a mall) serves the affluent Buckhead community. At this writing, it's undergoing a $140 million renovation and expansion, to add more shops, spacious promenades, and grand interior courts. A first-class restaurant, a restaurant complex, and a 12-screen movie theater are also underway. The 100-plus shops and restaurants at Phipp's are anchored by Lord & Taylor, Parisian (an Alabama-based department store), and Saks Fifth Avenue; the exclusive Ritz-Carlton Buckhead hotel is adjacent. Posh emporiums here include Gucci, Abercrombie & Fitch, Tiffany & Co., Mark Cross, Jaeger International, and Cashmeres of Scotland. You'll also find chic boutiques selling ladies and men's apparel, luggage, jewelry, furs, home furnishings, shoes, and specialty gifts. The ambience is sedately elegant, and there's usually something special going on—an art show, luxury car show, fashion show, or some other advertisement for the high life. Most stores are open Mon–Sat 10am–6pm, Thurs till 9pm. Some are also open Sun 12:30–5pm. **MARTA:** Lenox.

MALL AT PEACHTREE CENTER, Peachtree St. at International Blvd. Tel. 614-5000.

Part of the vast 14-block Portman-designed Peachtree Center complex, this downtown mall offers 70 shops, restaurants, and services on three levels. It's location couldn't be more convenient—three adjoining hotels even offer direct access to it via indoor passageways. It's a very complete shopping center, with quality boutiques featuring shoes and clothing for the whole family, luggage, jewelry, toys, books, photographic equipment, office supplies, pharmaceuticals, records, and imported gifts—all in a smart setting of

Italian marble, fountains, greenery, and polished bronze. There are branches of Muse's Department Store and Brooks Brothers. Services include florists, hairstylists, a Delta Air Lines desk, a travel agency, Federal Express and Purolater Courier, UPS, a dry cleaner, and an optician. As for dining, a food court dishes up everything from gyros to Mrs. Field's cookies, and full-service restaurants range from a chili parlor to the prestigious Morton's of Chicago (see Chapter 6, "Atlanta Dining"). Open Mon–Sat 10am to 6pm, with some stores open Sun noon–5pm. **MARTA:** Peachtree Center.

3. SHOPPING AROUND TOWN

BOOKS

In addition to the independent bookstores in Atlanta, the nationwide chain stores of **B. Dalton** and **Waldenbooks** are represented (see "Department Stores and Malls" above). Most important, Atlanta has **Oxford,** a truly great book emporium.

LATITUDES, Lenox Square Mall, 2393 Peachtree Rd. NE. Tel. 237-6144.

Latitudes offers a wide variety of reference books, atlases, globes, wall maps, and regional guides as well as travel accessories such as money belts and folding traveling irons. Open Mon–Sat 10am–9:30pm, Sun noon–5pm. **MARTA:** Lenox.

THE RENAISSANCE BOOKSHOP, Rio Shopping Center, 595 Piedmont Ave. at North Ave. Tel. 873-4161.

The Renaissance Bookshop has an extensive selection of new and back-list titles and a large inventory of remaindered books. In addition to best-sellers, the store features children's, gardening, cooking, crafts, interior decorating, and art books, as well as newspapers and stationery. Many books are discounted. Open Mon–Sat 11am–9pm, Sun 1–7pm.

OXFORD BOOKS, 360 Pharr Rd., between Peachtree and Piedmont Rds. Tel. 262-3333 or 800/476-3000.

The Oxford is the largest bookstore in the Southeast, and one of the best in the nation. It's a bibliophile's treasure trove, offering a vast selection of books on every subject plus sheet music, audio/videotapes, CDs, and out-of-town newspapers and magazines. It's also the scene of very frequent appearances by celebrated authors. Among those who have appeared to publicize new works (they sign books and give talks and/or readings) are Calvin Trillin, Mickey Mantle, Erma Bombeck, Jimmy and Rosalynn Carter, Armistead Maupin, Miss Manners, Quentin Crisp, and Bob Keeshan (better known as Captain Kangaroo). You can peruse your newly purchased books over soup and a sandwich at the Oxford Espresso Café on the premises. And while you're here, pick up a copy of the store's *Oxford Review,* a publication that includes book reviews and tells about upcoming author signings, writing workshops, poetry readings, lectures, songwriter's showcases, art exhibits, and other store-related events. Hours are Sun–Thurs 9am–midnight, Fri–Sat 9am–2am.

There's another immense store with vast inventory called **Oxford at Peachtree Battle,** 2345 Peachtree Rd. NE, at Peachtree Battle Ave., in the Peachtree Battle Shopping Center (tel. 364-2700). It, too, has an on-premises eatery, here called the Cup and Chaucer. Hours are the same as the above.

In the same shopping center is **Oxford Too** (tel. 262-3411), an additional 12,500 square feet of space housing a vast selection of used and remaindered books, records, tapes, and CDs, and a large comic collection. It's open Sun–Thurs 9am–11pm, Fri–Sat 9am–midnight.

A fourth **Oxford** store is at 1200 W. Paces Ferry Rd. and I-75 (tel. 364-2488). It offers a large selection of books in all categories, with special emphasis on books for children, home and garden, and travel. It's open Sun–Thurs 9am–10pm, Fri–Sat 9am–midnight.

WOMEN'S CLOTHING

See also "Department Stores and Malls," above, for more stores.

A PEA IN THE POD, in the Phipp's Plaza Mall, 3500 Peachtree Rd., at Lenox Rd. Tel. 261-0808.

This cleverly named shop features maternity clothes, but we're not talking T-shirts with an arrow pointing to your stomach and the word *baby.* These are gorgeous clothes—the kind you wore when you weren't pregnant. They run the gamut from really elegant tweed suits (perfect for board meetings) to evening wear and chic sports clothing. In fact, the clothes are so beautiful that women who are not pregnant shop here as well. Open Mon–Sat 10am–6pm, Thurs till 9pm. **MARTA:** Lenox.

SASHA FRISSON, 3094 E. Shadowlawn Ave. NE, between Peachtree and E. Paces Ferry Rds. Tel. 231-0393.

Without a doubt, the most high-fashion boutique in town. This is the stuff best-dressed lists are made of. Owners Emma Nassar and Laura Turner (she's Ted's daughter) carry only the smartest European and American designers—Moschino, Alberto Ferretti, and Liza Bruce of Italy; Thierry Mugler and Jacques Molko of Paris; Karl Lagerfeld, and others. Wonderful accessories and jewelry here, too. Prices are in the if-you-have-to-ask-it's-not-for-you category. This delightful and impeccably elegant boutique is located in a peach-brick 1930s house. There are other chic emporia occupying residential buildings on the same street if you feel like doing some upscale browsing. Open Mon–Sat 10am–6pm.

FACTORY OUTLETS

OUTLETS LTD. MALL, 750 George Busbee Pkwy., in Kennesaw. Tel. 424-9500.

Not quite as chichi as Tanger (below), Outlets is more of a bread-and-butter operation. Its 13 discount stores include a jeweler, two shoe stores, two clothing boutiques, All Stars Cards & Collectibles (baseball cards), and the General Bookstore (new and used books and college texts). If you're driving, take I-75N to exit 117, turn right on Chastain Road, right again on George Busbee Parkway. It's about 25 minutes from downtown. Open Mon–Sat 10am–9pm, Sun 12:30–5:30pm.

TANGER FACTORY OUTLET, 198 Tanger Dr., at exit 53 off I-85N in Commerce. Tel. 335-4537.

Tanger is a bargain-hunter's paradise, with 41 factory-outlet stores on a 22-acre property. Included are Oneida, Harvé Benard, Liz Claiborne, Corning, American Tourister, Farberware, Gitano, L'Eggs, Hanes, Bali, Maidenform, Van Heusen, and the Paper Factory, among others. Open Mon–Sat 9am–9pm, Sun noon–6pm.

FARMER'S MARKETS

ATLANTA STATE FARMER'S MARKET, 16 Forest Pkwy., Forest Park. Tel. 366-6910.

Not quite as exciting as the DeKalb market, the State Farmer's Market is still quite something to see—a vast 146-acre outdoor facility where stall after stall is piled high with produce. There are also vendors of meats, poultry, and fresh eggs; home-canned pickles, jams, and relishes; plants and flowers; and seasonal items such as pumpkins in October, holly and Christmas trees in December. It's a colorful spectacle. You can have a good meal at Davis Bros. Cafeteria on the premises. If you're driving, take I-75 south to exit 78; the market is on your left. Open 24 hours daily except Christmas.

DEKALB FARMER'S MARKET, 3000 E. Ponce de Leon Ave., Decatur. Tel. 377-6400.

Even if you have no intention of purchasing comestibles, this incredible market, started in 1977 by Robert Blazer, merits a visit. A mind-boggling array of food items from throughout the United States and 24 countries is temptingly displayed in a 140,000-square-foot pine-paneled building that harmonizes nicely with its wooded surroundings. It's about a 20-minute drive from downtown. International flags from Australia to Zaire are hung from the rafters. Tables are laden with mountains of produce from broccoli to bok choy, not to mention winter melons and water chestnuts, lily root, curry leaves, breadfruit, Jamaican jerk marinade, Korean daikon, a multiplicity of mushrooms, chick-pea miso, cheese fudge, a vast beer and wine section, dried fruits, plants and flowers, seafood, meat, poultry, every imaginable variety of fresh herbs and hot peppers, fresh-baked breads and pastries, stalks of sugarcane, 450 varieties of cheese, frog's legs, conch meat, quail, and so on. As you shop, you can nibble grilled red snapper, knishes, sections of grapefruit, Ecuadorian octopus, or whatever else is offered at sample tables throughout the facility. Open Mon–Fri 10am–9pm, Sat–Sun 9am–9pm.

CHAPTER 10

ATLANTA NIGHTS

1. THE PERFORMING ARTS
2. THE NIGHTCLUB SCENE
3. MORE ENTERTAINMENT
4. FILM & VIDEO

The Allman Brothers called it "Hot'lanta!" This is a city that sizzles after dark, with numerous music clubs featuring jazz, rock, country, and blues. It also offers a comprehensive cultural scene, including first-rate symphony, ballet, opera, and theater productions. And major artists headline regularly at Atlanta's many large-scale performance facilities.

To find out what's on during your stay, consult the "Weekend" section of Saturday's *Atlanta Journal-Constitution* or *Creative Loafing*, a free publication you'll see in stores, restaurants, and other places around town.

Tickets to many performances are handled by Ticketmaster. Call 249-6400 to charge tickets.

1. THE PERFORMING ARTS

MAJOR CONCERT/PERFORMANCE HALLS

ATLANTA CIVIC CENTER, 395 Piedmont Ave. NE, between Ralph McGill Blvd. and Pine St. Tel. 523-6275 for general information, 873-5811 for information on Atlanta Ballet performances.

Built in 1968 to attract major performers, the Civic Center offers a wealth of entertainment options in its 4,600-seat auditorium. It hosts headliners like Bob Hope, Frank Sinatra, Vanilla Ice, Roger Whittaker, Eddie Murphy, and Jay Leno. Broadway shows (with New York casts) sometimes come here. And the center presents traveling symphonies and opera companies, local dance companies, TV evangelists, fashion shows, Ravi Shankar, and closed-circuit boxing. Quite a mixed bag.

The Civic Center is the home of the Atlanta Ballet, a company founded in 1929 by Dorothy Alexander. It is the oldest regional ballet company in the United States. Today, under the artistic direction of Robert Barnett, it presents about six productions each season (Sept–Apr), including George Balanchine's highly acclaimed version of *The Nutcracker* every December.

Tickets to the ballet and other Civic Center performances are available through Ticketmaster (tel. 249-6400). Call the Civic Center or check local newspapers and magazines to find out what's on during your stay.

Prices: Admission varies with performances. Tickets for the Atlanta Ballet are $5–$35.75, with discounts for students and senior citizens.

Open: Hours vary with performances. **MARTA:** Civic Center (about 5 blocks away); buses go to the door. **Parking:** Entrances to paid lot on Pine St. or Ralph McGill Blvd.

COCA-COLA LAKEWOOD AMPHITHEATRE, Fair Drive at the Lakewood exit of I-85 on the Lakewood Fairgrounds. Tel. 627-9704; 249-6400 for tickets through Ticketmaster.

Opened in 1989, with Al Jarreau headlining, the $15 million Lakewood Amphitheatre accommodates 18,000, including 7,000 reserved seats and a sloping lawn that holds an additional 11,000. Needless to say, this vast facility is used for major shows. It offers a broad musical spectrum. Among those who have performed here are Rod Stewart, Alabama, Eric Clapton, Michael Bolton, Al Jarreau, George Strait, Bon Jovi, Jimmy Buffet, Elton John, Tom Petty, and the Allman Brothers. There are umbrellaed picnic tables on the grounds, and though you can't bring in food or drink, a wide variety of comestibles is available—imported beers, champagne, fruit and cheese, pizza, gourmet ice creams, and, of course, Coca-Cola. The amphitheatre is 3.5 miles south of downtown.

Prices: Prices vary with the performer. Most events are in the $10–$27 range.

Open: Early May to end of Oct; occasional events the rest of the year. Showtimes are 8pm, parking lots open at 5:30pm, doors open at 6:30pm. **MARTA:** Lakewood/Fort McPherson (shuttle buses take patrons to and from the station). **Directions:** I-75 or I-85 south to Lakewood Freeway exit (88E or 88W) and follow the signs. **Parking:** $5.

FOX THEATRE, 660 Peachtree St. NE, at Ponce de Leon Ave. Tel. 881-2100, 249-6400 to charge tickets via Ticketmaster.

Built in 1927, when movie theaters were conceived along lavish lines, the Fox is a Moorish-Egyptian extravaganza complete with arabesque arches, onion domes, and minarets. Its exotic interior reflects the Egyptomania of that decade—a phenomenon resulting from archaeologist Henry Carter's discovery of the treasure-laden tomb of King Tutankhamen. Throne chairs, scarab motifs, hieroglyphics, and falcon wings representing the Egyptian sun god are seen throughout the theater, and the auditorium evokes a Middle Eastern courtyard under a starlit azure sky. See Chapter 7, "What to See and Do in Atlanta," for details on the Fox's history, architecture, and interior design, as well as information on tours.

Every year there's an October-to-April "Best of Broadway"

season, featuring six major New York shows with star casts. It's followed by a summer Broadway series, so you can see hit shows like *The Will Rogers Follies, City of Angels,* and *Aspects of Love* almost year round here. In addition, a wide spectrum of headliners plays the Fox—Keith Richards, Kenny Rogers, Stevie Wonder, Ray Charles, Liza Minnelli, Gladys Knight, George Strait, Ben Vereen, and legions of others. There's a major film festival every summer (see the "Calendar of Events" in Chapter 2 for details). And the Coca-Cola International Series, September through April, offers entertainment ranging from the Opera Nazionale Italiano of Venice performing *Rigoletto* to Africa Oyé, a pan-African folkloric group. Other happenings range from dance-company performances to fashion shows to closed-circuit boxing.

Prices: Admission varies with the performance.

Open: Hours vary with the performance. **MARTA:** North Avenue.

ATLANTA-FULTON COUNTY STADIUM, 521 Capitol Ave. SW, between Fulton St. and Georgia Ave. Tel. 522-1967, 249-6400 to charge tickets via Ticketmaster.

Though this open-air circular stadium, with seating for 60,000, is primarily used for sporting events, it also hosts major rock shows. Among those who have appeared here are George Michael, Michael Jackson, Gladys Knight, and Ashford and Simpson. Call the above number for ticket information.

Open: Year round. Call to find out about concerts during your stay.

Prices: Vary with performers.

OMNI COLISEUM, 100 Techwood Dr. NW. Tel. 681-2100, 249-6400 to charge tickets via Ticketmaster.

The 16,000-seat Omni is the Southeast's showcase arena for sports and entertainment. In addition to shows like Walt Disney's World on Ice, The Ringling Bros. and Barnum & Bailey Circus, and Sesame Street Live, the facility hosts about 40 major concerts a year, featuring headliners such as Hammer, Hank Williams, Jr., Metallica, Prince, Michael Jackson, Bruce Springsteen, Elton John, and Bon Jovi. Call to find out what's on during your stay.

MARTA: Omni.

VARSITY PLAYHOUSE, 1099 Euclid Ave., near Washita Ave. Tel. 524-7354 for information; 249-6400 to charge tickets via Ticketmaster.

Built in the 1930s as a neighborhood movie theater, the Variety today offers an eclectic array of live entertainment. For example, in recent months they've presented the DeKalb Ballet; jazz artists McCoy Tyner, Kenny Kirkland, Sun Ra, and Tuck & Patti; Roger McGuinn; Roseanne Cash; the Count Basie Orchestra; and the play *Little Shop of Horrors*. There are also frequent album-release parties here. It's definitely worth checking out. While you're in Little

---

REAL TALK

Real Talk is a free, 24-hour service offered by Ticketmaster. It provides complete up-to-the-minute information on all sports and entertainment events going on in Atlanta at any given time. You can only use it in Atlanta. To access this information dial 728-8000. When asked, dial in the appropriate four-digit code and press the # button. You may listen to as many messages as you like by simply pressing in a new code. Four-digit codes are as follows:

Concerts 3900	Family Attractions 3904
Sporting Events 3901	Special Events 3905
Clubs 3902	Ticketmaster Locations 3910
Performing Arts 3903	Facility Locations 3911

To charge tickets via Ticketmaster, dial 249-6400.

Five Points, plan dinner at the Bridgetown Grill (see Chapter 6, "Atlanta Dining").

Prices: Most tickets are in the $5–$20 range; they vary with the performer.

Open: Year round, whenever shows are booked. **Parking:** There's a lot on Euclid Ave., near Colquitt Ave., charging $2 a night.

CHASTAIN PARK AMPHITHEATRE, in Chastain Park at Powers Ferry Rd. and Stella Dr. Tel. 231-5888 for information and to charge tickets.

This delightful 7,000-seat outdoor facility offers concerts under the trees from May to October. Everyone brings food; a picnic on the grass here is a tradition. Big-name performers are featured—stars like Kenny Loggins, Frank Sinatra, Liza Minelli, Harry Connick, Don Henley, and Paul Simon. It's hard to get tickets, so order as far in advance as possible (months ahead if you can). See also listing for the Atlanta Symphony Orchestra "Summer Pops Concerts" below.

Prices: Most tickets $23.50–$50.

THEATER

ALLIANCE THEATRE, Woodruff Arts Center, 1280 Peachtree St. NE, between 15th and 17th Sts. Tel. 872-SHOW for recorded information, 892-2414 for box office.

The Alliance originated in 1968 as the Atlanta Municipal Theatre; today, under the artistic direction of Kenny Leon, it is the largest resident professional theater in the Southeast. On two stages, it produces about 10 plays a year. Many well-known actors have played these stages, among them Armand Assante, Jane Alexander, Richard Dreyfuss, Tony Roberts, Jean Smart, and Morgan Freeman. Recent productions have included *A Streetcar Named Desire, Much Ado About Nothing,* Athol Fugard's *Playland* (a drama set in contemporary South Africa), *Once on this Island,* and Harold Pinter's *Betrayal.*

The Alliance Lunchtime Theatre series comprises six one-act plays ranging from vaudeville to Shakespeare. The plays are presented on the Main Stage on designated Tuesdays and Thursdays between November and May. And the Alliance Children's Theatre presents plays geared to youngsters such as *The Wind in the Willows* and *The Velveteen Rabbit* (the season is September through April).

There's parking in the Arts Center Garage on Lombardy Way between 15th and 16th streets. Consider dining at the Woodruff Arts Center's excellent restaurant, Chef's Grill, before or after the show (see Chapter 6, "Atlanta Dining").

Prices: For most productions, $17–$34. Discounts to students and seniors and "rush tickets" are often available on the night of the performance. Lunchtime Theatre admission, $3. Children's Theatre productions, $5.

Open: Sept–June; occasional productions during the summer.
MARTA: Arts Center.

SEVEN STAGES PERFORMING ARTS CENTER, 1105 Euclid Ave., two blocks west of Moreland Ave. Tel. 523-7647.

Seven Stages is a professional theater company "committed to providing the Atlanta community with issue-oriented plays whose themes provoke thought and discussion about social, political, interpersonal, or spiritual matters." Under the direction of Del Hamilton, it has been producing new and experimental works of international scope since 1979. Many worthy new works and new playwrights find a stage here, and both local and international acting groups supplement the resident company.

The center has two stages, the 100-seat Backdoor Theater and the 300-seat Main Stage. Past productions have included Odetta in *Woman's Voices: A Music and Letter Series,* Sam Shepard's *Buried Child* and *Geography of a Horse Dreamer,* an anti-Klan musical called *Bang, Bang Uber Alles* (protesting Klansmen demonstrated outside the theater), Rainer Werner Fassbinder's *Katzelmacher,* David Mamet's *Sexual Perversity in Chicago,* Samuel Beckett's *Quad,* and the American premiere of South African Adam Small's *Kanna—He is Coming Home,* an indictment of apartheid. Not everything done here is avant-garde or controversial, however; the company has performed Shakespeare, Molière, and Jacques Brel. Additional theater, dance, and music performances under Seven Stages' auspices take place at various Atlanta locations each year. And a gallery in the facility shows works of local artists.

Prices: For most shows, $10–$15; discounts available for students and seniors.

Open: Year round. **MARTA:** Inman Park. **Parking:** $2.

OPERA

ATLANTA OPERA, Woodruff Arts Center, 1280 Peachtree St. NE, between 15th and 17th Sts. Tel. 355-3311, 892-2414 for box office.

Under the artistic direction of William Fred Scott, the Atlanta Opera, founded in 1979, offers three fully staged productions each year at the Woodruff Arts Center's Symphony Hall. Principal performers are drawn from top opera companies from across the United States and Europe. Three to five performances are given of each opera. A recent season's productions included Bizet's *Carmen,* Donizetti's *Lucia di Lammermoor,* and Benjamin Britten's *Albert Herring.* There's a free season preview lecture/musical evening called "Opera Magic" on a selected date in April; call 355-3311 for information. Future plans call for a move to a new performance hall and a more comprehensive season, but the Atlanta Opera will most likely remain at Woodruff through 1994.

An excellent restaurant, the Chef's Grill, is located in the Arts Center (see Chapter 6, "Atlanta Dining").

Prices: Tickets $10–$62, with half-price tickets for seniors and students on the day of performance only. Tickets can be difficult to obtain; charge them in advance if possible.

Open: Late May through Labor Day. **MARTA:** Arts Center. **Parking:** In the Arts Center Garage on Lombardy Way, between 15th and 16th Sts. ($4).

CLASSICAL MUSIC

ATLANTA SYMPHONY ORCHESTRA, Woodruff Arts Center, 1280 Peachtree St. NE, between 15th and 17th Sts. Tel. 876-HORN for Concert Hotline recorded information, 892-2414 for box office.

The Atlanta Symphony Orchestra, under music director Yoel Levi, has evolved into one of the United States' most widely acclaimed orchestras. Complementing it is the 200-voice Atlanta Symphony Orchestra Chorus, enabling performances of large-scale symphonic-choral works.

The ASO's annual schedule is extensive. The main offerings from September to May are the **Master Season Series** and the **Champagne and Coffee Concert Series.** The Master Season concerts are held on selected Thursday, Friday, and Saturday evenings in the plush 1,762-seat Symphony Hall. This series comprises the orchestra's most highbrow performances, featuring many world-renowned guest artists and conductors. There are 24 different programs featuring the music of Bach, Rachmaninov, Mozart, Liszt, and others. The Champagne and Coffee Concert Series, featuring light classics, takes place on selected Fridays and Saturdays. Six Coffee Concerts performed Saturday mornings at 11am are preceded by coffee and pastries in the lobby at 10am and a preconcert lecture at 10:30am. And six nighttime concerts on Fridays and Saturdays at 8pm are followed by complimentary champagne. A recent season's offerings ranged from *A Night in Old Vienna* (Strauss waltzes, polkas, and so on) to *The Music of Richard Rodgers.* Also held during this season is a series of **Family Concerts.** Geared to children, they might include anything from a puppet-show version of Stravinsky's *Firebird* to *Peter and the Wolf.* They take place in Symphony Hall.

Summer Pops Concerts, in the 7,000-seat Chastain Park Ampitheater, begin at 8:30pm on Wednesday, Friday, and Saturday evenings between June and August. All seating is reserved. It's customary to bring elaborate picnics and wine. A recent season's "pops" performers included Roberta Flack, Phyllis Hyman, Tony Bennett, Johnny Mathis, Chet Atkins, Paul Anka, and The Manhattan Transfer. Another ASO warm-weather production is **Summerfest,** which takes place for three weeks in July in the informal setting of Symphony Hall Galleria. The six-concert series features popular classical music. Summerfest is always themed—for example, *Mostly Tchaikovsky* or *Mainly Mozart.*

There are free concerts in Piedmont and Grant parks on selected summer evenings. These run the gamut from full symphony performances to light classical repertoires. And Christmas season holiday concerts always include Handel's *Messiah.*

An excellent restaurant, the Chef's Grill, is on the premises (see Chapter 6, "Atlanta Dining").

Prices: Master Season tickets $16–$34, Champagne and Coffee Concerts $15–$34, Summer Pops $14.50–$32.50. Summerfest $16–$34. Family Concerts $10.

Open: Year-round season includes Sept–May performances at Symphony Hall in the Woodruff Arts Center and summer concerts in various Atlanta parks. **MARTA:** Arts Center. **Parking:** In the Arts Center Garage on Lombardy Way between 15th and 16th Sts.

ATLANTA CHAMBER PLAYERS. Tel. 651-1228.

The Atlanta Chamber Players have been delighting audiences both here and abroad since 1975. Their highbrow repertoire includes a wide spectrum of classical and contemporary masterpieces, and each year they commission new works by leading composers. The players give more than 100 concerts a year at various locations, most of them in Atlanta. Call to find out where they'll be playing during your stay.

Prices: Most concerts are $12, $7 for seniors and students.
Open: Fall-through-spring season.

ATLANTA BOY CHOIR. Tel. 378-0064.

This choir of 175 boys ages 5 to 14 has been delighting Atlanta audiences since 1956. A frequent guest at the White House, the choir has toured extensively both in the United States and abroad, always to great critical acclaim. In 1989 it won a Grammy Award. In Atlanta the choir sings at the lighting of the capitol Christmas tree early in

December and in local churches throughout the Christmas season. Five performances a year are given with the Atlanta Symphony Orchestra during its Master Concert season (Sept–May). And the choir frequently appears at other locations around town. Call the above number for schedule and ticket information.

Prices: Vary with each performance.

2. THE NIGHTCLUB SCENE

Two nationally famous clubs, the sophisticated celeb-studded **Limelight** and the **Hard Rock Café** are both planning to open branches in Atlanta at this writing. The Limelight will be located at 1150-B Peachtree Street in a baroque 1919 mansion with soaring 70-foot ceilings. The Hard Rock doesn't have a location as yet. One or both clubs may be open by the time you read this. Call 411 for phone numbers or check the newspaper to find out.

Just as these two places arrive to brighten Atlanta's nightlife, one or two others may well close their doors. Clubs come and go. Those listed below were the major ones operating at presstime.

KENNY'S ALLEY IN UNDERGROUND ATLANTA

Since so many nightclubs offering varying entertainment formats are grouped conveniently at Underground Atlanta, Kenny's Alley clubhopping is very popular.

DANTE'S DOWN THE HATCH, Kenny's Alley. Tel. 577-1800.

This is the original Dante's, the prototype for the Buckhead branch described in detail below. To enter, you literally go down a hatchway similar to any ship's descent to lower decks, except that its walls are lined with photographs of celebrity guests—Bill Cosby, Jimmy Carter, Rod Stewart, Count Basie, and others.

Owner Dante Stephensen earns kudos for highlighting the historic sites within his club. He's the only businessperson in the complex who seems to fully appreciate the historic significance of Underground. A sign informs visitors, for instance, that an exposed wall of the hatchway staircase is from the 1850s Planter Hotel and is the actual site of the hospital depicted in *Gone With the Wind*. An 1810 well on the premises was the water source for Atlanta's first fire department, and a steam engine on view powered the Frank E. Block Candy Company from 1868 to 1888. Like the Buckhead club, this is a fantasy ship moored in crocodile-infested waters (three live crocs swim in the moat). And there's plenty of nautical ambience—oak-plank floors, ship's ropes, steering wheels, and more. A singer and guitar player entertain on the "wharf," while the Brothers Three offer traditional jazz Monday through Saturday and another jazz trio does the same on Sunday. Sometimes well-known artists such as Phyllis Hyman come in and jam with the band. Fondue dinners are featured (see details in Buckhead listing).

Prices: For folk music on the wharf, there's a $1 cover charge; for jazz on the ship, cover is $5.

Open: For folk music on the wharf: Mon–Thurs 3–11:30pm, Fri–Sat 2–12:30am, Sun 2–10:30pm. For jazz on the ship deck: Mon–Thurs 8pm–midnight, Fri–Sat 8pm–1am, Sun 7–11pm. A jazz pianist entertains on the ship deck Mon–Sat 6:30–8pm. **MARTA:** Five Points.

BANKS & SHANE'S, Kenny's Alley. Tel. 577-4300.

Folk/bluegrass duo Banks Burgess (the banjo picker) and Paul Shane (on guitar) have been playing together since 1972. First at the original Underground, and later at their own club in Sandy Springs, they've delighted audiences with a unique blend of music and comedy, becoming something of an Atlanta institution in the process. Which is not to say they're just a local act; they've performed throughout the United States and abroad and appeared on national TV. You can see them here Thursday through Saturday night. Monday and Tuesday local pop artists perform. The setting is comfy and pleasant—floral-carpeted floors, pale-green walls lit by gaslight sconces, marble-topped tables. The dinner menu features entrées such as a 12-ounce New York strip steak, chicken teriyaki, and blackened shrimp over rice pilaf, all in the $12 to $15 range. Coffee liqueur drinks are a specialty.

Prices: Wed–Sat $5 cover for 8:30 and 10pm shows, $3 for midnight show; Mon–Tues $3–$12 cover, depending on the performer.

Open: Mon–Thurs till midnight, till 1:30 or 2am Fri–Sat. There are two or three shows per night. **MARTA:** Five Points.

BLUES HARBOR, Kenny's Alley. Tel. 524-3001.

If you like blues, you'll love Blues Harbor. It features nationally prominent artists such as Taj Mahal, James Cotton, Roomful of Blues, Duke Robillard, Matt "Guitar" Murphy, and Luther "Guitar Junior" Johnson. Dimly lit by candles, the club is vaguely New Orleansy in decor, with seating enclosed by black wrought-iron grillwork and a mural behind the bar depicting New Orleans at the mythical corner of Peachtree and Bourbon Streets. A very talented piano player, Johnny Rouse (*Atlanta* magazine called him the best in town) entertains during dinner and until showtime. The menu here lists items ranging from nachos and chicken wings to a full lobster or prime-rib dinner.

Prices: Cover charge $5–$6.

Open: Nightly, with three shows beginning at 9:30pm. Call for later showtimes. Dinner 6–10pm. **MARTA:** Five Points.

FAT TUESDAY, Kenny's Alley. Tel. 523-7404.

This New Orleans–concept club has a bar similar to a Mardi Gras float. Special machines behind the bar mix over 20 flavors of frozen daiquiris—margarita, peach colada (that's mixed with peaches, rum, ice cream, and coconut cream), white Russian, and more—and you can sample an ounce of any flavor on the house. Light fare (po' boy sandwiches, salads, gumbo) is also available. Rock and top-40 tapes are played at an earsplitting level. IDs are checked at the door: You have to be 21.

Prices: Admission is free. Drinks are $3.50–$5.25.

Open: Sun–Thurs till 1am, Fri–Sat till 2am. **MARTA:** Five Points.

CARIBBEAN SUNSET, Kenny's Alley. Tel. 659-4589.

Local reggae, calypso, Latin, and salsa groups provide the entertainment at this exotic island paradise. The tropical mood is set by a large, beautiful aquarium at the entrance. Inside, tie-dyed fabrics form a billowing canopy overhead, rustic stone walls are painted with trompe-l'oeil windows overlooking island scenery, the bar nestles under a bamboo eave, and there are neon-fronded bamboo "palm trees" amid the tables. A Caribbean menu offers items like jerk chicken wings and deep-fried Bahamian conch. There's live entertainment Wednesday through Sunday (bands come on at 9pm weekdays, 10pm weekends), recorded music other nights.

Prices: $5 cover weekends only.

Open: Fri–Sat till 2am, Sun–Thurs till 1am. **MARTA:** Five Points.

FANNY MOON'S OPERA HOUSE, Kenny's Alley. Tel. 521-2026.

In this large club, with southern state flags lining the walls, everyone sings along to Ruby Red's Dixieland band. Sometimes the band plays fifties rock tunes as well, and the music stops when major sporting events are aired on a 10-foot-square screen. Fanny Moon's is a casual place, on the pubby side, with checkered cloths on the tables. A western menu offers three-alarm chili, chili "dawgs," burgers, and sandwiches.

Prices: $1 Tues–Thurs, $2 Fri–Sat.

Open: Tues–Thurs till 1am, Fri–Sat till 2am. **MARTA:** Five Points.

MISS KITTY'S COUNTRY ROCK CAFÉ, Kenny's Alley. Tel. 524-4614.

This laid-back saloon offers high-energy country and southern rock music, featuring up-and-coming acts from all over the country, with occasional big names like Mo Bandy, David Allan Coe, Billy Joe Royal, Marty Brown, and Travis Tritt headlining or sitting in. It's a fun place. On the dance floor, folks are doing everything from the Texas two-step to dirty dancing. The staff is in western garb, and big crystal chandeliers overhead further evoke a wild-west saloon. More modern are 20 TV monitors airing everything from country-music videos to sporting events. The menu features chili, nachos, burgers, steaks, and ribs. Note the large Remington sculpture near the entrance.

Prices: No cover Sun–Thurs, $4 Fri–Sat.

Open: Mon–Thurs till 2am, Fri–Sat till 3 or 4am, Sun till 12:30am. **MARTA:** Five Points.

T-BIRDS DANCE CLUB AND CAFÉ, Kenny's Alley. Tel. 525-0991.

At this high-energy club, a DJ plays rock-and-roll tunes from fifties oldies through contemporary top-40. T-Bird's also functions as a restaurant, offering a largish menu of sandwiches, salads, and entrées like rotisserie chicken with homemade plum sauce and roast beef with mushroom gravy.

Prices: Cover $2–$3, Fri–Sat only.

Open: Open nightly 8pm–3am; the action really gets underway at about 10:30pm. **MARTA:** Five Points.

AROUND TOWN

DANTE'S DOWN THE HATCH, 3380 Peachtree Rd. NE, across the street from the Lenox Square Mall. Tel. 266-1600.

This wonderful jazz supper club is the realm of Dante Stephensen, a bona fide Atlanta character and former Aspen ski bum who makes his home in a posh private railroad car that was designed for the Woolworth family in the 1920s. He mans the decks of this well-rigged schooner, a fantasy 18th-century ship (actually afloat in murky waters) in a colorful seaport village. His aim was not to erect an exact replica but to create the period seagoing setting of everyone's imagination. It's a mix of antiques and nautical kitsch—200-year-old handstitched sails, oak paneling from English banks, pirate and sea captain mannequins, beveled-glass doors, 1892 leaded-glass panels from Lloyd's of London, centuries-old ship's lanterns and bells, Polish ship figureheads. Fish netting forms a canopy over the lower deck. There are many intimate seating areas—a velvet-curtained "bordello," a lighthouse, an English mahogany elevator, and a sail loft among them. Amber streetlamps and candlelight enhance the cozy ambience. The most romantic seating is in semienclosed private booths on the lower deck where the very talented Paul Mitchell Trio plays traditional jazz. Gladys Knight, who lives in Atlanta, occasionally stops in and sings with them, and it's not unusual for visiting musicians to sit in on sets. Mellow folk music is played on the "wharf."

Do plan to have dinner during the show. Fondues are featured. An imported cheese fondue is made with Emmentaler, Gruyère, and Swiss cheeses, flavored with Kirsch and Swiss wines, and served with French and honey-nut bread croutons, winesap apples, and fresh vegetables. Or you might opt for a Mandarin fondue of beef, chicken, pork, and shrimp served with four Chinese dipping sauces. Cheese platters and Chinese dumplings are additional specialties. And for dessert, there's delicious chocolate fudge cake served hot, or, if you order two days in advance, chocolate fondue with a gorgeous array of fresh fruit. Entrées, all including a large and tasty salad, are $13.50 to $18. An extensive wine list is reasonably priced. Reservations are suggested.

Prices: $4 cover for seating on jazz ship, no cover on the wharf.

Open: For folk music on the wharf: Mon 6–11:30pm, Tues–Thurs 6–8pm, Sun 5–7pm. For jazz on the ship: Tues–Thurs 8pm–midnight, Fri–Sat 6pm–1am, Sun 7–11pm. **MARTA:** Lenox.

RUPERT'S, 3330 Piedmont Rd., just north of Peachtree Rd. in the Peachtree Crossing Shopping Center. Tel. 266-9866 or 266-9834.

One of Atlanta's hottest clubs is Rupert's, a high-energy, live-music venue with state-of-the-art sound and lighting systems. Its interior is on the plush side, with gleaming mahogany paneling, silk wall coverings, mirrored columns, brass rails, and art deco lighting fixtures. Its clientele is upscale and chicly attired. There's a top-flight show every night—a 10-piece band and six versatile star-quality vocalists performing everything from Motown to top-40 tunes, from blues to funk—with a DJ filling in between sets. Singers who perform here have a big local following.

The dance floor is right in front of the stage, and there are five bars downstairs. Rupert's has a pretty good visiting-celebrity quotient. Jimmy Buffet, Rod Stewart, Alec Baldwin, Leif Garrett, Jennifer Grey, Cher, Donny Osmond (he got up on stage and did a few numbers), Chubby Checker (he also took to the stage and did the twist), Paul Anka, Mary Wilson, and Rob Lowe are among those who've partied here while in Atlanta. A large complimentary buffet is served from 6 to 8pm.

Prices: $7 cover Fri–Sat, $4 Tues–Thurs. No cover if you arrive before 8pm.

Open: Tues–Thurs till 2am, Fri–Sat till 3am. Call ahead weeknights; sometimes the club is closed for private parties. **Parking:** Valet parking is $2, but you can park in the shopping center lot free if you wish.

JOHNNY'S HIDEAWAY, 3771 Roswell Rd., two blocks north of Piedmont Rd. Tel. 233-8026.

Johnny's has been one of Atlanta's top night spots for over a decade. It's not glamorous, but the regular folks who frequent the club always seem to be having a super time. Ebullient owner Johnny Esposito, always on hand to greet his guests, is a well-known Atlanta character. The music is primarily big-band era, and so is the crowd. Tunes progress through the decades as the night wears on, but the music is always mellow.

This is a place for serious dancing, and most of the clientele can execute a pretty proficient two-step or tango. And though it's unpretentious, there are celebrities who hang out here when in town (Tommy LaSorda, Arnold Palmer, Jake La Motta, and burlesque queen Tempest Storm). A silver ball rotates over the dance floor, and you're likely to see Glenn Miller on the video monitors. A reasonably priced menu lists items ranging from deli sandwiches to snack fare such as nachos and buffalo wings to steak and prime-rib entrées. Sunday at 6pm you can have a free spaghetti dinner. Special events here include Johnny's Tomato talent contests (about 1,000 women in Atlanta carry cards identifying them as "Johnny's Tomatoes"), bocci tournaments, and sing-alongs. Dress is casual.

Prices: Admission is free, but there's a two-drink minimum (at tables only) after 8pm nightly.

Open: Sun–Fri till 3am, Sat till 4am. **Closed:** Christmas. **Parking:** Valet.

A SPORTS BAR

CHAMPIONS, at the Marriott Marquis, 265 Peachtree Center Ave., between Baker and Harris Sts. Tel. 521-0000.

Champions, in several cities nationwide, is the ultimate sports bar. It's decorated with neon beer signs and a hodgepodge of athletically themed paraphernalia and memorabilia—a baseball autographed by Willie Mays, a 1962 Patterson-Liston fight poster, Duke Snider's baseball mitt, and more. The circular oak bar is plastered with thousands of baseball cards under a laminated surface, and waiters wear striped referee uniforms. Twenty-one TV monitors, plus two large screens, air nonstop sporting events. (In those rare times when no game is on, they replay highlights.) During Monday-night football, a special table is set up for beer and hot dogs. But there's more to do than sit with your eyes glued to a TV set. You can test your skills on a five-hole putting green, play Street Shooter (a coin-op basketball game), or toss darts. Occasionally a DJ is on hand playing dance music. There are frequent promotions involving sports celebrities; they tend to stop in when in town. The menu features chili, nachos, pepperoni pizza, barbecued ribs, and burgers. Men outnumber women about five to one.

Price: No cover or minimum.

Open: Daily till 2am. **MARTA:** Peachtree Center.

3. MORE ENTERTAINMENT

DINNER THEATER

AGATHA'S MYSTERY DINNER THEATRE, 693 Peachtree St., at 3rd St. Tel. 875-1610.

Thespians manqué and Poirot aficionados: Here's a unique night on the town made to order for you. Agatha's presents comic mystery dramas, with everyone in the audience taking a small role in the play. The action takes place in the dining room during a five-course meal, including a buffet of hot hors d'oeuvres, soup, salad, a choice of five entrées, dessert, wine, and coffee.

When you sit down, you'll be given your lines or instructions. Many roles require finding and collaborating with other members of your performance group. The night I was here, I had to locate other "monkeys" in the room, compose a song with them, and perform it. Don't be nervous about it. Everyone's an amateur, and it's impossible to mess up. In most roles, you're part of a large group. Is it corny? You bet. But it's also an unbelievable amount of fun. Two talented professional actors—who are also the script writers—keep things moving along smoothly, and sometimes they're upstaged by would-be Barrymores in the audience. Productions are themed—for example, *The Maltese Chicken* or *The Wizard of Odds*—and new shows come on every 10 weeks. Use your little gray cells; all evidence points to the advisability of an evening at Agatha's.

Prices: $32–$43.75 per person for the show and a five-course dinner, including wine. Major credit cards accepted.

Open: Shows Tues–Sat at 7:30pm, Sun at 7pm. **Reservations:** Essential. **MARTA:** North Avenue. **Parking:** Limited free parking in the lot out back; paid garage nearby.

A DINNER TRAIN

NEW GEORGIA RAILROAD, depot at Zero Milepost Station in Underground Atlanta, 90 Central Ave., between Martin Luther King, Jr., Dr. and Decatur St. Tel. 656-0769.

This is Atlanta's answer to dinner on the Orient Express. Honoring Underground's site at the terminus of the Western & Atlantic Railroad, a vintage turn-of-the-century excursion train and several passenger cars have been restored to their former grandeur. These gorgeous cherry-paneled cars, with curtained windows, evoke a more luxurious era of rail travel. Waiters in black tie provide deft service, white-linen-covered tables are candlelit, wine and champagne cool in ice buckets tableside, and big-band-era music plays softly in the background. Don't bring the kids; the ambience is perfect for a romantic evening on the town or a convivial group of friends. Everyone dresses to the nines, which adds to the excitement and glamour of the evening. Dinner features a choice of three entrées: chicken marsala, filet of lemon sole stuffed with crabmeat, or prime rib (I urge the latter), along with a salad, vegetables, dessert, soft drinks, and coffee. Bring your own wine or champagne. There's free parking in a multistory garage at 90 Central Avenue, across the street from Underground; an elevator in the garage takes you to the train level. The trip takes about 2½ hours, and the route either circles Atlanta or goes to Stone Mountain. The dinner train is very popular. Make reservations as far in advance as possible.

Prices: $39.50 per person, plus tax. Bring your own wine.

Open: Departs at 7:30pm (boarding at 7pm) Thurs–Sat. **MARTA:** Five Points.

4. FILM & VIDEO

The **Image Film/Video Center,** 75 Bennett St. NW, off Peachtree Road between Collier Road and Colonial Homes Drive, Suite M1 (tel. 352-4225), offers regular screenings of work by the nation's most important independent media artists. Screenings might include animation programs (such as a showcase of works by Will Vinton of California Raisin fame), a gay and lesbian film festival, politically themed films and videos, or works of southern media artists. A wide gamut is covered, ranging from existentialist works to Dr. Seuss stories. IMAGE also sponsors numerous lectures and workshops related to film and video on subjects such as "An Introduction to Computer Graphics," "Beginning Screenwriting," and "VCR and Camcorder Basics." And, of course, there's the film festival in May (for details, see "Calendar of Events" in Chapter 2). Most films are $5.50, $3.50 for students and seniors.

INDEX

GENERAL INFORMATION

Accommodations:
 bed and breakfast reservation service, 51–2
 children, especially for, 63
 how to read the listings, 51
 maps: Buckhead, 79; downtown, 53;
  midtown-Georgia Tech, 66–7
 student discounts, 51
 tips for value-conscious travelers, 59
 see also Accommodations *index*
Agatha's Mystery Dinner Theatre,
  222–3
Airport, 40, 46
 transportation to and from, 40–1
Air travel to Atlanta, 30, 34
 tips for smart travelers, 31
Alliance Theatre, 213–14
American Association of Retired Persons (AARP), 28–9
Amtrak service, 30–1, 41
Area code, 46
Arriving in Atlanta, 40–1
Art galleries, 201, 204
Atlanta:
 famous Atlantans, 11–12
 Fast Facts, 46–9
 history of 3–11
 layout of, 41–4
 recommended books and films,
  12–13
 what's special about, 2
 what things cost in, 14–15
 see also specific topics
Atlanta Airport Shuttle Vans, 40–1
Atlanta Boy Choir, 216–17
Atlanta Chamber Players, 216
Atlanta Civic Center, 210–11
Atlanta Convention & Visitors Bureau
  (ACVB), 14, 34, 41, 51
Atlanta-Fulton County Stadium, 186,
  212
Atlanta Opera, 215
Atlanta Preservation Center, 184
Atlanta Symphony Orchestra, 215–16

Babysitters, 46
Banking, 47–8
Baseball, 186
Basketball, 186

Bed and breakfast reservation service,
  51–2
Bicycling, 188–9
Blues, 218
Bobby Dodd Stadium/Grant Field, 186
Books, shopping for, 202, 203–4,
  207–8
Brookhaven, 89–90
Buckhead, 44, 75–85, 111–25, 206
Business hours, 35
Bus travel:
 to airport, 41
 in Atlanta, 45
 to Atlanta, 31, 41
 sightseeing buses, 183–4

Calendar of events, 16–25
Calypso music, 219
Campgrounds, 87–8
Cars and driving, 31, 46
 rentals, 35, 46
Chamblee, 132–3, 199
Chastain Park Amphitheatre, 213
Children:
 accommodations liked by, 63
 attractions and activities, 176–83
 restaurants liked by, 100
City layout, 41–4
 map, 43
Classical music, 215–17
Climate, 15
Clothes:
 boutiques, 201
 shopping for, 208
Coca-Cola Lakewood Amphitheatre,
  211
Consulates, 35
Credit cards, 36
Currency and exchange, 35–6
Customs regulations, 33

Decatur, 44, 132
Dentists, 48
Department stores and malls, 205–6
Dinner theater, 222–3
Dinner train, 223
Disabled, tips for the, 28
Dixieland/Cajun music, 218–19
Doctors, 48

Documents needed by foreign visitors, 32

Downtown, 42, 52–63, 92–9, 184, 190–4
   maps: accommodations, 53; dining, 95; walking tour, 191
   walking tours, guided, 184

Drinking laws, 36, 48

Druid Hills, 88, 184

Elderhostel, 29

Emergencies, 36–7

Entry requirements for foreign visitors, 32–3

Factory outlets, 208–9

Families, tips for, 29–30, 31

Farmer's markets, 209

Fast Facts, 46–9
   for foreign travelers, 34–9

Film and video, 224

Fishing, 187

Folk/bluegrass, 217–18

Foreign visitors:
   Fast Facts for, 34–9
   getting to the U.S., 34
   preparing for your trip, 32–3

Fox Theatre, 184, 211–12

Gay men and lesbians, tips for, 29

Georgia Council for International Visitors, 33

Georgia's Stone Mountain, 86–8, 151–3

Georgia Tech area, 85–6

Golf, 187–8

Greyhound bus service, 211

Hairdressers, 48

Hartsfield-Atlanta International Airport, 40, 46

Hockey, 186

Holidays, 37

Hospitals, 48–9

Hot-air ballooning, 188

Image Film/Video Center, 224

Information, tourist, 14–15, 41

Inman Park, 184

Inoculations, 33

Insurance, travel, 33

Interpreters, 33

Island music, 219

Jazz, 220–1

Kenny's Alley, 217–20

Legal Aid, 37

Libraries, 49

Liquor laws, 49

Little Five Points, 44
   shopping in, 202–3

MARTA Rapid Rail (subway), 40, 45
   to airport, 40
   map, 43

Midtown, 63–75, 99–111
   accommodations map, 66–7; dining map, 102–3

Motor sports, 186–7

Music festivals and concert series, 215–17

New Georgia Railroad, 223

Newspapers and magazines, 49

Nightlife:
   big-band, 221–2
   blues, 218
   dinner theater, 222–3
   dinner train, 223
   Dixieland/Cajun, 218–19
   film and video, 224
   folk/bluegrass music, 219
   island music, 219
   Kenny's Alley, 217–20
   performing arts, 210–17; classical music, 215–17; concerts and performing halls, 210–13; opera, 215; theater, 213–15
   rock music, 219–20
   sports bar, 222

Omni Coliseum, 185–6, 212

Opera, 215

Organized tours, 183–4

Orientation
   arriving in Atlanta, 40–1
   Fast Facts, 46–9
   getting around, 45–6
   layout of city, 41–4
   tourist information, 14–15, 41

Peachtree Center, 190, 206–7

Performing arts, 210–13

Planning and preparing for your trip, 14–31
   calendar of events, 16–25
   foreign visitors, tips for, 32–3
   information and money, 14–15
   packing for your trip, 26–8
   tips for travelers, 28–9
   when to go, 15

Radio and television, 37–8

Rainfall, 15

Real Talk, 213

Recreation, 187–9

Restaurants:
   afternoon tea, 136
   breakfast/brunch, 134
   hotel, 134
   how to read the listings, 90
   Japanese breakfasts, 135–6
   for kids, 100
   late night/24-hour, 136
   light, casual, and fast food, 134

Restaurants (*cont'd*)
  local favorites, 133–4
  maps: Buckhead, 115; downtown,
    95; midtown, 102–3
  picnic fare, 136
  theater district, 134
  tips for value-conscious travelers, 96
  see also Restaurants *index*
River rafting, 188
Rock music, 219–20
Roller skating, 188–9

Safety, 38
Seniors, tips for, 28–9, 31
Seven Stages Performing Arts Center,
    214–15
Shopping, 199–209
  for antiques and gifts, 200
  art gallery, 201
  for body and bath, 200–1
  for books, 202, 203–4, 207–8
  Chamblee's Antique Row, 199
  for clothing, 201, 203
  department stores and malls, 205–7
  factory outlets, 208–9
  farmer's markets, 209
  for folk art, 204
  for furniture, 202
  in Little Five Points, 202–3
  for New Age items, 201–2
  in Stone Mountain Village, 204
  store hours, 35
  in Underground Atlanta, 205
  in Virginia-Highland district, 199–
    200
Sightseeing
  buses, 183–4
  Frommer's Favorite Experiences,
    147
  maps: Atlanta area, 166–7; Central
    Atlanta, 146–7; Georgia's
    Stone Mountain Park, 153
  organized tours, 183–4
  strategies for, 137–8
  see also Sights & Attractions *index*
Single travelers, tips for, 29
Sports, spectator, 185–7
Sports bar, 222

Stone Mountain Village shopping, 204
Students, tips for, 29, 51
Sweet Auburn, 42, 44, 131
  walking tour, 194–8
Swimming, 189

Taxis, 45–6, 49
Telephone, telegraph, telex, 38–9
Temperature, 15
Tennis, 189
Theater, 213–15
  dinner, 222–3
Time zones, 39
Tipping, 39
Tours:
  organized, 183–4
  walking: downtown, 190–4; guided,
    184; Sweet Auburn, 194–8
Train travel:
  to airport, 40–1
  to Atlanta, 30–1
  dinner train, 223
  Stone Mountain Scenic Railroad,
    151–2
Translators, 33
Transportation (public) in Atlanta,
    45–6
  arriving, 40–1
  information, 41, 49
Traveler's checks, 35–6
Travel insurance, 33

Underground Atlanta:
  Kenny's Alley in, 217–20
  shopping in, 205
  tourist information, 41
Varsity Playhouse, 212–13
Virginia-Highland district, 44, 125–31
  shopping in, 199–200

Walking tours:
  downtown, 190–4
  guided, 184
  Sweet Auburn, 194–8
Weather information, 48

Yellow Pages, 39

SIGHTS & ATTRACTIONS

Antebellum Plantation, 152
Antique Auto & Music Museum,
    151–2

APEX Museum, 147–8, 198
Atlanta Botanical Garden,* 158–9
Atlanta College of Art Gallery, 172

NOTE: An asterisk (*) after an attraction name indicates that it is an author's favorite.

Atlanta History Center,* 139–42; Atlanta History Center Downtown, 171, 193
Atlanta Museum, 172–3
Big Shanty Museum, 168–9
Callanwolde Fine Arts Center, 173–4
Carlos (Michael C.) Museum of Emory University,* 164–5
The Carter Presidential Center & Library, 153–4
Château Elan Vineyards, Braselton, 165–8
CNN Center, 155–6
Confederate Hall, 152
Cyclorama,* 148–50
Ebenezer Baptist Church, 148, 195
Fernbank Museum of Natural History,* 154–5
Fox Theatre,* 157–8
Georgia Pacific Center, 193
Georgia State Capitol, 159–61
Georgia's Stone Mountain Park,* 147, 151–2
Grant Park, 175–6
Guided walking tours, 184
Hammonds House, 173
Heritage Row, * 162–3
Herndon (Alonzo F.) home, 171–2
High Museum of Art, * 156–7; at Georgia-Pacific Center, 170–1
Kennesaw Mountain/National Battlefield Park, 169–70
Lasershow, 151
McElreath Hall, 139

Martin Luther King, Jr., Birth Home of, 142–3, 195
Martin Luther King, Jr., Center for Non-Violent Social Change,* 143–7, 194
Martin Luther King, Jr., National Historic Site, 146
Memorial Hall, 152
Mitchell (Margaret) House, 175
Museum of Atlanta History, 142
Oakland Cemetery,* 150
Piedmont Park, 175
Rhodes Memorial Hall, 174–5
Stone Mountain Scenic Railroad, 151
Swan House, 139–40
Swan Woods Trail, 142
Tullie Smith Farm, 140–2
Underground Atlanta, 161–2
Woodruff Park, 193
The World of Coca-Cola, 163–4
Yellow River Wildlife Game Ranch,* 147

FOR CHILDREN ESPECIALLY
Center for Puppetry Arts,* 178–9
Fernbank Science Center, 181
Scitrek (Science and Technology Museum of Atlanta), 180–1
Six Flags Over Georgia, 181–2
White Water, 182–3
Wren's Nest,* 177–8
Yellow River Wildlife Game Ranch,* 147, 179–80
Zoo Atlanta,* 176–7

ACCOMMODATIONS

BUCKHEAD
Beverly Hills Inn (B&B*), 85
Days Hotel at Lenox (M$), 81
Holiday Inn Buckhead (M), 81–2
JW Marriott at Lenox (VE*), 76–7
Lenox Inn (I), 84
Nikko Atlanta, Hotel (VE*), 75–6
Residence Inn Buckhead (M*), 63, 82–3
Ritz-Carlton Buckhead (E*), 77–8
Swissôtel (E*), 80–1
Terrace Garden Inn (M*), 83–4

DOWNTOWN
Atlanta Hilton & Towers (VE), 52–4

Best Western American Hotel (M), 59–60
Comfort Inn (M), 60
Days Inn Downtown (M), 60–1
Hyatt Regency Atlanta (VE), 54–5, 63
Marriott Marquis (VE*), 55–6
Plaza Hotel by Howard Johnson (M), 61
Quality Inn Habersham (M), 61–2
Ramada Hotel Downtown (M), 62
Ritz-Carlton Atlanta (VE*), 57–8
Travelodge Atlanta Downtown (I), 63
Westin Peachtree Plaza (VE*), 58–9

KEY TO ABBREVIATIONS: B = Budget; B&B = Bed-and-Breakfast; CG = Campgrounds; E = Expensive; I = Inexpensive; M = Moderately priced; VE = Very Expensive; $ = super-special value; * = an author's personal favorite

DRUID HILLS/EMORY UNIVERSITY/BROOKHAVEN
Budgetel Inn (*B*), 89–90
Courtyard by Marriott (*M*), 88–9
Emory Inn (*M*), 89

GEORGIA'S STONE MOUNTAIN
Evergreen Conference Center and Resort (*E**), 86–7
Family Campground (*CG*), 87–8
Stone Mountain Inn (*I*$*), 87

GEORGIA TECH
Comfort Inn (*I*), 85–6

MIDTOWN
Ansley Inn (*B&B*), 72

Biltmore Inn (*I$*), 69
Cheshire Motor Inn (*B$*), 71–2
Days Inn Peachtree (*I*), 69–70
La Quinta Inn (*I*), 70–1
Marriott Suites (*VE*), 64
Quality Inn Midtown (*I*), 71
Residence Inn Midtown (*M**), 68
Shellmont Bed and Breakfast Lodge (*B&B**), 73–4
Sheraton Colony Square (*VE*), 64–5
Woodruff Bed & Breakfast (*B&B*), 74–5
Wyndham Hotel Midtown (*E*), 65–8

OFF I-20
Econo Lodge (*B*), 90
Motel 6 (*B*), 90

RESTAURANTS

AFTERNOON TEA
Hotel Nikko, 136
Ritz-Carlton Atlanta, 136
Ritz-Carlton Buckhead, 136

AMERICAN
The Buckhead Diner, Buckhead (*M**), 120–1
Delectables, downtown (*B*), 98–9
Gorin's, midtown (*B*), 110–11
Gorin's Diner, midtown (*B*), 111
Mick's, downtown (*I*), 130–1, 134
Mick's, Underground Atlanta (*M*), 96–7
Murphy's, Virginia-Highland (*B*), 130–1, 134
The OK Cafe, Buckhead (*I**), 123–4, 136
R. Thomas, midtown (*I*), 109–10, 134, 136
The Swan Coach House, Buckhead (*I**), 124
Thumbs Up, Decatur (*B*), 132, 134
The Varsity, downtown (*M*), 99, 133

BREAKFAST/BRUNCH
Bridgetown Grill, 135
Chef's Café, 135
Evergreen Conference Center and Resort, 135
OK Cafe, 135
Ritz-Carlton Atlanta, 135

Ritz-Carlton Buckhead, 135

CAJUN
French Quarter Food Shop, midtown (*I*$*), 107–8

CANTONESE
Honto, Chamblee (*I**), 132–3

CARIBBEAN
Bridgetown Grill, Virginia-Highland (*I**), 128–9

CLASSIC EUROPEAN
The Hedgerose Heights Inn, Buckhead (*VE**), 114–16

COASTAL
Indigo Coastal Grill, Virginia-Highland (*M**), 126–7

CONTEMPORARY AMERICAN
Chef's Café, midtown (*M**), 101–4
Chef's Grill, midtown (*M**), 104, 134
Chow, Virginia-Highland (*M*), 126
City Grill, downtown (*VE**), 92–3
The Country Place, midtown (*M**), 104–5
Dailey's, downtown (*E**), 94–5
The Peasant Restaurant & Bar, Buckhead (*M*), 121–2

KEY TO ABBREVIATIONS: *B* = Budget; *B&B* = Bed-and-Breakfast; *CG* = Campgrounds; *E* = Expensive; *I* = Inexpensive; *M* = Moderately priced; *VE* = Very Expensive; *$* = super-special value; *** = an author's personal favorite

CONTINENTAL
The Pleasant Peasant, downtown (M), 97

CROSS-CULTURAL
Partners Morningside Café, Virginia-Highland (M), 127–8

EUROPEAN HAUTE CUISINE
The Dining Room, Buckhead (VE*), 113–14

FRENCH/FRENCH NEW AMERICAN
103 West, Buckhead (VE), 117–18
Pano & Paul's, Buckhead (VE*), 118

HOTEL DINING
Nikolai's Roof, Atlanta Hilton (E), 134
Ritz-Carlton Buckhead Dining Room (VE), 134
Sun Dial, downtown (I-E), 134

ICE CREAM
Gorin's, midtown (B), 110–11

ITALIAN/PIZZA
Fellini's Pizza, Buckhead (B), 124–5
Pricci, Buckhead (E), 119–20
Rocky's Brick Oven Pizzeria (I*), 110, 134

JAPANESE
Hotel Nikko-Cassis (breakfast), 135–6
Kamogawa, Buckhead (VE*), 116–17
Westin Peachtree Plaza, downtown (breakfast only), 135

JEWISH DELI
Stage Deli, Buckhead (M*), 122–3

LATE NIGHT/24-HOUR
OK Cafe, 136
R. Thomas, 136

"NEW AGE" ITALIAN
Bice Ristorante, midtown (VE), 100–1

NEW AMERICAN CREOLE
Taste of New Orleans, midtown (M), 105–6

PICNIC FARE
DeKalb Farmer's Market, 136
Partner's Pantry, 136

SEAFOOD
Fish Market, Buckhead (E), 118–19

SOUTHERN/SOUL FOOD
The Beautiful Restaurant, Sweet Auburn (B), 131
The Colonnade, midtown (I), 106–7, 133
Mary Mac's Tearoom, midtown (I), 108–9

STEAKS & SEAFOOD
Bone's, Buckhead (VE*), 111–12
Chops, Buckhead (VE*), 112
Morton's of Chicago, downtown (VE), 93–4

TEXAS BARBECUE
The Rib Ranch, Buckhead (B), 125

THAI
Surin of Thailand, Virginia-Highland (I*), 129–30

Now Save Money On All Your Travels by Joining
FROMMER'S ™ TRAVEL BOOK CLUB
The World's Best Travel Guides at Membership Prices

FROMMER'S TRAVEL BOOK CLUB is your ticket to successful travel! Open up a world of travel information and simplify your travel planning when you join ranks with thousands of value-conscious travelers who are members of the FROMMER'S TRAVEL BOOK CLUB. Join today and you'll be entitled to all the privileges that come from belonging to the club that offers you travel guides for less to more than 100 destinations worldwide. Annual membership is only $25 (U.S.) $35 (Canada and all foreign).

The Advantages of Membership

1. Your choice of three free FROMMER'S TRAVEL GUIDES (you can pick two from our FROMMER'S COUNTRY and REGIONAL GUIDES and one from our FROMMER'S CITY GUIDES).
2. Your own subscription to **TRIPS AND TRAVEL** quarterly newsletter.
3. You're entitled to a **30% discount** on your order of any additional books offered by FROMMER'S TRAVEL BOOK CLUB.
4. You're offered (at a small additional fee) our **Domestic Trip Routing Kits.**

Our quarterly newsletter **TRIPS AND TRAVEL** offers practical information on the best buys in travel, the "hottest" vacation spots, the latest travel trends, world class events and much, much more.

Our **Domestic Trip Routing Kits** are available for any North American destination. We'll send you a detailed map highlighting the best route to take to your destination—you can request direct or scenic routes.

Here's all you have to do to join:
Send in your membership fee of $25 ($35 Canada and foreign) with your name and address on the form below along with your selections as part of your membership package to FROMMER'S TRAVEL BOOK CLUB, P.O. Box 473, Mt. Morris, IL 61054-0473. Remember to select 2 FROMMER'S COUNTRY and REGIONAL GUIDES and 1 FROMMER'S CITY GUIDE on the pages following.

If you would like to order additional books, please select the books you would like and send a check for the total amount (please add sales tax in the states noted below), plus $2 per book for shipping and handling ($3 per book for all foreign orders) to:

FROMMER'S TRAVEL BOOK CLUB
P.O. Box 473
Mt. Morris, IL 61054-0473
1-815-734-1104

[ ] YES. I want to take advantage of this opportunity to join FROMMER'S TRAVEL BOOK CLUB.

[ ] My check is enclosed. Dollar amount enclosed＿＿＿＿＿＿*

Name＿＿＿＿＿＿＿＿＿＿＿＿＿＿＿＿＿＿＿＿＿＿＿＿＿＿＿

Address＿＿＿＿＿＿＿＿＿＿＿＿＿＿＿＿＿＿＿＿＿＿＿＿＿＿

City＿＿＿＿＿＿＿＿＿＿＿＿＿＿ State＿＿＿＿ Zip＿＿＿＿＿＿

To ensure that all orders are processed efficiently, please apply sales tax in the following areas: CA, CT, FL, IL, NJ, NY, TN, WA and CAN.

*With membership, shipping and handling will be paid by FROMMER'S TRAVEL BOOK CLUB for the three free books you select as part of your membership. Please add $2 per book for shipping and handling for any additional books purchased ($3 per book for all foreign orders).

Allow 4-6 weeks for delivery. Prices of books, membership fee, and publication dates are subject to change without notice.

FROMMER GUIDES

	Retail Price	Code		Retail Price	Code
Alaska 1990–91	$14.95	C001	Jamaica/Barbados 1993–94	$15.00	C105
Arizona 1993–94	$18.00	C101	Japan 1992–93	$19.00	C020
Australia 1992–93	$18.00	C002	Morocco 1992–93	$18.00	C021
Austria/Hungary 1991–92	$14.95	C003	Nepal 1992–93	$18.00	C038
Belgium/Holland/Luxembourg 1993–94	$18.00	C106	New England 1992	$17.00	C023
Bermuda/Bahamas 1992–93	$17.00	C005	New Mexico 1991–92	$13.95	C024
Brazil 1991–92	$14.95	C006	New York State 1992–93	$19.00	C025
California 1992	$18.00	C007	Northwest 1991–92	$16.95	C026
Canada 1992–93	$18.00	C009	Portugal 1992–93	$16.00	C027
Caribbean 1993	$18.00	C102	Puerto Rico 1993–94	$15.00	C103
The Carolinas/Georgia 1992–93	$17.00	C034	Puerto Vallarta/Manzanillo/Guadalajara 1992–93	$14.00	C028
Colorado 1993–94	$16.00	C100	Scandinavia 1991–92	$18.95	C029
Cruises 1993–94	$19.00	C107	Scotland 1992–93	$16.00	C040
DE/MD/PA & NJ Shore 1992–93	$19.00	C012	Skiing Europe 1989–90	$14.95	C030
Egypt 1990–91	$14.95	C013	South Pacific 1992–93	$20.00	C031
England 1993	$18.00	C109	Switzerland/Liechtenstein 1992–93	$19.00	C032
Florida 1993	$18.00	C104	Thailand 1992–93	$20.00	C033
France 1992–93	$20.00	C017	USA 1991–92	$16.95	C035
Germany 1993	$19.00	C108	Virgin Islands 1992–93	$13.00	C036
Italy 1992	$19.00	C019	Virginia 1992–93	$14.00	C037
			Yucatán 1992–93	$18.00	C110

FROMMER $-A-DAY GUIDES

	Retail Price	Code		Retail Price	Code
Australia on $45 a Day 1993–94	$18.00	D102	Israel on $45 a Day 1993–94	$18.00	D101
Costa Rica/Guatemala/Belize on $35 a Day 1991–92	$15.95	D004	Mexico on $50 a Day 1993	$19.00	D105
Eastern Europe on $25 a Day 1991–92	$16.95	D005	New York on $70 a Day 1992–93	$16.00	D016
England on $60 a Day 1993	$18.00	D107	New Zealand on $45 a Day 1993–94	$18.00	D103
Europe on $45 a Day 1993	$19.00	D106	Scotland/Wales on $50 a Day 1992–93	$18.00	D019
Greece on $45 a Day 1993–94	$19.00	D100	South America on $40 a Day 1991–92	$15.95	D020
Hawaii on $75 a Day 1993	$19.00	D104	Spain on $50 a Day 1991–92	$15.95	D021
India on $40 a Day 1992–93	$20.00	D010	Turkey on $40 a Day 1992	$22.00	D023
Ireland on $40 a Day 1992–93	$17.00	D011	Washington, D.C. on $40 a Day 1992	$17.00	D024

FROMMER CITY $-A-DAY GUIDES

	Retail Price	Code		Retail Price	Code
Berlin on $40 a Day 1992–93	$12.00	D002	Madrid on $50 a Day 1992–93	$13.00	D014
Copenhagen on $50 a Day 1992–93	$12.00	D003	Paris on $45 a Day 1992–93	$12.00	D018
London on $45 a Day 1992–93	$12.00	D013	Stockholm on $50 a Day 1992–93	$13.00	D022

FROMMER TOURING GUIDES

Amsterdam	$10.95	T001	New York	$10.95	T008
Australia	$10.95	T002	Paris	$ 8.95	T009
Barcelona	$14.00	T015	Rome	$10.95	T010
Brazil	$10.95	T003	Scotland	$ 9.95	T011
Egypt	$ 8.95	T004	Sicily	$14.95	T017
Florence	$ 8.95	T005	Thailand	$12.95	T012
Hong Kong/Singapore/			Tokyo	$15.00	T016
Macau	$10.95	T006	Turkey	$10.95	T013
Kenya	$13.95	T018	Venice	$ 8.95	T014
London	$12.95	T007			

FROMMER'S FAMILY GUIDES

California with Kids	$16.95	F001	San Francisco with Kids	$17.00	F004
Los Angeles with Kids	$17.00	F002	Washington, D.C. with		
New York City with Kids	$18.00	F003	Kids	$17.00	F005

FROMMER CITY GUIDES

Amsterdam/Holland 1991–92	$ 8.95	S001	Miami 1991–92	$ 8.95	S021
Athens 1991–92	$ 8.95	S002	Minneapolis/St. Paul 1991–92	$ 8.95	S022
Atlanta 1991–92	$ 8.95	S003	Montréal/Québec City		
Atlantic City/Cape May 1991–92	$ 8.95	S004	1991–92	$ 8.95	S023
Bangkok 1992–93	$13.00	S005	New Orleans 1993–94	$13.00	S103
Barcelona/Majorca/			New York 1992	$12.00	S025
Minorca/Ibiza 1992	$12.00	S006	Orlando 1993	$13.00	S101
Belgium 1989–90	$ 5.95	S007	Paris 1993–94	$13.00	S109
Berlin 1991–92	$10.00	S008	Philadelphia 1991–92	$ 8.95	S028
Boston 1991–92	$ 8.95	S009	Rio 1991–92	$ 8.95	S029
Cancún/Cozumel/Yucatán 1991–92	$ 8.95	S010	Rome 1991–92	$ 8.95	S030
Chicago 1991–92	$ 9.95	S011	Salt Lake City 1991–92	$ 8.95	S031
Denver/Boulder/Colorado			San Diego 1993–94	$13.00	S107
Springs 1990–91	$ 7.95	S012	San Francisco 1993	$13.00	S104
Dublin/Ireland 1991–92	$ 8.95	S013	Santa Fe/Taos/		
Hawaii 1992	$12.00	S014	Albuquerque 1993–94	$13.00	S108
Hong Kong 1992–93	$12.00	S015	Seattle/Portland 1992–93	$12.00	S035
Honolulu/Oahu 1993	$13.00	S106	St. Louis/Kansas City		
Las Vegas 1991–92	$ 8.95	S016	1991–92	$ 9.95	S036
Lisbon/Madrid/Costa del			Sydney 1991–92	$ 8.95	S037
Sol 1991–92	$ 8.95	S017	Tampa/St. Petersburg		
London 1993	$13.00	S100	1993–94	$13.00	S105
Los Angeles 1991–92	$ 8.95	S019	Tokyo 1992–93	$13.00	S039
Mexico City/Acapulco			Toronto 1991–92	$ 8.95	S040
1991–92	$ 8.95	S020	Vancouver/Victoria 1990–91	$ 7.95	S041
			Washington, D.C. 1993	$13.00	S102

Other Titles Available at Membership Prices—
SPECIAL EDITIONS

	Retail Price	Code		Retail Price	Code
Bed & Breakfast North America	$14.95	P002	Marilyn Wood's Wonderful Weekends (within 250-mile radius of New York City)	$11.95	P017
Caribbean Hideaways	$16.00	P005			
Honeymoon Destinations	$14.95	P006			
			New World of Travel 1991 by Arthur Frommer	$16.95	P018
			Where to Stay USA	$13.95	P015

GAULT MILLAU'S "BEST OF" GUIDES

Chicago	$15.95	G002	New England	$15.95	G010
Florida	$17.00	G003	New Orleans	$16.95	G011
France	$16.95	G004	New York	$16.95	G012
Germany	$18.00	G018	Paris	$16.95	G013
Hawaii	$16.95	G006	San Francisco	$16.95	G014
Hong Kong	$16.95	G007	Thailand	$17.95	G019
London	$16.95	G009	Toronto	$17.00	G020
Los Angeles	$16.95	G005	Washington, D.C.	$16.95	G017

THE REAL GUIDES

Amsterdam	$13.00	R100	Morocco	$14.00	R111
Barcelona	$13.00	R101	Nepal	$14.00	R018
Berlin	$11.95	R002	New York	$13.00	R019
Brazil	$13.95	R003	Able to Travel		
California & the West Coast	$17.00	R102	(avail April '93)	$20.00	R112
Canada	$15.00	R103	Paris	$13.00	R020
Czechoslovakia	$14.00	R104	Peru	$12.95	R021
Egypt	$19.00	R105	Poland	$13.95	R022
Florida	$14.00	R006	Portugal	$15.00	R023
France	$18.00	R106	Prague	$15.00	R113
Germany	$18.00	R107	San Francisco & the Bay		
Greece	$18.00	R108	Area	$11.95	R024
Guatemala/Belize	$14.00	R109	Scandinavia	$14.95	R025
Holland/Belgium/			Spain	$16.00	R026
Luxembourg	$16.00	R031	Thailand	$17.00	R114
Hong Kong/Macau	$11.95	R011	Tunisia	$17.00	R115
Hungary	$12.95	R012	Turkey	$13.95	R116
Ireland	$17.00	R110	U.S.A.	$18.00	R117
Italy	$13.95	R014	Venice	$11.95	R028
Kenya	$12.95	R015	Women Travel	$12.95	R029
Mexico	$11.95	R016	Yugoslavia	$12.95	R030